Dreaming the Actual

SUNY series in
Modern Jewish Literature and Culture

Sarah Blacher Cohen, *editor*

Dreaming the Actual

Contemporary Fiction and Poetry
by Israeli Women Writers

Selected, Edited, and with Introductions by
Miriyam Glazer

STATE UNIVERSITY OF NEW YORK PRESS

Published by
State Univesity of New York Press, Albany

Cover illustration © copyright Hedva Harechavi

Production by Kristin Milavec
Marketing by Anne M. Valentine

For information, address the State University of New York Press,
State University Plaza, Albany, NY 12246

Library of Congress Cataloging-in-Publication Data

Dreaming the actual : contemporary fiction and poetry by Israeli women
    writers / selected, edited, and with introductions by Miriyam Glazer.
        p.   cm. — (SUNY series in modern Jewish literature and
    culture)
    ISBN 0-7914-4557-7 (hc. : alk. paper). — ISBN 0-7914-4558-5 (pbk.
    : alk. paper)
        1. Israeli literature—Women authors—Translations into English.
    I. Glazer, Miriyam, 1945– . II. Series.
    PJ5059.E1 D74   2000
    892.4'0809287'0904—dc21   99–041322
                                                                            CIP

10 9 8 7 6 5 4 3 2 1

For Avigail

" . . . Tovat sei'khel v'y'faht to'ar . . . "

. . . cleaving
to a dream of the actual,
breathing touch
spinning the self
and the shadow.

—Leah Aini, "One Girl's Dance"

Contents

Acknowledgments   xv

Introduction   1

Part I Short Stories
And She Is Joseph *by Nurit Zarchi*   17
Madame Bovary in Neve Tsedek *by Nurit Zarchi*   24
Invisible Mending *by Ruth Almog*   33
A Piece of Cake for Saul *by Mira Magen*   50
If Nella Could Do It *by Shulamith Gilboa*   58
The Fruit of Paradise *by Leah Aini*   68
Rest *by Leah Aini*   76
"It's Greek to You," She Said to Him *by Savyon Liebrecht*   81
Hunger *by Nava Semel*   99
Schlaffstunde *by Yehudit Katzir*   124
Two Hours on the Road *by Shulamith Hareven*   148
Gerbera Daisies at Half-Price *by Mira Magen*   163
Apples in Honey *by Yehudit Hendel*   182
Photograph *by Ronit Matalon*   193

Introduction to Selected Short Stories by Orly Castel-Bloom   200

A Thousand Shekels a Story *by Orly Castel-Bloom*   202
The Woman Who Went Looking
    for a Walkie-Talkie *by Orly Castel-Bloom*   206
The Woman Whose Hand Got Stuck
    in the Mailbox *by Orly Castel-Bloom*   209

xi

A Special Section: Stories Translated from the Russian   212

    Monologue of a Life Model *by Dina Rubin*   217
    Rough Casting *by Elena Makarova*   226

Part II   Poetry
Yona Volach: In Memoriam   243
    Hebrew   245
    I Have a Stage in My Head   248
    Tefillin   249
    When You Come Sleep with Me   251
    The Life You Have   253
    Bird   254

Dahlia Ravikovitch   256
    Real Love Isn't What It Seems   258
    An Unusual Autumn   260
    Hovering at a Low Altitude   262
    Blood Heifer   265

Hedva Harechavi   267
    1 x 2   268
    And It Is Still That Way   274
    Already Night, Already Day   276

Raquel Chalfi   278
    Reading the I Ching   279
    Night Hair   282

Maya Bejerano   284
    I Made a New Memory for You   285
    States of War   287
    From "The Hymns of Job"   289

Esther Ettinger   298
    Excerpts from the Sabbath Dream Book   300
    Micrographic Manuscript, Miniature (I)   302
    Micrographic Manuscript, Miniature (II)   303
    The Glass   304
    Believe Me   306

Chava Pinchas-Cohen   308
    Remembering Our Fathers   309
    Her, Me, and Yochanan   312

My English Teacher   314
The Yearning of Karakashian   315
The Ineffable Name   317
Journey of a Doe   319

Hamutal Bar Yosef   326
Jaffa, July 1948   327
Reflections on a Dove   328
In the Library   331
An Angel on the Beach   333

Agi Mishol   334
Estate   335
The Sacred Cow of Hardship   337
Gravity, Death   339
Shopping   340

Devorah Amir   342
After Fall, 1956   343
I Have Longings for My Dead   344
What Seeps In   345
Thoughts about Sari's Jump   346
The "Nightingale" of Uncle Yair   348

Leah Aini
One Girl's Dance   349
Liquidation   350
In Their House   351
Shower   352
The Empress of Imagined Fertility   354

Nidaa Khoury   355
Death Is Your Salvation   356
People of Fire   358
People of Pomegranates   359
People of Figs   360
People of Olives   361

A Special Section: American Israeli Poets Writing in English   362

Shirley Kaufman   364
Déjà Vu   365
Stones   367
Security   369
Job's Wife   371
The Mount of Olives   372

Linda Zisquit   373
    From "Unopened Letters"   374
    After Years of Feasting and No Sacrifice   376
    A Word before the Last about Loss   377

Rachel Tzvia Back   378
    Notes: From the Wait   380
    Untitled   382
    Abu Salim, Healer   384
    Gaza, Undated   386
    After Eden   388

Karen Alkalay-Gut   389
    From "Between Bombardments: A Journal"   390
    Kitzbuhl Church   393
    Public Outcry   394
    Transportation   396

Acknowledgments

Little did I realize the scope of what I so readily agreed to undertake that sunlit August afternoon in Jerusalem when a group of poets whose work had been included in my earlier collection, *Burning Air and a Clear Mind: Contemporary Israeli Women Poets,* urged me to create a new anthology in light of the radical changes in Israeli women's literature since 1981. In the years that followed, how many more new and gifted writers of both prose and poetry I was to encounter! What an intensely active literary scene! Working on *Dreaming the Actual* was more than a matter of hundreds of hours spent in my Santa Monica, California, study; over the years, I have come to cherish the many afternoons and evenings passed in intent discussion with poets, writers, translators, as well as with critics of Israeli literature, in my sister Phyllis Glazer's lovely Tel Aviv garden, in writers' homes, as well as in Jerusalem's and Tel Aviv's lively cafés. And not only in studies, gardens, living rooms, and cafés. As I doubt either of us will ever forget, as my sister Alyne and daughter Avigail snorkelled away, my niece Sigalit Bat Haim and I ensconced ourselves in the cooling waters of the Red Sea in the Sinai desert, sharing our interpretations of the poetry of Yona Volach as Sigalit prepared for her role as a literature professor in the Habimah Theatre production of "Yona, Yona," and I prepared the Volach translations for my book.

I am grateful for the literary adventures—and I am even more grateful to the colleagues, writers, friends, and members of my family who were so willing to be of help. The enthusiasm of Professor Sarah Blacher Cohen for this project encouraged me all along the way. Professors Aryeh Cohen, Baruch Link, Tova Oren, Eliezer Slomovic, and Ziony Zevit—

my warm, responsive, and profoundly appreciated colleagues at the University of Judaism—continually shared their rich Jewish learning in Talmud, Midrash, Bible, and Hebrew language and literature with me. Ora Band worked with me on the early stages of this project. Haim Dov Beliak helped me unravel the Hebrew of more than one story, and Professor Zilla Goodman helped me unravel poems. Marina Bereznyak was a pleasure to work with on a translation from the Russian, as well as Gal Keidar, on translations from the Hebrew. Adva Klein, my student, was of special help, and remarkably efficient, patient, and persevering. Randi Sherman was invaluable to me in the preparation of the manuscript. I thank you all.

I owe a debt of gratitude to the Institute for the Translation of Hebrew Literature for their patient responses to my many faxes over the years and for their support of this project, as well as to the College of Arts and Sciences of the University of Judaism, which not only provided the intellectual environment in which this project could flourish, but also, and crucially, generously supported my research over the years and the publication of this book. I extend my thanks for the generous support of the Lucius M. Littauer Foundation, as well to Luis Lanier, and to Mark Borowitz, whose contributions helped to subsidize the book's publication.

I greatly appreciate Mariana Barr's patience with my seemingly endless queries and I value her own passion for poetry as well as gift for language—not to mention the long hours she spent poring over my translations. I am grateful to David Dortort and Professors Esther Fuchs, Mark Shechner, and Maeera Shreiber for taking the time to read and critique my Introduction. And I appreciate so very much the many writers and translators whose work is included here and who not only sat with me for hours of discussion but guided me to other writers. I am especially grateful to writers Karen Alkalay-Gut, Shirley Kaufman, and Nava Semel. I also want to thank Professors Yael Feldman and Michael Gluzman for making their critical work and insights available to me. I trust that the loyal, wonderfully attentive and insightful adult students in my Thursday morning University Women Continuing Education class at the University of Judaism, who served as the "proving ground" for the translations here, know how much I value our many classes together these last seven years.

Above all, I am grateful to members of my much-beloved family. My daughter, Avigail Glazer-Schotz; my parents, Harry and Ida Glazer; my sisters, Ilsa Glazer, Alyne Bat Haim, and Phyllis Glazer, and my niece,

Sigalit Bat Haim, have been consistent voices of loving encouragement. Indeed, only Alyne and Phyllis's expansive hospitality made my long and frequent stays in Israel possible. Yarden and Zohar Oron made those stays a special delight. I feel blessed *sheh kakha lo b'olamo*.

Introduction

War insinuates itself in every pore.

— Maya Bejerano, "States of War"

. . . the telling of the individual story and the
individual experience cannot but ultimately involve
the whole laborious telling of the collectivity itself.

— Fredric Jameson[1]

There goes Shmaryahu again to bring the Jews of the
world to Israel, and here comes Shmaryahu again,
still without the Jews of the world. Ada can no
longer bear the awfulness of hope.

— Shulamith Hareven, "Two Hours on the Road"

The idea of producing a new collection of fiction and poetry in translation that would articulate the end-of-the century literary sensibility of Israeli women writers was kindled in my conversations with writers during the tumultuous month of July 1992. Thanks to both the Jerusalem Foundation and my own University, I was spending that summer as a visiting scholar in the evocative setting of Jerusalem's *Mishkenot*

---

1. In "Third World Literature in the Era of Multinational Capitalism," quoted by Homi K. Bhabha, "DissemiNation: Time, narrative, and the margins of the modern nation," *Nation and Narration*, ed. Homi K. Bhabha (London: Routledge, 1990), p. 292.

1

Sha'ananim—the "Tranquil Dwellings" near the old windmill of Yemin Moshe, in what before the Six Day War of 1967 had been an impoverished neighborhood of nineteenth-century stone houses on the edge of the Jordanian border. As we talked of the active engagement today of Israeli women writers with the profoundly changed Israeli cultural scene, outside my room, in the distance, was the parched Judean wilderness veiled by its perennial haze; the room itself faced Mount Zion, traditionally the site at once of King David's tomb, the hall of the Last Supper, and the spot in which *Dormition Sanctae Mariae*: the Virgin Mary fell into eternal sleep.

But for a host of reasons this backgrounding of our conversation by the aura of hushed eternality at *Mishkenot Sha'ananim* was anomalous amidst the rest of Israel. For one, the country was bursting with noisy creative exuberance from the Galilee to the Negev. Two hundred thousand people flocked to the small town of Karmiel, near Haifa, for a Dance Festival. Another one hundred thousand—among them Lubavicher Hasidim driving "Mitzvah Tanks," teenage soldiers with Uzis, and Ethiopian Jews who set up booths to braid hair into corn-rows—were attending the Music Festival in the southern desert town of Arad. Thousands more from all over the world were participating in the international film festival in Jerusalem. The festivals, too, though, seemed anomalous, for that same month had witnessed a major political upheaval. The Likud government of Yitzhak Shamir had been overthrown and, in what seemed then to herald a significant reversal in Israeli politics, Labor had returned to power. In an odd concatenation of contexts, in his opening speech to the *Knesset*, the Parliament, on July 13, newly elected Prime Minister Yitzhak Rabin *(z"l)* signalled a radical shift in Israel's official self-apprehension and stance toward the world by drawing on the biblically resonant words of the pre-State poet Rachel. *"A concerted, stubborn, and eternal effort of a thousand hands: Will it succeed in rolling the stone off the mouth of the well?'* The answer is within us," said Rabin, "the answer is us, ourselves":

> No longer are we "a people who dwells alone," and no longer
> it is true that "the whole world is against us." We must over-
> come the sense of isolation that has held us in its thrall for
> almost half a century.

And even as the country was sorely split between those who celebrated, and those who bitterly bewailed, Labor's victory, just over the

"Green Line" the fifty-sixth month of the Palestinian uprising, the *Intifada*, was raging. That July, in Gaza, Bethlehem, Hebron, and in villages and refugee camps throughout the West Bank, there were molotov cocktails, tear gas and rubber bullets, full curfews and partial curfews, closures, arrests, barrages of stones, injuries, raids, deaths. By the fifty-sixth month of the *Intifada*, more than one thousand Palestinians had already been killed.

"Oh the miraculous holy land/ Oh the land of hardship, of gallows," writes the poet Maya Bejerano in her "Hymns of Job." For the kind of wrenching and conflictual disparities so inescapably vivid that summer were no aberrations for Israel. From its earliest days to the moment of this very writing today, the country has been a bevy of contradictions, controversies, paradoxes. Disjunctions and disparities have flowed through the nation's arteries; they seem to exist in its very heart. A former military hero tries to inspire a revisioning of his country's self-perception by drawing on words of a woman poet who for decades had been depicted by (mostly male) critics as producing only "personal lyrics"—and is assassinated moments after publicly singing, for the first time in his life, a song celebrating peace. "Operation Solomon" heroically rescues thousands of Ethiopian Jews from starvation, suffering, and discrimination, only to have hundreds discover, upon their arrival in Israel, that hegemonic religious authorities are unwilling to consider them "Jews." Jerusalem *shel l'matah*, Jerusalem of the earth, is simultaneously the site of a serene transtemporal spirituality, bitter intra- and inter-religious squabbles, displaced neighborhoods, and violently contested heaps of stones: a capital city self-enclosed in its own volatile subcultures remote from the tenors of Haifa, Tel Aviv, or Beersheva, and all four from those of the villages in the Galilee, the scattered agricultural settlements, or the dusty forlorn towns of the Negev.

One of the most multilingual and culturally hetereogeneous countries in the world, Israel, in the words of one observer, defies all "standard categorizations." It is at once "First World" in its dominant ideologies and economic ranking and "Third World" in the preponderance of its peoples' ethnicities; it partakes at one and the same time of the "East" and the "West."[2] A Mediterranean country the size of Rhode

---

2. See the cogent analysis of Ella Shohat, "Antinomies of Exile: Said at the Frontier of National Narrations," in Michael Sprinker, ed. *Edward Said: A Critical Reader* (Oxford: Blackwell, 1992), pp. 124–125.

Island, with a population smaller than that of Los Angeles County, that repeatedly garners world headlines; a vividly robust country of artistic sophistication, technological brilliance, and military might; of serious poverty and great wealth; spiritual questing, fierce secularism, alongside religious and political fanaticisms; brutality; ethnic, religious, and racial discrimination; suicide bombs; despair, closures, arrests. And alongside its immense vitality, deaths, constantly—in too many and too frequent traffic accidents, in "exchanges" on the Lebanese border, in bus explosions, and in suicide bombings in the open air market and shopping promenade in downtown Jerusalem, in a major mall and popular cafe in Tel Aviv. *War insinuates itself in every pore,* wrote Maya Bejerano, as Israelis huddled behind gas masks and, unimpeded by "secure borders," Iraqi missiles exploded on the city streets. In Israel, even the century one lives in is slippery: though for most of its population that summer was "July 1992" on the calendar, for thousands of the country's devout inhabitants it was existentially and actually either the Hebrew month of Tammuz in the year 5752, or the Muslim Moharram, 1413.

For some time now, postmodern theorists have taught us to be wary of structuring differences in terms of binary oppositions, and to become aware both of what such constructions mask as well as what they reveal. They have shown us that to construct a binary is to occlude the complex diversities, the multifoliate meanings, the hetereogeneities within each term. As critics have come to see, binaries veil distinctions even as they claim to be identifying them and create discursive oppositions where instead there are striking if uneasy and unacknowledged similarities. In this sense, Israel is a quintessentially appropriate cultural landscape for a postmodernist to unravel, for it is so profoundly and pervasively a site where imagined binaries implode and conflictual diversities are the order—and disorder—of the day. Such diversities have always been the pulsebeat of Israel, but whereas once they were muffled, today they are inescapable.

To grasp the change between the Israel that once was and the Israel that is today, dissolve, for a moment, to a scene in Talbieh, Jerusalem, where I was living in the 1970s. Growing restless watching the 8:00 news on my black-and-white TV, I stepped out onto my living room balcony and looked across the street at the balconies of my neighbors. Everyone beneath their vine and fig tree: seen through the open shutters of *their* living rooms, all my neighbors (Ashkenazim, Sephardim, ex-Palmach heroes, Holocaust survivors, "secularists," or "religious") were glued to the same news program on the sole and state-sponsored channel of their identically placed TVs.

How considerably less uniform and more untidy the media landscape is today. A hotly debated commercial Channel Two was established in the 1990s, and Israeli homes opened to cable and the international STAR TV. On its own, of course, this new flood of programming from Turkey, Morocco, Russia, and western Europe—the soap operas from Spain, films from Egypt, Jerry Seinfeld, and CNN—did not erode the imagined cohesion of Israeli culture, nor was that culture ever really cohesive. But the medium is the message. So long as only a single state-sponsored if officially "independent" channel was all that was available on Israeli television (unless one was among the fortunate few whose receiver occasionally picked up Amman), night after night the illusion was quietly reinforced that Israelis were a people sealed off from the rest of the world: a people, as some ideologues insisted, stubbornly and dourly fated to "dwell alone." Watching the same lone broadcasts at the same moment, the television viewers of the country could suspend their workaday awareness of the quarrelsome diversity of their own social, cultural, religious, and political affiliations and imagine themselves instead a homogeneous society, a virtually real "us." With the news delivered nightly by a suited-and-tied Ashkenazi male with an air of authority and no *kippah*—a signal that he was not a religiously observant Jew—the television audience was beckoned to identify with a national vision that was likewise male-centered, secular, Ashkenazi, and clothed, like the newscaster himself, in the costume of the "West." That vision also served as the gauge for identifying the errancy of any dissenting eye, occluding any differently constituted collective, whether Levantine, female, religious, or Arab.

The once-dominant and media-reinforced "virtually real" experience of unity had significant implications for the reception of writers and works who did not share it. Thus, for example, as Ammiel Alcalay has brilliantly demonstrated, in the process of Israeli cultural formation, the experience and narratives of Sephardic, Levantine, Arab, and Persian Jews, as well as that of Christian or Muslim Arab-Israelis, were eliminated from consideration as participant voices in the "collective."[3] And so, in general, were women's. In a series of articles published in the Hebrew literary journal *Moznayim* in 1989, for example, writer Amalia Kahana-Carmon addressed the refusal to hear the voices of women within the

---

3. Ammiel Alcalay, *After Jews and Arabs: Remaking Levantine Culture* (Minneapolis: University of Minnesota Press, 1993). See especially chapter four, pp. 220–284.

"collective" on the Israeli literary scene, suggesting that that refusal was a legacy of Jewish religious tradition. Jewish prayer stresses the welfare and destiny of *ahm yisrael*, the nation and people of Israel, rather than the singular "I"; but in Orthodox synagogues, men alone are seated in the central arena and bidden to pray aloud as the voice of the people. Consigned to a separate gallery, women pray only *sotto voce*. In such synagogues, then, says Kahana-Carmon:

> Someone else, acting in the name of all Israel, speaks also on [women's] behalf. And so, anything that is likely to happen to the woman seated in the women's gallery will be defined ahead of time as peripheral, a hindrance, and a deviant incident. Likewise, it will not be a regular part of the shared course of events; it will be subordinate to the main events conducted in the central arena. . . .

Though modern Hebrew literature has been primarily secular, it has become for both the writer and the reading public a similarly constructed "national synagogue of the mind":

> In fact, for [secularists] there may be no other synagogue today. [No matter who the protagonist is in a literary work by an Israeli male, his] story will be an expression of the collective situation, of the average Israeli in light of past tradition, and so of general interest. As for the female, if she does not act the role of his partner but is a character in her own right, her tale will always be the "true life story" of a woman and her destiny, and the attitude of readers will be: come let us see if she knows how to write a story. . . .[4]

This exclusion of women's experience from notions of the "collective" was also noted in a different vein at the end of the 1980s by scholar Esther Fuchs. Mapping the evolution of Israeli literary criticism, Fuchs pointed out that only in the previous decade, and possibly as a result of the debacle of the Yom Kippur War (1973), did critics' "fastidious insis-

---

4. Published in English as "The Song of the Bats in Flight," in *Gender and Text in Modern Hebrew and Yiddish Literature,* eds. Naomi B. Sokoloff, Anne Lapidus Lerner, and Anita Norich (New York: Jewish Theological Seminary, 1992), pp. 237–240.

tence on separating politics from poetics" begin to give way to a "new recognition of the inseparability of life and art." Even so, their perspective remained entirely male-centered:

> "Experience" in the new theories means male experience, "politics" refers to the procedures of male ruled governments and male dominated parties. A quick glance at recent theories about contemporary Israeli fiction reveals that most of them tend to marginalize or altogether ignore female experience and female writing.[5]

But just as black-and-white images and a single channel have given way to full-living-color and the choice of programming from all over the world, so in today's Israel the illusion has dissolved that only one kind of voice—secular, Ashkenazi, male (and middle-class)—can render into words the pulsebeat of the nation. In that sense, Rabin's 1992 call to the nation to overcome the "sense of isolation that has held us in thrall," was actually a translation into political terms of what was already happening both technologically and culturally, as images from all over the world were being telecast daily into my once-neighbors' homes. With a population freely switching channels among a multiplicity of electronically transmitted alternative narratives, the past illusion of a collectively unifiable

---

5. In *Israeli Mythogynies: Women in Contemporary Hebrew Fiction* (Albany: State University of New York Press, 1987), p. 3. Fuchs's book is a cogent analysis of the masculinist biases of both Israeli fiction and the criticism of modern Hebrew literature. See also Yael Feldman, "Gender/Indifference in Contemporary Hebrew Fictional Autobiography," *Biography: An Interdisciplinary Quarterly* 11, 3:189–209.

As Michael Gluzman has amply demonstrated, as late as 1990 the marginalization by many critics of women's poetry in Israel, and their relegation to "silence and invisibility," were reflected in critical descriptions of the development of Hebrew poetic modernism, which fail to consider the contributions of the early poets Rachel, Esther Raab, Yocheved Bat Miriam, and Leah Goldberg. See Michael Gluzman, "The Exclusion of Women from Hebrew Literary History," *Prooftexts* 11 (1991): 259–278.

The marginalization of women poets as *women* poets could become almost parodic. After the death of Yona Volach, one of Israel's more avant garde poets David Avidan opposed the assessments of Volach as one of the greatest Hebrew poets of the century, arguing that as a *woman* poet she was on a separate "woman's track" on which there was little competition because of the dearth of women's poetry. For a discussion of her response to Avidan and his subsequent reaction, see Fuchs, pp. 7–8. Having lived in poverty for many years, Avidan himself died in desperate circumstances in 1994, provoking national discussion about government support for writers.

sensibility has faded, and the often cacophonous differences of ideology, ethnicity, gender, religious stance, and class, exposed. That exposure has intensified the destabilizing rumpus that is Israeli politics. But it has also meant an exciting new polyphony in Israeli literature, inspiring a more insistent challenging of what Alcalay has called "the covenant of consensus represented by officialdom's sanctioned versions of the past" (p. 231). If, as Hebrew University sociologist Erik Cohen has argued, the Six Day War of 1967, in which all of Western Mandatory Palestine came under Israeli control, paradoxically initiated the conditions "for an existential and ideological crisis in Israeli society,"[6] in the twenty-first century, Israel has tumbled head-first into a postmodern and post-Zionist age.

As an anthologist of Israeli women's literature born and raised in America, centered in both Israeli and Jewish American culture and women's literature for the last two decades, who also—thanks to long residence in Israel—holds the passports of both countries and journeys often between them, I feel like a nomad. To prepare this anthology has meant becoming a "Hebrew" in its originary meaning of *ivriya*, a boundary crosser, laying out the wares I've carried from one of my worlds before another, aware of the myriad ways those wares can be ordered in their new American context—and at the same time of how their valence has altered now that they are rent from their Israeli cultural matrix and their own discursive world. More than their valence: for the wares, of course, are words. Shaped into stories and poems, those words have undergone what translation theorists Jose Lambert and Clem Robyns have called a "migration-through-transformation," for literary translation involves a recontextualization to suit a different linguistic and cultural code.[7] But the reverse, a "transformation through migration," has also occurred, for translated, edited, organized, and published in an American anthology, the works are cast in a new light and themselves seem to change. That is partly because written at different times and by different authors, the stories and poems that comprise the body of *Dreaming the Actual* (like any anthology of literature) are now relocated in apposition with one another, situated where they never intended to be. They are like a group of expatriates from the cities, towns, and villages of one

---

6. "Israel as a Post-Zionist Society," in *The Shaping of Israeli Identity: Myth, Memory, and Trauma*, eds. Robert Wistrich and David Ohana (London: Frank Cass, 1995), pp. 203, 208.

7. See Edwin Gentzler, *Contemporary Translation Theories* (London: Routledge, 1993), p. 186.

country, belonging to different social classes and ethnic groups, who now discover themselves dwelling together in the same neighborhood in a foreign land. As diverse as they seemed to be back in their homeland, they realize now that compared to the locals, they have more in common with one another than they would ever have imagined if they had never left home.

An expatriate community does not "represent" its members' native land—nor should *Dreaming the Actual* be seen as "representing" contemporary Israeli women's literature. Rather, by its very nature, the anthology constitutes that literature differently, offers it anew. It seeks to offer short stories and poems that in their original are both beautifully written and revelatory: significant in themselves and in the role each plays in each author's work, as well as in the compelling, illuminating, thought-provoking, and even disorienting vision that they can convey to English-language readers. For my intention in compiling this collection has been more than to expose English-language readers to recent literature by Israeli women writers. As an inveterate boundary crosser myself, what has interested me is the kindling of an intricately nuanced conversation between the two cultures in both of which, in such different ways, I, too, belong. Ideally, that conversation will inspire readers in the States to reflect back upon American culture even as they more deeply apprehend Israeli. For at their best, translations of powerful literary works can stretch the boundaries of one's own cultural and aesthetic assumptions, one's own linguistic associations, in the process of pondering the seemingly strange, even occasionally awkward, twists and turns the works-in-translation have required of one's language. To read a literary translation can mean awakening to the richness of English and the possibilities of one's own life in a new way.

In any anthology, the order in which the literary works are offered is also as vital a player as the works themselves. *How* literary works are set in the new neighborhood of an anthology colors both the way they are seen as well as, potentially, the perspectives of the seers. For example, literary anthologies often arrange the works they include in the order in which those works were originally published, in the order in which the writers were born, or perhaps in alphabetical order, according to author; quainter anthologies rather tendentiously order them according to "theme." Though we often assume that such chronological or alphabetical arrangements are simply "objective," ideologically neutral, in reality they are not so at all. Structuring the ways in which we view, "place," and comprehend individual works and discern their web of connectedness with one another, such arrangements have hermeneutic implications; that is, they influence how we interpret what we have read. In certain ways, too, a chronological arrangement according to the authors' dates of birth or the works' date of publication alone ducks the problem of interpretation. For such an arrangement can serve as a kind of refuge. Erecting a framework exterior to and independent of the content of the works, a chronological arrangement creates and shelters an often unadmitted narrative of its own. It is as if there were an absentee landlord other than the anthologist who, having predetermined where all the residents should live, moved away, taking no responsibility for the relationships that ensue.

Still, there is a kind of chronological order unfolding in *Dreaming the Actual*. For though most of the literary works here were written in the 1990s, many of them reach beyond their era. Their settings range from ancient times to the present moment, engaging the conflicts of contemporary life even as they wrestle with the burdens of history. The difference is that, just as the opening story, Nurit Zarchi's "And She Is Joseph," responds to traditional midrashic commentaries by spotlighting issues of gender and imagining the biblical Joseph as a woman, so in *Dreaming the Actual* as a whole the literary imagination of women writers is gathered together in the "central arena" instead of occupying the peripheral "gallery." As the stories and poems travel the spectrum of twentieth-century history, they inscribe and portray the many perspectives of women: poor, working-class, affluent; religiously observant and thoroughly secular; living in sophisticated city centers, crowded slums, small towns, or rural villages. The voices heard in this book are those of schoolgirls, young women on the verge of puberty, adolescents, twenty- or thirty-somethings, the middle-aged, and old. And their countries of origin, reflecting those of the writers themselves, cross the too often embedded and volatile Ashkenazi-Sephardic divide, ranging from North Africa, Poland, Hungary, Russia, Germany, English-speaking countries, and the Levant, to Palestine/Israel itself.

Because the stories have been organized to the extent possible in the *chronological order of the era in which they are set*, to read through the first section of book is like embarking on a journey through Israeli history, from the Bible to pre-State Palestine, the days of the British Mandate, the early years of the State, the post-Six-Day-War and then much more troubled post-Yom-Kippur-War period, to the still more radically different contemporary moment. With the poetry following as a kind of polyphonic accompaniment, it is a journey that lingers in corners and on paths often overlooked by the more generally familiar Israeli story. For, gathered together, juxtaposed with one another, and seen in one another's light, the literary works of Israeli women writers vividly articulate "the Other Side of the Story,"[8] a multivoiced "alternarrative" to the once male-dominated Israeli narrative. *There are as many faiths as there are people*, says poet Maya Bejerano. Richly varied in tone, content, and style, the alternarrative by women writers voices both a highly charged and newly constituted collective story.

Like the literature by women of many countries, the works here portray the travails of young women's coming-of-age, the unease of sexuality, the complexities of consciousness, the webs of connectedness between people, spiritual conflict, the deprivations of poverty, the anxieties of memory, the pain of loss, the enmeshments of family, the intimacies of marriage, as well as creative triumph, and, ultimately, the power and challenges of writing itself. One source of the uniqueness of the alternarrative of Israeli women writers lies in the specific ways these portrayals are wrought. But another source of uniqueness lies in the manner in which the writers probe the singular reality of Israel itself, the "story behind the story" of Israeli ideologies, Jewish religious beliefs, public political dramas, and collective traumas. Over and over again, sometimes overtly, sometimes more subtly, the writers explore the resonance for women's and men's lives of the country's profoundly rooted self-image as the Jewish homeland. At the heart of many of the works, too, is a troubled exploration of the aesthetic, emotional, and spiritual consequences of living generation after generation, and year after year, within the shadows cast by war. And, finally, whether or not they are religiously observant in their personal lives, living in a *Jewish* state and writing in a multilayered, allusive, Hebrew, many of the writers draw upon the deep well of the traditions, theologies, and ancient texts of Judaism to enrich their work.

That so many of the stories and poems are entwined in the drama of Israel as "homeland" should come as no surprise. Since its formal establishment in the late nineteenth century, one of the most passionate obsessions and values of the Zionist movement, and therefore, subsequently, of the State, has been putting an end to the ancient exile of the

---

8. I am indebted here to the insights of Molly Hite in *The Other Side of the Story: Structures and Strategies of Contemporary Feminist Narratives* (Ithaca: Cornell University Press, 1989). My departure from Hite's work lies in the importance I see in acknowledging that while Israeli women writers are presenting the "Other's" side of the collective story, there is no unanimity in the versions of "the story" that they tell. There is no *single* "Other side." Rather, the *diversity* of these "Othered" voices is one of its most salient features.

Jewish people in the global diaspora and launching their ingathering and
return to their destined "home." More so perhaps than any other coun-
try, Israel since 1948 therefore has been and is a nation of immigrants.
The very language embeds the value of immigration: a Jew immigrating
to Israel makes "an ascent" *(aliyah);* one who leaves the country was (at
least until the less passionately Zionist present) pejoratively called a
"descender" *(yored, yoredet).*

But the women writers trouble these traditional notions of the Zi-
onist cause. In their narrative reconstructions of the lives of women, the
writers force us to grapple with the gendered differences experienced
both in "exile" and "at home." From Israeli-born Nurit Zarchi's story
"Madame Bovary in Neve Tsedek," based on the life of the pre-State
writer Devora Baron, to the stories set in contemporary Israel by recent
Russian immigrants Dina Rubin and Elena Makarova, the narrative gaze
focuses on the wrenching emotional, cultural, social, and aesthetic dis-
placements that the "return" to the "homeland" has also meant. Simi-
larly, but from a different perspective, Shulamith Hareven's "Two Hours
on the Road" suggests that the national obsession with immigration has
been lived very differently by Israeli men and women. While the husband
of the story has long been a Zionist emissary charged with bringing "the
Jews of the world to Israel," only to return home, trip after trip, "still
without the Jews of the world," the wife has been leading her own life
at home and has grown more accustomed to his absence than his pres-
ence. Indeed, the story hints of the fruitlessness of imagining that the
Jews of the world will *ever* come to Israel. In the process, it provokes the
disturbing question whether the most significant consequence of main-
taining that fantasy isn't in its providing a rationalization for the failures
in intimacy for public men.

The power of retelling Israel's story through the perspective of women
is also evident in the many ways in which the writers portray living with
war: World War II and the still palpable emotional devastation of the
Shoah, the 1948 Independence War, the 1956 Sinai War, the Six Day War
of 1967, the 1973 Yom Kippur War, the Lebanon War, the *Intifada.*
"Most of my childhood was spent in the shadow of war," says writer
Esther Ettinger, in words that echo the experience of thousands of oth-
ers. "My parents named me 'Esther' after my late grandmother, not
knowing if anyone else in my family was alive or dead." The legacy of
the *Shoah* lurks in many of these works, haunting one generation after
another. In Nava Semel's "Hunger," for example, that legacy is passed
from an aged mother to her adult daughter through the obsessive stock-
piling of food. In Leah Aini's poem "Shower," even the simple act of

combing one's hair conjures up images of a grandmother whom the Nazis gassed to death. In Aini's story "Rest," the ghosts of the *Shoah* pierce the air as a woman survivor screams in the night. In Esther Ettinger's poetry, they appear between the lines of old manuscripts. In Yehudit Katzir's powerfully evocative "Schlaffstunde," images of Anne Frank and her attic, and of Adolf Hitler, flow through a young woman's remembrance of the erotically charged games she played as a girl, almost three decades after the end of World War II.

In the poems and stories of Israel's women writers, the anguish of the country's recent wars also enacts itself: not on battlefields, but deep in the psyche. That anguish beats like a ceaseless drum in "Apples in Honey," which takes place in a dream-like military cemetery where year after year a widow returns to mourn the loss of her eternally young husband. It is felt on city streets, as a lone woman obsesses over buying a walkie-talkie. It is in a son's bedroom, empty because he will never come home; in an apartment where a mother tapes the windows in case of bombings; in a woman photographer's secret crossing of a forbidden border to face the death of her country's "enemy," a woman who was the photographer's friend. As the writers reveal, war is not an "event" that has closure; it is lodged in the soul and in the abyss of the psyche. It seeps into the most intimate moments of sexuality. It permanently scars the heart.

Finally, for those who write in Hebrew, the language has to be purposively "thin" *not* to at all resonate with Judaic history; echoes from the Bible, the Talmud, the Midrash, and the liturgy thus also suffuse many of these works. But in the alter/narrative of *Dreaming the Actual*, allusions to traditional religious texts metamorphosize into a language that *"women who live in this land know but men born here do not speak,"* in the words of poet Chava Pinchas-Cohen. Judaism comes alive in these texts in profoundly female ways: through the awakening of spiritual vision between mother and daughter; through women's celebration of the Sabbath; in the act of giving birth. Drawing on the book of Job, Maya Bejerano envisions harsh angels as a harassed mother awakens and feeds her children in super charged Tel Aviv. The experience of the covenant at Sinai is seen through the eyes of a woman hanging out the family laundry. Spiritual vision arises as a young woman witnesses an aged one feeling desperately useless, and as poets and authors describe mourning the dead or facing the violence of the *Intifada*.

In radically diverse ways as well, the writers fasten on the relationship of Judaism to female sexuality. The late iconoclastic and often gender-bending poet Yona Volach erotically challenges the presumed remote, masculine, power of the Jewish God. In "Tefillin," for example, Volach conflates the (traditionally exclusively male) ritual of "binding oneself" tightly to God through the wearing of black leather phylacteries with a violent, sadistic\masochistic sexuality. In Ruth Almog's complexly textured "Invisible Mending," the artistic consciousness of a young girl on the verge of puberty is forced to angrily engrave the words of the prophet Jeremiah even as she wrestles with her own father's death. Mira Magen's "Gerbera Daisies at Half Price," a far different story, compares the paradoxical differences in the ways women experience their body in the sophisticated urban secular world, on the one hand, and the more crowded, more claustrophobic, religiously Orthodox one, on the other. If Jewish tradition is central to many of these stories and inscribed in the very language of the poetry, it is a Judaism infused with engendered experience, with the spiritual, emotional, and sexual sensibilities of women.

Clearly, as their stories and poems draw on and portray Jewish tradition and their country's past, Israeli women writers are writing women's experience in, revising and revisioning the national understanding of the *collective* story. Yet while many commentators on the Israeli scene readily concede that the old "covenant of consensus" has been lost, they often also fail to see that these newer works have generated new interpretations of shared national experience, a different sense of "nation." Instead, the new abundance of women writers has been interpreted as evidence of the culture's "openness" to the "personal," as if, despite the subject matter of their work, women writers still cannot be considered contributing voices in what Kahana-Carmon called "the national synagogue of the mind." But just as the pre-State poet Rachel, so long regarded as writing only personal lyrics, was recognized by the late Prime Minister Rabin as eloquently articulating an urgent national imperative, so the voices of Israel's women writers should be heard today as both dismantling the illusory opposition between "personal" and "collective" entirely and, crucially, speaking to the fallacy of the opposition to begin with. The more the alter/narrative of this collection unfolds, the more evident it becomes that in contemporary Israel any notion of a "secure border" between individual selves and society is a chimera. The stories and poems reveal that all aspects of collective life—whether historical, social, cultural, political, or religious—permeate even the most intimate, most minute, corners of the private self: one's sexuality, memories, capacity to love, one's dreams. In American culture, where the value of the "personal" has so long taken precedence over acknowledgment of the intimate impact of the collective, what Israel's women writers most eloquently and insistently ask us to do as readers is to reconsider how we all perceive the contours and contents of our own lives.

Part I

Short Stories

Introduction to Nurit Zarchi's "And She Is Joseph"

A poet and much-heralded author of more than forty children's books for which she has won Israel's most prestigious awards, Nurit Zarchi published *The Mask Maker,* her first collection of stories for adults, in 1993. Many of the stories in the collection involve disguises, metamorphoses, and changing sexual identities and draw on a rich well of spiritual, religious, mythological, and narrative lore. "And She Is Joseph," centered on the evocative character of the biblical Joseph, is among them.

According to ancient commentators and spinners of midrash, Joseph, son of Jacob and his beloved wife Rachel, was a "paragon of beauty" who "dressed his hair" and "touched up his eyes so that he would appear good-looking."[9] "Now Israel [Jacob] loved Joseph more than all his children because he was the son of his old age," says the Bible, "and he made him a coat of many colors" (Gen. 37:3). Joseph is a dreamer, hated by his brothers not only for their father's favoritism toward him but also for telling them his dreams—among them that "the sun and moon and the eleven stars made obeisance" to him (Gen. 37:9). Seizing an opportunity,

---

9. See, for example, the commentary of the medieval Rashi [Rabbi Solomon ben Isaac], 1040–1105, in *Chumash with Targum Onkelos, Haphtaroth and Rashi's Commentary*, ed. Rabbi A.M. Silbermann. Trans. Rabbi A. M. Silbermann and Rev. M. Rosenbaum. Vol. I. Bereshith [Genesis] (Jerusalem: Silbermann Family, 1934), p. 180.

they cast him into a pit and sell him for "twenty pieces of silver" to passing Ishmaelites who in turn take him to Egypt and sell him to Potiphar, an officer of Pharoah. Joseph refuses the advances of Potiphar's wife and is consequently betrayed by her and cast into prison. Only his gift for dream interpretation saves him; his former cell-mate, the chief butler, remembers the young Hebrew when Pharoah finds himself now troubled by indecipherable dreams. Only years later and after much suffering are Joseph and his brothers reconciled. For the moving scene to which Zarchi alludes at the end of her story, in which Joseph cries out, "Cause every man to go out from me," see Genesis 45:1. For a fuller sense of the sources from which Zarchi weaves her own gender-bending midrash, readers might want to consult all of Genesis 37 and 39–48.

"Most people associate fantasy with things that are impossible: people who fly, seas that talk, trees that walk," Zarchi has written. But in literature, she goes on, the use of fantasy is a way of conveying an otherwise elusive reality: fantasy, writes Zarchi, "tries to achieve in prose what metaphor does in poetry."[10]

Nurit Zarchi was born in Jerusalem in 1941 and grew up on Kibbutz Geva. She lives in Tel Aviv.

---

10. In "Three Impossible Things Before Breakfast," *Modern Hebrew Literature* 16 (Spring/Summer 1996): pp. 7–9.

And She Is Joseph

Nurit Zarchi

A man stands and peeps inside; through the opening he sees something strange: his wife is combing his son's long hair. She gathers it up and braids it, then she quickly stuffs the braids underneath the cap covering his head.

But the son isn't his son.

The man closes his eyes and opens them again: it's night, the darkness is blue, the breathing of the bulls is audible in the dark, a donkey brays with a dry, sawing sound, the hanging gourds knock into each other in the wind with a hollow noise.

No, it's not a mirage. This son, the son born to his wife in his old age, is a girl.

The man isn't angry, he knows that his wife did this out of her love for him, she wanted to please him, she wanted to believe that he had an heir.

For many years his wife was unable to bear him a son. Again and again she consulted doctors, witches, and soothsayers, and in the end, when she gave birth, she tricked him and pretended that the baby was a boy.

Now he understands why she had insisted on giving the child a name from the word which means "to add"; in other words, something which bears the seed of something else inside it, and signifies neither male nor female but both.

19

The man bends a little so they won't see him. He goes on watching.

Now, in the light of the lamp which the mother lights, the little girl looks just like a boy. He doesn't know what she sees in the light of the flame. From where he is standing, his wife's lips seem to be moving. He hears only an unintelligible murmur, and sees her face close to her daughter's face, concentrated and clouded. Is it so hard, the sight she sees before her in the flame?

Like many other men, he has never believed in magic, and he had forbidden his wife to practice it, and so she has been doing it in secret and teaching her daughter everything her father had strictly forbidden her to know.

Before they were banished from the Garden of Eden, Adam and Eve had not known themselves as male and female. Learning this was part of their punishment.

The man turns, his shoulders bowed, and walks away. He would never tell his wife that he had discovered her secret, because his soul was bound to hers, and because she was about to die, a death which ended the life of a woman who obtained her wish too late in life and at a cost greater than life.

And the coat: a person never sees himself as anything but himself, neither male nor female, both male and female, and which you are is decided only between you and the person facing you. But how can so vital a fact be decided by the eyes of the beholder?

Her father watches her anxiously, he keeps her secret like a vow, and does not reveal what he knows even to her. A lie within a lie. In their father's tents her brothers walk around too, all those sons born to other mothers, and they watch Joseph from a distance with a curiosity in which hatred mingles with fear, like chickens watching each other to pounce and peck until they draw blood.

How strange he is. They do not know the secret and will never discover it, even though it is so close and almost exposed to view.

The air jumps, the air dances, as it does early in the morning when it is still too opaque to define the points of the spires and the domes of the roofs, and it moves and shifts as if all possibilities are emerging to greet the eye of the beholder, for everyone knows that the sun is a masculine sign whereas the moon—the moon is female, and at night she draws the surface of the sea toward her and the plants and seeds sprout out of the earth to reach her. They all want to come close to the moon, for she is the midwife, while the power of the sun is direct and naked and lies within the world itself.

In the heart of the swept courtyard of the compound, Joseph stands pale-faced and tells her dream to her brothers sitting flushed around the campfire: the sun and the moon bowed down to me, she says, and thus she reveals to them the secret hieroglyphics of sleep. The brothers laugh but their faces are angry. Their father listens anxiously. Once more he realizes what he has long known: people always hear a story as if it is about them, whereas in truth the dreamer dreams only of himself.

The brothers sit around the campfire in silence. The night is soft and dark, and sparks explode and fly up towards the stars.

"What is this dream?" they demand resentfully.

Joseph stands a step away from the fire, her figure still shrouded in darkness. Only her white face, her forehead round as the dome of a synagogue, is revealed, as if the flames bursting out of the fire have peeled away its darkness. How can she answer without falling into a trap? Whatever she says they won't believe that she doesn't feel superior to them, not even by a single sheaf of wheat. Joseph doesn't know if her secret is an advantage or a disadvantage, and so she keeps it to herself and does not risk revealing it, for if she were loved for what she was, she would not have to walk about disguised as somebody else.

None of the brothers takes the trouble to make room for her around the fire. And so she sits down behind the back of one of them, hugging her kid with the little bell around its neck, who follows her wherever she goes.

The brothers go on talking as if she isn't there. But when they have nothing left to talk about, they remember her, and say, "And what about that dream you didn't want to tell us about before?"

Joseph loved her dreams, which were both clear and strange and which surprised her too by showing her what lay deep within her.

The moon and the stars—but of course they weren't the moon and the stars, because the dreamer never destroys the darkness under his closed lids in order to see the world as it is.

She finishes telling her dream, and silence falls. The fire smolders, a lamb bleats nearby. But what is that other sound, a sound which comes closer all the time, filling them with dread?

"I'll go and see where it's coming from," said the oldest brother and he slipped away from the bright circle of darkness.

And so the deed was done. A moment later, when the eldest brother returned, they couldn't tell him how it had happened. One of them said contemptuously: "That dreamer"—and they couldn't remember who he was.

"Let's take his kid and roast it on the fire."

"No!" shrieked Joseph and clasped the kid to her with all her strength. The brothers ran after her and she ran round the fire with the kid in her arms—the heat was so close it almost charred her eyebrows. "All right," said the brothers, "if he loves this animal so much, we don't have to roast it, we can have a little fun with it instead," and one of them dragged the kid roughly out of her arms. The kid fled for its life and the brother ran after it in the dark of the field, caught it, and threw it to his brothers.

"Stop it! Stop it!" Joseph screamed and ran. Many years later it occurred to her that perhaps it was all her fault; if she hadn't fallen into that pit they would never have dreamed of casting her into it.

So, what actually happened to that little girl?

Did her father extricate her in secret, since he had been following her all the time behind the backs of the brothers? Being a man gifted with divine insight, perhaps he guessed what human beings in their depths were capable of doing to each other—especially brothers. And perhaps after he rescued her from the pit, the father confessed to his daughter that he had always known that she was a woman, the daughter of his beloved whom she so closely resembled, and he was relieved to be able to reveal his feelings to her and love her.

As for the story of the Joseph who appeared many years later in Pharaoh's palace in Egypt—as the German novelist wrote, that was probably a political story about a very distant relative who found his way to the royal court, achieved high office there, rescued the relations of his relations, could not restrain himself when he met them again, and wept, like any man meeting kinsfolk from the land of his fathers after living for years in a foreign land.[11]

But if it was true that Joseph the girl was rescued from the pit not by her father but by Ishmaelites, and that everything really happened the way it is said to have happened, and in her wisdom she knew how to hide the fact that she was a girl, then a woman, and nobody ever found out, then we can imagine her lying on her bed, and in the nights when life came to meet her, either after the story with Potiphar's wife,[12] which is

---

11. *The German novelist:* the allusion is to Thomas Mann's four-part novel, *Joseph and His Brothers* (1943).

12. See Gen. 39: 1–8. Serving in the house of Pharoah's officer Potiphar, Joseph is seduced by Potiphar's wife, but he refuses to sleep with her.

now easy to understand, or years later when she lay in bed next to a man or a woman who had already fallen asleep at her side—sustaining her courage by reading ancient books, and preserving her secret. The secret of her double life, that existence which was wakeful sleep or sleep in wakefulness, to which she owed her ability to read the signs of what lies beyond, dream signs intended to solve the riddle of our waking lives.

In any case, in this entire story we are not afforded a single moment of relief in which Joseph reveals his secret to his readers or to anybody else. Except perhaps for the moment when he cries: "Cause every man to go out from me," and remains by himself, weeping and remembering what might have happened and did not happen. Was he a man or a woman? And the enigma for which there is no answer: was it the solution or the riddle? Which is real life? Joseph the dreamer, interpreter of dreams, did not know.

(1993)
—*Translated by Dalya Bilu*

Introduction to Nurit Zarchi's "Madame Bovary in Neve Tsedek"

Like "And She Is Joseph," "Madame Bovary in Neve Tsedek" is from Zarchi's short story collection, *The Mask Maker*. It, too, inscribes and explores the uses of fantasy in literature, and imaginatively re-engages Hebrew literary tradition, in this case, the life and work of Dvora Baron (1887–1956), the only major woman fiction writer of the pre-State years, who, in addition to writing short stories, translated Flaubert's *Madame Bovary* into Hebrew.

Some acquaintance with Baron enhances the experience of reading Zarchi's story. Baron was born in Uzda, a small Lithuanian town in the district of Minsk; the daughter of the Rabbi of Uzda, she was permitted to study the sacred texts at a time when Jewish girls were rarely educated. After her father's death, she worked as a private tutor in the houses of the wealthy. She joined Zionist circles and left for Palestine in 1911. But after Baron came to Palestine, her stories continued to be set in the cramped and oppressive Jewish world of eastern Europe. Their subjects were often the lonely, bitter, crippled lives of women, portrayed mostly as passive victims, their defeats and tragedies exacerbated by the indifferent cruelties of Jewish religious law.

Baron worked as the literary editor of the Labor Zionist newspaper *Hapoel Hatza'ir* ("The Young Worker"), and married the paper's editor, Yosef Aharonovitch, who was also a leader of the Labor Zionist movement. They had a daughter, Zipporah. When Aharonovitch resigned from the newspaper in 1922 to become director of the Bank Hapoalim

("Workers' Bank"), Baron resigned as well. But she also disappeared from the public world: from 1936 until her death twenty years later, she never left her Neve Tsedek house. For decades, critics described Baron as having had a "long and serious" but always unnamed "illness." In all likelihood, in ways reminiscent of the tragic invalidism of gifted Victorian women, what Baron suffered from was anorexia and agoraphobia. Cared for by her daughter, Baron stayed in bed, nearly starved herself, and saw only a few literary acquaintances, the situation Zarchi's story depicts.

Her contemporaries' reception of her short stories is exemplified by a letter written to her by the novelist Yosef Brenner. "It is true that your literary 'net' is spread over a limited sphere of life," wrote Brenner, "but in this limited sphere you show your own specific talent. You have a style all your own, you have your own imagery and your fine Hebrew soul. Your compassion is very delicate." In the Introduction to the 1969 English translation of Baron's collection of stories, *The Thorny Path*, one can perceive the prism of values through which Baron's work was seen. "At least on the surface," writes literary critic A. B. Yoffe, her style is "masculine in nature, but it is suffused with a sensitivity that can be felt between the lines, it is, however, a sensitivity that differs from that of other women writers because it is inspired by her very nature, the nature of a modest daughter of Israel." Elsewhere, he describes her style as "disciplined, sober and realistic, without embellishment, restrained and enclosed in a well-defined artistic frame"; perhaps, one might add, an artistic frame as "restrained and enclosed" as Baron's life itself became.[13]

Zarchi transmutes these aspects of Baron's life and work into a narrative that suggests the painful drama within Baron's own mind as she was translating Flaubert's novel into Hebrew in the context of the male-dominated ideological fervor among Labor Zionists in the pre-State days—an era, as Zarchi writes, in which "little attention was given to woman's body (or to any other part of her)." But what most characterizes the protagonist in Zarchi's story is that odd detail: her feet have "no soles." How is she ever to "plant" herself firmly on the ground of Palestine if her feet have no soles? How is she ever to feel "rooted"? Or is the *refusal* really to belong, the insistence upon never leaving her own home, crucial to the freedom of her imagination, necessary for her own creativity?

---

13. See Dvora Baron, *The Thorny Path,* ed. Itzhak Hanoch. Trans. Joseph Shachter (Jerusalem: Israel Universities Press, 1969), pp. vii, x–xii.

Particularly in light of the "rootlessness," of the sense of displacement, that reverberates through so many of the works in this collection, these questions, if unanswerable, seem central.

One final note: the neighborhood of Neve Tsedek, where the story takes place, was the first neighborhood of the new town of Tel Aviv; it was built on the shore of the Mediterranean outside of the adjacent Arab city of Jaffa.

Madame Bovary in Neve Tsedek

Nurit Zarchi

Like other eras marked by a passion for philosophizing, in the pre-State days no one gave the physical body—least of all woman's—much weight. That might be why, when the woman disembarked at Jaffa port, even the longshoremen didn't notice that below the hem of her dark dress, her legs ended in feet with no soles. This, after all, was a time for *philosophical* passion; we need to grasp the blindness in such a spirit, seeing this woman as among the species of creatures that culture implants somewhere between imagination and biology—like the Unicorn, the Virgin's Child, Mephistopheles, and the Loch Ness monster.

She was found a home on the sands of Tel Aviv. Before long she was joined by the editor of a newspaper known for its stand on social and humanitarian issues. The newspaper published her stories, which the editor found enchanting. Before he drowned (not surprisingly, given the traditions of the deep sea), his wife bore him a daughter who was ordinary in every way. No sooner was she able to stand on her own two feet than she was given the task of looking after her mother, whose only food was the seeds and grains the girl gleaned from other neighbors' gardens, or the shore. Claiming that her mother was her teacher, she never went to school.

When the father went abroad to collect contributions from diaspora Jews for the Building of the Land, mother and daughter stayed behind in their wooden house on the beach, where they lived as if on an island of their own. No one came by or came in, except for the authors and poets who wrote for the newspaper and were used to congregating in their house once a week. Like hummingbees circling a flower, they would surround the woman as she lay like a vision in her bed, all covered-up and thin as a black wasp, her hair pulled back to expose her sallow heart-shaped face, the white collar of her dress accentuating the black fire in her eyes that blazed with either malice or melancholy. The girl, too, fluttered around like a dark butterfly with a wounded wing, pouring tea for the guests in tin cups. They were all men—except for one English-woman who had had a complicated love affair with the man who brought her to the country and then abandoned her. She hadn't returned to her own country, to her parents' house, either because she was too proud or for some other reason.

It was too dark for the guests to make out the sea beyond the window. But the clamor of the waves echoed in the house, now rising, now falling, as if the little house itself were a shell or an ear, as if the din of the ocean had forced its way in to mask secrets or to make revelations, beyond reason.

In the midst of this the visitors chatted about Hebrew Literature and the unique destiny it was to fulfill in the renewal of the land. Lisbeth, the English poet whom the *yishuv*[14] called Elisheva,[15] tried to outtalk the noise of the sea and the voices of the men. She said that Literature needs fictions of its own—the truths of poetry might not be truth in the real world at all. Poetry was an attempt to capture the flow of nothingness, the abyss that everything hovers over, the void in the very bowels of words: existence as it was before the First Day. The men around the bed vigorously protested. It's blasphemy to conceive of poetry as merely a sort of hovering over emptiness, they retorted. For here we are now, in the midst of the Real, bidden to strengthen it, to forge a new literature and a new world, to replace the old empty individualism. And why? To create the New Man! What is literature after all, if not a mirror in which man as he once was can see himself revealed?

"A toast to the man of our era!" exclaimed one of the writers, raising his empty tin cup. All the men raised their cups and called out,

---

14. *Yishuv:* The early Jewish population in pre-State Israel (Palestine).

15. *Elisheva* was born Elizabetha Zirkova in 1888 in Russia, to a Russian father and Irish mother. After her mother died, she was raised in her English aunt's home in Moscow, where she began moving in Jewish circles, learned Hebrew, and began translating from Yiddish and Hebrew into Russian. In 1920, she married Simon Bikhovsky, a writer and active Zionist, and together they settled in Palestine in 1925 (Bikhovsky died in 1932). Elisheva remained in Israel, and died in Tiberias in 1949.

"To the life of the collective, salvation of the self!" And so the evening ended.

"Are you writing to Rabinowitz, by any chance?" Zatzkis, Ben Zion, Ziskind, and Zarchi[16] asked her, one after the other, before they went out onto the sand. "Send him our best regards, and remind him that we're standing watch."

Though vaguely embarrassed, Lisbeth sent her regards too. She didn't want it to seem that she nursed a grudge against all men just because one man had broken her heart.

But the woman felt no need to justify not writing the letter. In her heart of hearts she believed that all husbands were their wife's hangman, as well as the other way around. She harbored a memory of a garden of raspberry bushes and a wild thicket, spreading down to the banks of the river that had powered her father's flour mill. She and her brother had played there before her mother died. Later, she would join him to study the books at night that he studied by day. Though their room had had just one little desk, one chair, and a bed, it had been enough. Only after her brother died too and she came to these shores, stepping onto the soil of this land, did she feel that the soles of her feet had been left behind. Or perhaps . . . she had never had any?

The sea had calmed. She dimmed the flame of the oil lamp whose shadows fell on the tense face of her daughter sleeping in the armchair, she who was born to a sadness not of her own making but nonetheless too powerful to avoid. The woman returned to the table, opened the window, and looked outside. The sea was utterly still. No casual passerby would know that this sliver of darkened land was in fact a sea. She mulled over the words of her visitors. What is the "now," she wondered, what is the "here," what is the collective? Wars, plagues, disappointments—aren't they all, in their essence, the same sorrow: the sorrow you have the capacity to suffer—and isn't that then the greatest anguish you will be forced to bear on this earth? And time, what is time, if not little links of pain forged by each and every moment? She dipped her quill in the ink bottle and began to write.

But this evening, more than ever before, perhaps because the men's words still hovered in the empty air of the room, she sensed the still-lingering presence of the stories of the past: the little town, her father's flour mill, her grandmother the rebbetzin,[17] her spotted cow. She had to

---

16. The names all refer to established pre-State writers, including the renown *Shai Agnon* (*Zatzkis*), *Alexander Ziskind*, and *Israel Zarchi*, father of the author.

17. *Rebbetzin:* Rabbi's wife.

be wary of these men. She had to stay cloistered in this little house guarding her world, which was so fragile, so delicate, that one word alone could burst its bubble. These are not just embers of denial, she thought, but words striking her mind like jolts of electricity, and even a single dead word could uproot the source of the flame and turn the brain into a charred limb.

She knew that her stories would come back to her, but not tonight. She felt her mind turning grey in her skull, orphaned from itself, heavy and lifeless, like a stone or a dead fish. Then she opened the door and sat down on the bench on the patio.

A tiny fishing boat, obviously belonging to Arabs, cast a very thin strip of light, as if filtered through the net of an eyelash.

"Bon soir."

Someone came out of the sea and sat down next to her. It was a matronly woman, and she introduced herself.

"Je suis Madame Bovary."

The woman looked around suspiciously. Madame Bovary! Of all people! The very character viewed by the *yishuv* and the editorial board as the symbol of decadence, of emotional bankruptcy! Why did she have to materialize here and sit down next to her, on the bench! The woman turned to her, hating the sense of obligation she felt. But the truth was that she had often fantasized meeting Bovary—to give her some practical advice. She would tell her, first of all, that her choice of lovers lacked both taste and discernment. Even though she was the kind of woman who obsessed about bearing children, she could have shown more imagination when indulging her talent for falling in love. Experience should have taught her that real hunger is never satisfied . . . though now that Bovary had risen out of the sea and was sitting next to her, and she finally had the chance to speak her mind, she hesitated. What was the point?

Madame Bovary sat wrapped up in a black cloak like a monk. But instead of speaking the words in her heart, the woman said only, "Madame, what do you want from me?"

Bovary was shaken by the rude tone, the one the *yishuv* used toward women they considered useless citizens—women who longed for lost lovers during nights when the dry desert wind destroyed all hope of sleep; for dimly lit salons, pianos, the touch of silk on their smooth white thighs, for bitter tears for no reason. But Madame didn't respond. She didn't even remove the dark hood hiding her face. For a moment the roar of the sea masked the maliciousness in the woman's voice.

" . . . What's that myth of love of yours in which you so foolishly cast yourself as goddess—and among men ten times cleverer than you, cunning foxes in their own petty lives? And what of desire . . . " she whispered, for in those days they scarcely spoke of such things. "If you craved high drama why cast a village pharmacist as your leading man? Or a bank clerk? And what a pathetic ending you chose for yourself!"

"L'amour," said Madame. The word fluttered, momentarily defied the smooth Jaffa sand, and was swallowed up. "Who can begin to describe life without love?"

She raised her head proudly as she uttered the words, like a heroine at the guillotine.

"I simply had to fall in love with one fool or another. How could I leave it in the hands of the author! How could I trust him to reward me with a hero worthy of all that he himself had stored up in me, my talent, my strength, my abundance? What if my own imagination helped out a bit, just to assist him? When all is said and done, the heroine too has a certain responsibility to the story."

The sea thundered like the wind through cornstalks. The two women stared at one another. Then Madame Bovary lowered her head and murmured, "If you must know the truth, here it is. None of it was up to me. Gustave led me by the nose."

"You shouldn't blame someone if you let him live your life for you," the woman retorted harshly. "But to let him get rid of you just because his imagination wore out is too much. You didn't have to go along with it. You should have realized that as a man he was never on your side."

The little boat appeared at the seashore, its flares waving in the wind so that it was hard to know what direction it was taking, whether it was drawing in closer or sailing farther out to sea.

"What would you have had me do?" said Madame. "We're all actors parroting the dialogue scripted for us by nature, culture, the times, God. Call it catechism, justice, reincarnation, fate. Like the nun in the joke—she confesses to her priest about the man who appears in her erotic fantasies and the priest sneers, 'You just have to wake up, madame. Both your dream and your heroes are all your own creation.'"

She's right, the woman thought to herself, without admitting it out loud. We cannot awaken from our dreams. Only priests pretend and fanatics are foolish enough to believe otherwise. But if that's the case, and dreaming is our true nature, how can we ever escape it? She was perplexed.

The two sat in silence.

"But the rage," the woman said abruptly, remembering what it had once been like to be filled with hope. "Isn't that a power even stronger than imagination?"

She turned to Bovary with a new attentiveness. "You should have revenged yourself on the fat, impotent man who toyed with you as if you were he, pretending that it was your lie and not his own limitations that caused your downfall—the man who killed you off. Why didn't you resist?"

Madame rose from the bench, her expression darker than night. "I never could," she said. She raised the hem of her dress. Under it, bared, were her feet. Without soles.

She disappeared.

The woman sat there a long time while the dark air grew as thin as the silver paper children smooth out with their fingernails till it becomes transparent, and the white morning light pushed through.

Despite everything, she told herself as she stood up, I won't let anyone drag me along as if I feel no rage. Not even fate. I will set myself in the center of my rage and stand fast like Honi[18] in his circle. And even if the sole of the foot is only imaginary, we have to cultivate it with love. Let imagination belong to whomever it belongs—the writer or the hero of the story. Because no one can claim that the soles we walk on in our imagination, even if they contradict the story line, are any more or less real than the story itself.

She went into the house, took the book she had been reading from the table, got into bed, and leaned it up against the slate on her knees. She began to translate from French to Hebrew:

"This wonderful scene, carved deep in Emma's memory, seemed to her more beautiful than anyone could ever imagine."

(1993)

—Translated by Miriyam Glazer

---

18. *Honi:* According to the Talmud, Honi-Who-Makes-Circles was a miracle worker during the time of the Second Temple (first century B.C.E.) who, during a drought, drew a circle and stood within it, exclaiming to God that he would not move from the circle until it rained; rain then began to fall. One Talmudic account of his death suggests that (like Rip Van Winkle) he went to sleep for seventy years, awaking to discover that no one recognized him. When people refused to believe he was Honi, he prayed in grief for his own death and died.

Introduction to Ruth Almog's "Invisible Mending"

Literary critic Erich Auerbach once characterized the narratives of the Hebrew Bible as "fraught with background." Modern Hebrew obviously radically differs from the language of that ancient text, yet in reading a richly textured contemporary Israeli short story, one can begin to feel the same way. In the "fraught background" of "Invisible Mending," Ruth Almog's narrative of a young girl, Hefzibah, growing up in pre-state Palestine and faced at once with her father's death and her own dawning sexuality, is an intermeshing of ancient texts, as well as sociopolitical, economic, sexual, psychological, familial, artistic, and religious tensions. Her mother worries that she won't return home from visiting Hefzibah's father in the hospital because the British have imposed a curfew. Her grandmother cleans houses for "well-to-do neighbors":

> (the ones her mother had in mind when she said that in Palestine all the parvenus had made it big, while people of culture and learning were starving) [and] Hefzibah believe[s] that if it hadn't been for Hitler, her grandmother would have servants of her own and wouldn't have to clean house for other people and maybe her father would still be alive. It's this country that killed him, she thought, and maybe it's true that mother shouldn't have given my jumper to invisible mending. (p. 29)

The "invisible mending" is double-edged: the young adolescent girls in her religious school cruelly obsess over whether Hefzibah has defied

33

Jewish religious law by having had her jumper repaired after its corner had been ripped in accordance with traditional Jewish mourning ritual. Though these children distinguish between themselves and the ultra-Orthodox whose young men attend *yeshivot* in Jerusalem, they nevertheless use the fine points of religious law as a way to torment her, while her harassed mother argues, "But you have nothing to wear . . . and winter clothes are awfully expensive."

In school, Hefzibah is also oppressed by her teacher who, blind to her love of drawing, relentlessly carps at her for inattentiveness. He demands that she copy out Psalm 82 "a hundred times" as punishment. Particularly because his name, "Mr. Levy," identifies him as a "Levite," that is, as a descendent of the priestly tribe singled out by the Torah, the words of the psalm inflicted upon Hefzibah serve as a bitterly ironic narrative comment on the misuse of authority in the name of religion:

> How long will you judge unjustly, and accept the persons of
>   the wicked?
> Defend the poor and fatherless: do justice to the afflicted and
>   needy.
> Deliver the poor and needy . . . (lines 2-3)

Given the context, the conflicts, and the conclusion of the story—which draws on the rage of the prophet Jeremiah against the Israelites—perhaps it is not far-fetched to suggest that there is a symbolic resonance in Hefzibah's own name. For "Hefzibah" is biblical, deriving from Isaiah's promise of salvation for the people of Israel in Isaiah 62:

> *For the sake of Zion I will not be silent,*
> *For the sake of Jerusalem I will not be still . . .*
> *Nevermore shall you be called "Forsaken,"*
> *Nor shall your land be called "Desolate";*
> *But you shall be called "I delight in her,"*
> *And your land, "Espoused."* (Isaiah 62: 1, 4)

In Hebrew, the words "I delight in her" are "Hefzibah." It is as if the pain enacted in Almog's story has been "invisibly mended" by the healing power of narrative art.

Indeed, all through "Invisible Mending," Hefzibah draws. Creativity is the only true freedom, Ruth Almog has said, "one that transcends gender, class, and national divisions." Born in the town of Petach Tikva in central Israel in 1936, Almog describes herself as having studied in a religious elementary school and attending synagogue with her father on Friday nights. Later she went to Jerusalem to study in a teacher's seminary, and began auditing classes at Hebrew University in Bible and English Literature while also drawing and writing. After her army service, she studied theatre and literature at Tel Aviv University with the hope of learning to write plays. Disappointed, she switched to philosophy, learning Greek in order to study the classics. She gave up her academic career after earning her M.A., choosing instead to concentrate on her writing. Her primary interest today is the Jewish mystical tradition—Kabbalah and Hasidism—but her "real passions" are mythology and folklore.

Ruth Almog works as Assistant Literary Editor of Israel's leading newspaper, *Ha'aretz*. She believes that the deepest challenge for her as a writer is to undermine the schism long perceived as conventional and endemic in Israeli writing: the schism between the traditionally masculinist collectively engaged, politically oriented writing, on the one hand, and the more inward, "private," writing of women, on the other. Indeed, literary critic Yael Feldman has suggested that Almog's well-received 1987 novel, *Roots of Light*, is the first novel written by an Israeli woman that succeeds in doing precisely that; Almog says the novel is at once in the genre of coming-of-age fiction, as well as "political, historical, and psychological."

Her earlier novels include *The Exile* (1970), *The Stranger and the Foe* (1980), and *Death in the Rain* (translated into English, and published by Red Crane Books, Santa Fe, 1993). *Invisible Mending,* the eponymous collection from which the selection here was taken, was published in Hebrew in 1993.

She lives in Tel Aviv with her husband, poet and author Aharon Almog, and her daughters.

Invisible Mending

Ruth Almog

Because the geography teacher Mr. Levy had talked about the Yarkon, Hefzibah locked herself in the Girls' Room during the morning recess.

At the beginning of the lesson, the teacher had announced that the class was going to study the Yarkon and "when we finish, we'll make a field trip to the headwaters of the river to see for ourselves how things run." While the class laughed and the teacher said they wouldn't be able to visit the Fortress of Antipatris because the area was still mined, images rose in her memory of a visit she had made with her mother and brother to the Yarkon Hospital in Tel Aviv four years earlier. The images seemed remote and disjointed, as it some opacity screened them from her. Still, though, they were acutely vivid, burdening her with a painful guilt. A strong light spilled into the room through the south-facing windows—it was early afternoon—and the whiteness of the walls dazzled her. The glare cast her into another probing of the dark night before that visit to the hospital, when she had been startled out of her sleep and didn't understand what the commotion was all about and why her father's bridge partners were in the house. Later she was able to discern the doctor passing by her bed in the foyer leading to her parents' bedroom and she realized vaguely that something serious had happened. Hefzibah asked herself now if she had gone back to sleep that night, and remembered that the next day the British had declared a curfew, scheduled to start at four in the afternoon and include the entire country. Before climbing into the ambulance, her

36

mother told her that she wasn't sure she'd get back by four and that Hefzibah should take care of her little brother and give him lunch. Hefzibah recalled the terrible tension wracking her the whole day and so she switched back to thinking about the white room. The dazzling light made her focus on the black spot on the pillow: thin straight hair parted on the left and combed over the right temple.

"The mills on the river, Hefzibah!" The voice of Mr. Levy, the teacher, suddenly burst upon her and she turned her head toward him, eyes glazed, curtained by those distant images. She said nothing.

"You're not paying attention again, Hefzibah," he chided her. Hefzibah lowered her eyes and returned to the scenes in her mind. It was fifth grade, she remembered, and her home teacher, Dr. Eisner, who was their neighbor and her parents' friend, had left at the end of that year and moved with his family to the new Rasco housing project on the outskirts of Tel Aviv, right next to the Yarkon. When she visited him with her little brother during summer vacation, the bus passed that same hospital and she remembered being struck then by some kind of momentary fear that froze the flow of her exhilaration. The family was happy to see them and Dr. Eisner, her former teacher, took them and his own children rowing on the Yarkon. Her brother was very frightened and wouldn't let go of her hand.

Esther Strauss, who was her best friend and sat next to her, nudged her suddenly and she heard the teacher ask, "Have any of you ever gone rowing on the Yarkon?" But Hefzibah didn't raise her hand, and her eyes returned to the glaring light, to the dazzling whiteness. She remembered how frightened she had been of looking at him—he was so strange, so unfamiliar, covered up to the neck with a stiff starched sheet, his head on the pillow: the black spot where his hair was, his white face, the bluish hue of his cheeks. Hefzibah recalled clearly that she had been more interested in the good-looking boy lying on the next bed than she had been in her father, and her pencil sketched the memory on the piece of paper on her desk: a room, a row of beds, a head on a pillow. Only the face escaped her. She couldn't understand how she forgotten it so quickly—after only two weeks—and she asked herself why the features were so blurred: the eyes, the nose, the lips, the wrinkles. Everything had been sucked into an elliptical void that resembled an ancient theatrical mask, like the Greek one she had once seen in a book. The book's title slipped her mind.

Mr. Levy, said, "Hefzibah, instead of paying attention you have been doodling the whole time." Hefzibah said, "I'm not doodling, Mr. Levy,

I'm drawing." The teacher lost his temper and said, "Talking back again, are you? Copy Psalm 82 one hundred times for tomorrow."[19] Hefzibah shrugged her shoulders, reminded that Dr. Eisner, her fifth grade teacher, had been sympathetic, had never reprimanded her. On the contrary, he would tell the class jokingly that Hefzibah could do anything, even listen and draw at the same time. It really didn't bother him that she drew during class. That's why Hefzibah showed him the journal she kept in which she had written about Impressionism and why Van Gogh cut off his ear, and where she had copied her own poems and even a little story about three old women in a secluded house. But she was sure Mr. Levy wouldn't appreciate things like that and there was no point in explaining them to him.

During the recess, then, Hefzibah locked herself in one of the bathroom stalls. She pulled down the cover of the toilet seat and sat there, her face crushed in her hands. She sifted through memories, trying to capture the features of the face on the white pillow in her parents' bedroom when her mother had sent her in to look at him for the last time. But now, returning to the room, she couldn't see anything. Her mind couldn't catch hold of any likeness and she was angry with herself and decided that as soon as she got home she would look at the photograph album and then close her eyes and summon up his picture over and over until it was engraved in her mind indelibly and could never again be so thoughtlessly lost. The door to the Girls' Room opened and Hefzibah heard someone come in, turn on the faucet, and speak. She recognized the voice of Bracha Shvili and heard her say, "Did you notice that she was wearing the jumper from the funeral?"

"Yes," said the voice of Shula Reisser. "So what?"

Bracha Shvili said, "She mended the place where the rabbi tore it.[20] That's not done."

"Is it forbidden?" asked Shula Reisser.

"I'll have to check that," said Bracha. "I'll ask the Talmud teacher." Meanwhile someone else came in and now Hefzibah heard Esther Strauss, her best friend, saying, "Did you hear how Hefzibah laughed out loud? She should be ashamed of herself."

They left the Girls' Room and Hefzibah's hand went up to her heart, fingering the spot where the rabbi had rent her jumper.

---

19. Psalm 82: The psalm includes the words, "How long will you judge unjustly? Defend the poor and fatherless; do justice to the afflicted and needy. . . . "

20. Traditional Jewish mourning practice includes *Kri'ya,* or rending of one's garment.

She usually sat in class next to her best friend, Esther Strauss, but now she took the seat next to Eli Weiss. And during the lesson, when Mr. Levy, the teacher, was explaining the characteristics of the idyll, Eli Weiss wrote in her notebook:

Your eyes exude a verdant light
Just like two sparkling emeralds.

Hefzibah read the lines and smiled. Suddenly, Mr. Levy said, "Hefzibah! What are you doing over there? Take your things and come sit here." He pointed to the empty seat in front of him.

Hefzibah took her time changing seats and the teacher bellowed at her, "Hurry up! You're wasting the whole lesson." Hefzibah gathered her things together sullenly. Eli Weiss whispered, "Why does he always pick on you?" She winked at him unobtrusively and he returned a shy smile. When she finally sat down in front of the teacher, she saw that Eli was flushed with anger and pleasure. Toward the end of the hour she tore a page out of her notebook, wrote a few words on it, folded it, and tossed it to the back. Mr. Levy shouted, "That's too much! You're going to stay after school tomorrow for two hours. Tell your parents—I mean your mother—not to worry."

Hefzibah thought, *The whole class noticed his mistake.* She was seething with anger and she said, "But, Mr. Levy, you've already given me a punishment . . . "

"No 'buts,' " he broke in. "Psalm 82 a hundred times and two hours after school and if that won't help, you'll have to bring your par . . . your mother."

Hefzibah thought about Dr. Eisner and about the fact that no other teacher had understood her since he left. She remembered that on the way to visit the Eisners with her brother, the bus had passed mounds of red earth carved out on either side of the road as if by a knife. She remembered that he had kept her journal for a few days and when he came over to return it, he told her parents, "You have no idea what kind of girl you have." And after that, her memories returned to the hospital and to the white room and the sharp light and the boy lying in the bed next to her father's and she thought, "I was more interested in the boy than I was in my father. Now I keep telling myself that I was afraid to look at him. But that's not true. I was simply indifferent. I didn't want to know."

During recess, Hefzibah stood on the terrace, leaning over the ledge, watching the boys and girls in the yard playing ball or jumping rope. Dr.

Moskowitz, the Talmud teacher, had taken out a chair and sat down in the sun. Hefzibah saw Bracha Shvili walk over to him, bend down, and say something. Her hand moved up her jumper and she fingered the place where the rabbi had rent it. Only by actually touching it could you tell there was a defect in the weave.

Shula Reisser came over to her. "Look at that pair of love-birds," she said, motioning with her head toward the corner of the yard. Hefzibah saw Mr. Levy and Bracha Shvili standing and talking together. "Disgusting," said Shula. "First she sucks up to Dr. Moskowitz and then to Mr. Levy."

"I see that it's been repaired," she went on, pointing to the top of the jumper.

"Yes. My mother gave it to invisible mending," said Hefzibah.

"Is that allowed?" asked Shula.

"I never asked the rabbi," said Hefzibah contemptuously. "I like this jumper. Maybe you think I should have walked around with it torn till doomsday?"

"You should find out if it's allowed," said Shula, annoyed.

"And if it's not allowed, so what? What's it your business? Why can't everybody stop watching me like a hawk all the time?"

"You'd better watch out," said Shula. "Everybody's talking about you. They say you laugh too much."

Hefzibah walked away and, standing by herself, again leaning on the ledge and watching the children play, she realized that there was no one in the world she could talk to: Esther Strauss, her best friend, was just a hairbrain, and Eli Weiss was still a baby and didn't understand a thing.

Now Bracha Shvili approached her. She fixed her eyes on the jumper and said, "They fixed it for you. You can't see a thing."

"Invisible mending," said Hefzibah.

"Hefzi," said Bracha Shvili softly, "they say it's wrong. I asked Dr. Moskowitz. He teaches Jewish law. He should know. He says it's forbidden."

"And the fact that you're so palsy-walsy with Mr. Levy, that's not forbidden? He's a married man with a wife and children in Jerusalem," Hefzibah carped.

Bracha Shvili turned red. "Why are you always insulting people?"

"Look who's talking about insults," said Hefzibah.

The next day Hefzibah gave Mr. Levy the pages on which she had copied out Psalm 82 a hundred times.

"I hope that you know the psalm by heart now," he said.

Hefzibah didn't answer and he said, "Don't forget. You're staying after school today for two more hours. Did you tell your mother?"

"Yes," Hefzibah lied. "How can you be sure I won't slip out in the middle?" she asked.

"I'm staying with you, that's how. What did you suppose?"

"So then you're also being punished," she laughed.

"No," he smiled, "I'll be correcting homework."

First she took her sandwiches and ate them in silence. Then she took out a pad of drawing paper, a small glass, and some tubes of gouache. "I'm just going to get some water," she told Mr. Levy. Then she painted for two hours without saying a word, inwardly abusing and vilifying the teacher the whole time, pouring out her wrath in strong colors, frenziedly covering the paper with paint, one coat on top of the other, page after page.

Suddenly the teacher said, "You can go. The two hours are over."

Hefzibah screwed on the tops of the tubes, cleaned and dried her brush, and put everything into her schoolbag. As she was leaving, Mr. Levy said, "I didn't know you paint."

"I only doodle," she said.

Outside she saw Bracha Shvili. She's waiting for him, she thought, and hid behind a wall to see what would happen. Mr. Levy came out of the school and Bracha Shvili went up to him. They exchanged a few words and then left together.

Crazy nut, thought Hefzibah. What can she possibly see in that revolting man? As for him, she thought, he punishes me on the slightest pretense and goes for walks in the evening with Bracha Shvili, while he has a wife and children in Jerusalem.

Hefzibah sat in the kitchen picking over the rice. She put the chaff and the tiny stones on one side, and the rice on the other, until there was a small white mound. Her mother was standing near the kitchen counter changing the wick in the kerosene cooker. Hefzibah's grandmother, who had just finished cleaning house for their well-to-do neighbors (the ones her mother had in mind when she said that in Palestine all the parvenus had made it big, while people of culture and learning were starving), came in and asked if they needed any help. Hefzibah believed that if it hadn't been for Hitler, her grandmother would have servants of her own and wouldn't have to clean house for other people and maybe her father would still be alive. It's this country that killed him, she thought, and maybe it's true that mother shouldn't have given my jumper to invisible mending.

Out loud she said, "You know, the girls say that it's against Jewish law to mend the rip."

"But you have nothing to wear," her mother answered, "and winter clothes are awfully expensive."

Hefzibah was late meeting her friends. "Where is everybody?" she asked the boy waiting for her.

"They left," he said.

"Where to?"

"Nowhere in particular. Just strolling—in couples."

"Eli wasn't here?"

"He went off with Rickey," the boy said.

Hefzibah's heart sank. What a traitor, she thought. He didn't even wait for me.

"Come on, let's go over to the park," said the boy, "maybe they're there."

They walked up the hill in silence. The silence weighed on Hefzibah and she said, "Are you from Jerusalem?"

"No."

"Then where did you go to school before?"

"The *yeshivah*,"[21] he answered.

"Your people are that religious?" she asked, stunned. He didn't look like that—like those ultra-Orthodox from the *yeshivah*.

"No."

Hefzibah had no more questions and the boy was silent. They reached the top of the hill and Hefzibah said, "I don't see them anymore. I'm going home."

The boy walked her home and quickly took his leave. In the front yard of the house a lantana bush grew wild around the fence, creating a small arbor. When she was small, she had played there with her brother. Now she made out a large grey hulk crouching in the foliage. She began to run toward the house. The figure detached itself from the bush and ran after her, massive and floundering.

"Mother! Mother!" Hefzibah screamed.

Her mother appeared at the door. "Get out of here, do you hear me, or I'll call the police!"

He always lay in ambush for her there, fat crazy Shalom, trying to catch her and kiss her. When he passed her on the street, he'd shout after her,

---

21. *Yeshivah:* School dedicated to the intensive study of Jewish sacred texts.

Pretty Hefzi is going to wed
Crazy Shalom with the hole in his head,
or
Shalom is crazy, Hefzi is good.
The rabbi will marry them because he should.

Hefzibah found him repulsive and terrifying. Her mother always said, "One day I'll lose all my patience with you and go to the police." But she never did. She pitied him and his parents. "If I go to the police," she said, "they'll lock him up for good and finish him off with electric shocks."

Saturday afternoon, Hefzibah went to the girls' club. She didn't pay attention to what the leader was saying. Later the boys joined them and they began to play guessing games. Hefzibah sat on the side, not taking part. Eli sat next to Rickey and didn't look at her even once. When evening fell and the Sabbath was out, they went inside for folk dancing. Hefzibah stood around watching. She loved dancing. Bracha Shvili came over and stood next to her.

"Why aren't you dancing?" Hefzibah asked her.

"I'm not in the mood," answered Bracha Shvili.

Someone called for a *krakowiak*[22] and Hanoch pulled out his harmonica to play. Hefzibah noticed that Eli picked Rickey for the dance.

Bracha Shvili said, "Eli and Rickey are going together."

Hefzibah didn't say a word and Bracha Shvili said, "Somebody saw them kissing. On a bench on Rothschild Boulevard. That Rickey'll give it to anyone who asks."

"He's just a big baby," said Hefzibah. She watched the dancing couples spin around before her eyes. She thought she better go home and learn the chapter of Jeremiah by heart. Otherwise Dr. Moskowitz would punish her. But she didn't feel like going home alone. She was afraid that crazy Shalom would be waiting for her behind the lantana bush. She figured that if she waited till the dancing was over, she'd find someone to walk her home.

A gallery ran along the walls of the club about halfway to the ceiling and Hefzibah decided to go up and sit there by herself in the dark. When she entered the darkened gallery, she was surprised to see someone on one of the benches. She stopped, ready to turn back and retrace her steps, when the voice of Bracha Shvili, a little choked and hoarse, called to her, "Come over here, Hefzi."

---

22. *Krakowiak:* A lively Polish folkdance.

"Why are you sitting here alone in the dark?" Hefzibah asked, surprised. "Come and sit down," said Bracha Shvili and Hefzibah sat down next to her, asking "What's the matter? Why are you crying?"

But Bracha Shvili didn't answer. Only choked sobs escaped. "Stop it! That's enough!" said Hefzibah, a little frightened, put off by this display of uncontrolled grief.

"I love him so much," Bracha Shvili sobbed. "I really don't know what to do. When he goes home to his wife and children I feel completely lost."

"But how can you? He's an old man. I can't understand what you see in him," said Hefzibah.

Bracha Shvili took Hefzibah's hand and began caressing it.

"I can't stand it anymore," she moaned. "I can't begin to tell you how crazy I am about him."

And then, before Hefzibah's darkening eyes, Bracha Shvili began to sway back and forth, her eyes closed and her voice whispering, "I love you, I love you so much. I can't live without you."

Hefzibah studied her in her anguish, trying to figure out what to do. Suddenly Bracha Shvili embraced her and whispered in her ear, "You won't leave me. You're mine alone." And then she kissed her passionately on the mouth. Hefzibah pushed her away savagely, disgusted. "You're out of your mind!" she mumbled harshly, getting up and running down stairs.

"Hefzi, Hefzi, wait for me!" the voice importuned her, but Hefzibah didn't stop. When she reached the bottom she immediately joined the circle of dancers, now in the middle of a tempestuous *hora*.[23] They stamped their feet and clapped their hands at a furious tempo, their voices emitting a frenzied gibberish: *"Ho! Ya! Ho! Ya! Lefti!, befti! belabelabefti, tchingileh, mingileh, loof, loof, loof!!!"* The fervor drove the nausea out of her system and she gave herself up to the beat, oblivious to everything.

Only later, when the circle of dancers dissipated and the frenzied *"Ho! Ya! Ho! Ya!"* stopped throbbing against her temples, did she realize what she had done. She left the club immediately. Hefzibah walked rapidly, her knees shaking, as she tried to blot it all out. Still, her mind kept churning up the terrible question, "What will they say? What will they say?" Every so often she took a long deep breath to fortify her battery of counterarguments, such as: "It's my own business. It doesn't

---

23. *Hora:* Israeli folk dance.

concern anyone else." But the question was overpowering, attacking her with renewed force.

When she reached the fence, she examined the yard carefully and, seeing no one, entered quietly, stealing past the thicket of the lantana bush. She kept as close as possible to the opposite hedge, her head a little bent, fighting the urge to look back at the dark shadow of overgrown foliage. But when she was halfway to the door, an obese body sprang out, stamping like a clumsy tottering bear, and fell upon her. He grabbed hold of her with his coarse, heavy hands, murmuring, "Hetzi, my beauty, the joy of my life. I've caught you!"

"Mother! Mother!" Hefzibah screamed, but his moist lips were already on her face, his hands red-hot tongs piercing the flesh of her arms.

In the square of light of the opened door, she saw her mother for half a second, standing and looking and suddenly running down the steps, waving a broom and shouting, "Get out of here! Now! Or I'll call the police!" The demented man let Hefzibah go and disappeared into the overgrown bushes, an obscure mass sinking into the mouth of darkness.

Hefzibah broke into a loud wail and her mother took her in her arms and helped her into the house. In the foyer she held onto her a little longer, caressing her head and saying, "Daddy would have broken all his bones, only we have no daddy. Tomorrow I'll tell the landlord he has to uproot that whole bush and I'll go over and talk to that maniac's parents."

On Sunday[24] the seat next to Eli Weiss was empty again and Hefzibah decided to sit there. Eli Weiss wrote her a letter of apology during class. He explained that he loved her, only her, that Rickey had provoked him, and that his biological urge had gotten the better of him.

On the note she returned she wrote only, "Hope you had a good time." That's all.

While passing the note to Eli she felt the teacher's menacing glance on her and she understood that if she wasn't careful she might be punished again. When the bell rang, Eli Weiss got up but Hefzibah stayed seated. She took the Book of Jeremiah out of her schoolbag and began to learn the assigned chapter by heart. The classroom emptied out slowly and in the end only a few girls remained, among them her best friend Esther Strauss, Bracha Shvili, Shula Reisser, and Leah Katz. Hefzibah was reading under her breath and her lips were moving:

---

24. Sunday is a normal school day in Israel.

O Lord, I will dispute with thee, for thou art just;
  yes, I will plead my case before thee.
Why do the wicked prosper
  and traitors live at ease?
Thou hast planted them and their roots strike deep.[25]

And while she was still absorbed in the Bible, memorizing the passage, she was suffused by the fear that a dangerous presence was approaching, throbbing in the air, spinning toward her and crying, *"Ho! Ya! Ho! Ya!"* She tried to ward off the feeling of oppression and went back to the text:

Thou art ever on their lips,
  yet far from their hearts.
But thou know me, O Lord, thou hast seen me;
  thou has tried my heart toward thee to thyself . . .

But some commotion deflected her from the passage and she noticed that her friends had gathered around her, randomly, in a horseshoe. Then all of a sudden, as if in a phantasmagoria, she saw Bracha Shvili spinning toward her, her arms outstretched. And before she realized exactly what was happening, she felt the full force of an open hand strike her cheek. Hefzibah raised her hand to her face, utterly nonplussed, and heard Bracha Shvili saying, "It's forbidden to repair the tear. Dr. Moskowitz says it's a terrible sin."

Esther Strauss, her best friend, came up close and, pointing her finger at her shouted, "You were dancing the *hora* last night at the club!"

---

25. See Jeremiah 12:1–2. These lines and the passage from Jeremiah that follows have also been translated as:

> "You will win, O Lord, if I make claim against you,
> Yet I shall present charges against You:
> Why does the way of the wicked prosper?
> Why are the workers of treachery at ease?
> You have planted them, and they have taken root,
> They spread, they even bear fruit.
> You are present in their mouths,
> But far from their thoughts." (Jere. 12: 1–2)

See *Tanakh-The Holy Scriptures:* The new JPS Translation according to the Traditional Hebrew Text (Philadelphia: Jewish Publication Society, 5748 [1988]), pp. 795–796.

Bracha Shvili took her cue from that. "You should be ashamed of yourself! You slut!"

"Are you out of your minds?" said Leah Katz. "Leave her alone! What do you want from her?"

"You shut up, you scaredy-cat," said Shula Reisser.

Hefzibah bent her head over the Bible on her desk and the tiny black letters grew before her eyes, crying out:

Thou hast planted them and their roots strike deep,
they grow up and bear fruit . . .

But Bracha Shvili swung again, striking her on the other cheek. "Stop! I'm going to call the teacher!" cried Leah Katz, but Shula Reisser caught hold of her and said, "Shut up! You're not going anywhere right now! We've got to show her a thing or two. What does she think she's doing laughing all the time? Dancing a hora? Sending her jumper to invisible mending!"

"She has to be punished!" cried Bracha Shvili, but Esther Strauss insisted, "That's enough."

"She's got to be punished!" shouted Bracha Shvili, grabbing hold of Hefzibah's hair and pulling. Esther Strauss pushed her away, "That's enough. Stop it!" But meanwhile Shula Reisser had edged closer, holding a scissors.

"Gimme the scissors!" shouted Bracha Shvili and to Hefzibah she said, "Invisible mending, huh? We'll show you how it's done, Hefzibah."

She grabbed the front of Hefzibah's jumper. Hefzibah resisted and from the back Esther Strauss caught hold of Bracha Shvili and pulled her away. The moment she was free, Hefzibah ran to the door. But Bracha Shvili, still holding the scissors, ran after her and caught her from behind.

"She's liable to kill her!" screamed Leah Katz.

At that moment Hefzibah turned around and with all the force she could muster, punched Bracha Shvili in the face.

"She broke my nose," Bracha Shvili howled.

"Serves you right!" said Hefzibah, and Esther Strauss, her best friend, took the scissors out of Bracha's hand. The sound of the bell, metallic and heavy, jolted them. They looked at one another, their faces flushed and angry, and Hefzibah was aware that the prolonged ringing was slicing through her like the knife that had cut the top of her jumper not so many days past in that strange, remote place, just before she bent down to pick up a handful of moist red earth.

A sudden light suffused the room. Boys and girls burst through the door and on the threshold stood Dr. Moskowitz. He waited until everyone was standing in place and then he walked up his desk and announced, "Be seated."

He read out the names from the roll book and when he finished he said, "I hope you've all learned the chapter by heart. Hefzibah, please begin."

Hefzibah sat with her trembling hands folded under her chest. The seat underneath her was hot and sticky. For a moment she didn't understand what he wanted but Eli Weiss, sitting next to her, nudged her and she began:

> *O Lord, I will dispute with thee, for thou art just;*
> *yes, I will plead my case before thee.*
> *Why do the wicked prosper*
> *and traitors live at ease?*

And Eli Weiss continued:

> *Thou hast planted them and their roots strike deep,*
> *they grow up and bear fruit.*

Hefzibah raised her hand and asked permission to leave the room. The teacher gave her permission. As she walked out, she felt the blood sticky between her thighs. Thank God the jumper is thick and dark, she thought. Outside, she unlocked her bike with shaking hands, gave it a push, mounted, and rode home. The house was empty and silent. Hefzibah washed herself, changed her clothes, and placed a thick wad of cotton in her underpants. "Why did it come early?" she asked herself, and she answered out loud without knowing quite why:

> *If you have raced with men and they have worn you down,*
> *how then can you hope to vie with horses . . .* [26]

She folded up her bloodstained jumper, wrapped it in newspaper, went out into the yard, and stuck it into the garbage can.

---

26. *If you have raced with men and they have worn you down, how then can you hope to vie with horses:* These and the lines that follow are a continuation of Jeremiah 12.

As she rode her bicycle up the street to school to pick up her schoolbag, crazy Shalom came toward her from the opposite direction, calling out:

> *Pretty Hefzi is going to wed*
> *Crazy Shalom with the hole in his head.*

Hefzibah got back to school during the recess and, ignoring all the eyes digging into her, went straight into the classroom. Her schoolbag was where she had left it, under the desk, and she took out her English notebook to study the new vocabulary. Esther Strauss, her best friend, came up to her and in a muted voice said, "Good thing you changed your clothes. That wasn't right, that invisible mending. It's forbidden."

Hefzibah fixed her eyes on the words in the notebook in front of her,

My heritage cries out against me like a lion in the forest.

(1993)
—*Translated by Dalya Bilu*

Introduction to Mira Magen's
"A Piece of Cake for Saul"

While reading the stories in Mira Magen's first collection *Well-Buttoned Up*, one Israeli critic found himself recalling the Beatles' "Eleanor Rigby" and the BBC production of George Eliot's *Silas Marner*. For many of the characters in Magen's stories live in worlds hemmed in by tradition and find themselves observers rather than active participants in the life around them. So, for example, set in the kitchen of a home in rural Israel (on a *moshav*, or semi-collective settlement), "A Piece of Cake for Saul" evokes a world view far from that of an urbane, secular, contemporary Israeli city. In the small, traditionally religious, universe of this story, women who spend much of their day in the heat of cooking gaze through the window above their kitchen sink at their neighbors' lives, observing, judging, marking deviations from the norm that they never let others forget. But, as is characteristic of Magen's style, the richness of language and of narrative detail counterpoints the repression inherent in the women's lives. Evoking such images as the fragrance of cinnamon, houses that seem as if they are "bathed in milk," the hue of dark red fabric in the sunlight, six fresh radishes in the sink, a raisin "swollen with heat," the narrative bristles with eroticism here as in many of the other stories in the collection.

Published in 1994, *Well-Buttoned Up* quickly appeared on the bestseller list, and Magen was praised as a "talented new author" by critic Eitan Ben-Natan. Magen's background is an unusual one for an Israeli writer. A registered nurse at Hadassah Hospital on Mount Scopus in

Jerusalem, Magen is an Orthodox Jew and the mother of three children who was urged by literary friends to seek publication for her stories. *Well-Buttoned Up* has since won a prize from Israel's Ministry of Education, and been translated into German; "A Piece of Cake for Saul" appeared in the Czech journal *Trafika*.

A Piece of Cake for Saul

Mira Magen

Sometimes the sky here is like the downy feathers of little chicks, flying high, and the more you want it to be lower and closer to you, the higher it soars, and the more you stretch out your fingers and shout until your vocal cords burst, the more the sky is like the downy feathers of little chicks, weightless.

Momma will serve tea soon. Two saccharin tablets will shoot up spinning and fizzling to the top of Malkeleh's cup. Her sugar has been high lately. Of course, she can live on lettuce and boiled beans, but when it comes to swollen, sizzling apples in crust, she prefers an extra injection of insulin in her thigh to a nervous and disappointed stomach. They drink tea before or after harsh words, never during. Soon they'll finish talking. Well, Momma has actually been finished for a while, she's silent, but even though Malkeleh Cooperstock is inhaling the fragrance of the hot cinnamon, her mouth watering, she's restraining herself because she still has things to say and she left everything half finished so she could come and say them.

You know, she's past her prime for a girl, she says to Momma, and I don't have to tell you that what's overripe falls to the ground and rots.

The light outside is strong, a good light for choosing material for a dress. At Marcel's store they're taking the fabrics out into the sun now because you can tell the difference between olive green and bottle green in the sunlight. Sammy drags out bolt after bolt and Marcel arranges them by color. I would gladly sew something for myself this summer in a soft viscose, but so many things have been said about me here that the words bunch up on one another, creating a barrier between me and the fabrics. For years I've been walking down the other side of the street, seeing the fabrics only from a distance, and sometimes something shines from inside the store, the glitter of Sammy's chain, maybe, or the sparkle in his eye; I don't know and I don't stop to find out.

In the middle of cooking, Malkeleh had buttoned her thin wool coat over her housedress and walked three short blocks to come to talk to Momma. She doesn't leave her house without wearing that coat until the end of May. I'm in my room, and if it weren't for the young goldfinches chattering on the branches of the plum tree, I would have heard every word. Even without seeing Malkeleh I know that she hasn't unbuttoned her coat yet, with its smell of fresh-crushed garlic and jellied chicken feet trapped in the lining from pressing heavy pots against her housedress when she carries them from the counter to the stove and uses her sleeve as a mitt when she mixes something in the red-hot frying pan or drains the noodles. She looks out of the window over the sink, all day long, squinting to see in between the splattered oil stuck on the panes, watching the fields of blue lupines that extend beyond the yard. This season the blue is as vivid as the blue of the hat she bought the year of Saul's bar mitzvah.

Ten years already, but people don't forget, Malkeleh says, it's stuck on your daughter like a birthmark. Even if you leave to go live in the city, she won't get rid of it because things like that spread like wildfire.

Momma doesn't answer. Maybe she's thinking about Rosie Klein, who already married off her youngest daughter. On the Days of Awe[27] six feathers, one on each of the hats worn by Rosie and her five daughters, will bend in the wind, blowing through the round windows of the synagogue. Only my head will be bare among all those women who have already reached the height of at least five-feet-five.[28]

Malkeleh is so crazy to marry off Saul that she's even willing to stop knowing what she knows about me. She tells Momma that she has to put a new hole in his belt every week; everything falls off him because there's no happiness in him.

---

27. *Days of Awe:* Rosh Hashanah to Yom Kippur (New Year to the Day of Atonemnt), usually in early autumn.

28. "Only my head will be bare," i.e., only she will still be unmarried.

We were thirteen when he said show me what you have in your mouth, and I turned my face toward the sun and opened my mouth as wide as I could and showed him the small wire braces on my teeth. He was fascinated and tried to look deeper down behind my teeth, bending and stretching his thin neck to stare into the black hole of my throat all the way to its pink center. Later he picked some lupines and handed me three blue blossoms on their stems; I noticed that his fingers were soft and white like mine and they had forgotten to iron one of his sleeves, which was wrinkled like the neck of a turtle. The other one was smooth, with a sharp fold along its length. The sky, as high as the raspberry bushes that grew near the fence, brushed our cheeks. Saul skipped across the field like a grasshopper bearing his joy the way someone might bear a young bird. I pulled petals from the flowers saying yes, no, yes, no, and I knew that when I grew up I would have a boyfriend whose hands were like nutshells, brown and hard.

The end of April. The house smells of onions fried in soybean oil even though the windows are wide open. Malkeleh unbuttons her coat. Momma says that soon it'll be summer and Malkeleh says that soon there will be plums and she can make jam and how the time flies, another year, and then another. Momma starts to say something about the sudden *khamsin*[29] that caused the loquats to ripen early, as if the conversation were a water-filled canal that could easily be diverted, trying so hard to avoid the subject of how quickly time passes. But Malkeleh doesn't want to waste any more time now because the apples smell different when they're not hot, and they have to get to the point while the cake is still steaming and the raisins are still swollen with heat. Later they'll cool off and collapse like burst bubbles.

I'm ready to forget what these eyes have seen, she says, though I remember it as if it were yesterday. There were six fresh radishes in the sink. I peeled one of them and looked out the window. Everything up to the fence was a kind of bluish-purple color, as if someone had spilled ink on the field and all of a sudden your daughter . . . she was only fifteen.

Malka, not again, Momma says. She hasn't forgotten how I came into the house that day wearing a dark red dress, my cheeks the color of pickled beets. Marcel had told me to come at noon to pick out material because sunlight shows true colors and fluorescence lies. We walked out of her shop onto the dirt road in front of the grocery. She

---

29. *Khamsin:* The dry desert wind, like the California Santa Anas.

held big bolts of cloth up against me, and Sammy held a mirror up in front of me, sending a blinding circle of light that danced on the grocery walls. The dark is best for you, makes you look like an actress, Sammy said, returning the fabrics to the shop. The sun ignited a small fire on the golden disk dangling from his neck and released white sparks from his pinkie ring. He sat on a bolt of pink satin, moving his head back and forth in time to the rhythm of the music coming from the radio, spitting salty pumpkin seed shells into a garbage pail. Marcel placed a tape measure around my waist and wrote in her notebook, then she placed the tape measure around my hips and wrote, and then measured from my shoulder to my waist, and finally, she encircled my chest with the tape but she needed only a small section of it, and most of the tape measure just dangled in the air. Sammy bent to look at the numbers in the notebook and said you should eat more. A man has to have something to grab onto.

Only a very few people in our farm community wore short pants like his. Sammy's legs looked brown and hard against the pink satin, and his fingers looked like big peanuts moving in time to the rhythm of the song on the radio. I never saw Saul's legs because he always wore long pants with shoes and socks. Malkeleh stuffs him with so many jellied chicken feet that I once dreamt his toenails were covered with skin.

All the windows are open, the leaves of the plum tree are fluttering and the wind ruffles the birds' feathers, and still it's stuffy. There's no air and the smell coming from Malkeleh's housedress is spreading through the rooms. Momma says, enough Malka, enough of this already, and turns on the electric kettle. But Malkeleh Cooperstock did not turn off the gas in the middle of the day or walk three blocks just for apple cake.

Your daughter is as hard and closed as an olive pit, she says, and Momma doesn't say a word. She too saw how Saul turned as red as the fully opened petals of a rose when we walked past him last Saturday. He greeted us, his eyes looking down at the pebbles scattered on the road near the synagogue, and I couldn't do anything about how the sun made my hair look golden or how the wind blew it around my shoulders and made turquoise-colored waves on the pretty dress I was wearing.

It really could work. He's serious and responsible and she's a smart cookie, you can't put anything over on her, says Malkeleh. They called me "Cohen's little tramp" when it happened, but since then the wedding canopy has been folded up and stored away in the synagogue, all the spring chickens have been married off already, and Saul is still single and blushes every time he sees me. Malkeleh brings Momma plum jam and always greets us with the kind of serious and weighty "hello" usually reserved for the neighborhood doctor.

The dress was clear, deep, red, the color of kiddish wine. Marcel spread it out on the counter and said that I would look like a princess in it. The whole store filled with a red glow from the fabric; even Sammy's eyes were like buttons of blood. Marcel put one sleeve on the other and folded the dress lengthwise, and she pinned a note on it, saying how much we had already paid and how much we still owed. Sammy said a person could go crazy from the smell of fabric all day long, and he walked out of the store after me. The light outside was the way it is now, the kind that makes the leaves transparent and the houses look as if they were bathed in milk. Sammy's legs were golden brown against the yellow gravel.

So listen, Malkeleh says. I was peeling the radishes and all of a sudden I saw your daughter in her blue school dress disappear into the raspberry bushes with you-know-who. Momma breaks into a spasm of small coughs, tapping her feet on the floor, each in a different rhythm, and Malkeleh waits patiently for Momma's coughing to subside so she can go on with her story. They came out of the bushes fifteen minutes later and all of a sudden her dress was red, such a dark red color that all the blue flowers paled next to it. I was so upset that the radishes fell right out of my hands. The switch on the electric kettle clicks, Momma opens and closes the oven noisily and coughs, but Malkeleh doesn't wait for the coughing to stop and asks, how could you let her wear red? She says she's amazed that Momma let me wave a red flag in front of a bull . . . Momma slices the cake and the banging of the knife on the glass dish cuts through Malkeleh's words and I can't hear what she says or how Momma answers her. Even now, after so many years, I can still smell the raspberries in this oppressive air. I stood among the leaves and saw Cooperstock's forehead moving behind her window, pressing up against it and then disappearing.

Sammy said, I'm dying to see you in that dress, you don't see a fifteen-year old girl wearing a dark red dress every day. Long spikes of wheat grew up near the raspberry bushes, and the black tassels growing out of their golden florets brushed against Sammy's legs. He put his pinkie, the one with the ring, into one of the beards and the bristles scratched it and I took off my blue dress and put it down on the raspberry bush and very carefully took the new, dark red dress out of its bag. The thin black tassels brushed against my naked shoulders and he said, I never saw such white skin, and he helped me pull up the zipper ever so carefully from my waist to my neck and I let him tie the belt in the back and the collar bow in front.

Marcel is right, a princess, he said, and I pursed my lips and pranced around like a model. The dress caught on a branch. When I stepped out from behind the bushes, the bill was still pinned to the hem of the dress, but it was crumpled and torn across the line showing how much we had already paid. Momma asked if I had gone crazy and she said, leave it for the holidays, who wears such an expensive dress for everyday? Her eyes widened and her mouth fell open, and she was shocked at how well the dark red suited me. It's too beautiful, she said, and her mouth stayed open and my face burned as if the dress were on fire.

Later on they called me "Cohen's little tramp" and the air grew suffocating, like the chicken houses after the feed has been scattered, and the spaces in the house seem to shrink and the distance between the roofs and the sky seemed to have expanded. All these years the dark red dress has remained as it was. Only people experience things and change from minute to minute, from hour to hour; fabric stays the same. The light from the window illuminates the material and the leaves of the plum tree weave delicate lacy shadows on it. I can barely close the zipper now. The dress stretches almost to the bursting point across my chest, squeezes my waist, and reaches only to a spot above my knees. I take a wide turn around the room, just as I did then among the spikes of grain.

Malkeleh bends over the cake and says oy vey because of the sugar and after the second oy vey she stops and asks why all of a sudden the kitchen looks so red and why the tiles look like Santa Rosa plums. She stops sucking the cinnamon off the apples, turns around, and sees my long legs at the door and the dark red fabric ballooning out above my knees touching both sides of the door frame.

Take a piece of cake for Saul, I tell her, picking up the largest slice to put in a plastic bag for him. A raisin falls and rolls onto her coat, coming to stop on her knee where it sticks like a beauty mark. Malkeleh Cooperstock doesn't move her knee, as if the raisin were a butterfly she didn't want to startle. Ever so slowly she extends two fingers to pick up the raisin and gently places it whole and still swollen with heat into the bag holding the piece of cake for Saul. Then she closes it tightly, tying it with a double knot.

(1994)
—*Translated by Sondra Silverston*

Introduction to Shulamith Gilboa's "If Nella Could Do It"

The stories in Shulamith Gilboa's collection *The Fourth Lie* (1993), from which "If Nella Could Do It" is taken, are all set in a moshav—a semi-collective settlement—in rural Israel before 1967, an Israel, indeed, remote from and neglected by the Israeli present. Like the village in Mira Magen's "A Piece of Cake for Saul," Gilboa's moshav is a claustrophobic world; it's a hothouse of gossip, frustration, sad ironies, small and large deceptions, strangled desire and violence. "I ask very little of life," says the young adolescent narrator whose voice weaves its way through the collection, "The possibility of breakfast when you're not hungry, someone to talk to, a book to read. Nothing more." Sensitive to the subterranean tensions that surround her, she describes the madness, betrayals, and loneliness that stalk her community, where most of the people have been severed from their past and where a rape may or may not have taken place. For in a village in which each character has his or her own version of the truth, what really happened and what didn't happen remain ultimately obscure, with only the voice of the young girl serving as witness.

Born in Tel Aviv in 1943, married and the mother of three children, Shulamith Gilboa is editor of the literary supplement of the daily newspaper *Yediot Aharonot*. She holds an M.A. in Philosophy from Tel Aviv University. She has published literary reviews, essays, and poems, as well as an earlier collection of stories, *Either Winter or Its End* (Sifrat Hapoalim, 1982). *The Fourth Lie* (Hakibbutz Hameuchad) was her second book.

If Nella Could Do It

Shulamith Gilboa

Nella's dream was not unattainable. Just look at her. After seven years, she opened a boutique on Hafetz Hayim Street in Petach Tikva. *Nella's Fashions*, written in wavy gold letters on a red background, scream out: I did it. In spite of the mudslingers and their slander. They can all drop dead.

She sits behind a cash register in her spike heels, staring at the passersby on the other side of the decorated store window, her profile multiplied in the wall mirrors. You won't find jeans here, or anything else that's a hundred percent cotton. Artificial silk, viscose, chiffon, various percentages of polyester. There was something here for every woman's pocketbook, but there was absolutely nothing masculine, stiff, pseudo-casual.

Nella doesn't make apologies. Those who want to, will find something, those who are puzzled will understand, and those who are satisfied will return. You shouldn't run after people. They're like mercury, she once told Shimon. If you grab hold of them, they slip out of your fingers. But if you walk slowly alongside them, you'll get it all. And Nella's "all" changed over the years.

When you sit behind a cash register, life takes on different proportions. There are receipts. Totals. You can assume that a particular item will bring in a particular price. Nella doesn't like surprises. An article of clothing is not a squash that gets gnawed by bugs if you forget to sulferize in time. An article of clothing is the essence of the contemporary experience,

59

she would have said if the words had come to her. But the words always came to her too late, and they sounded different.

Hafetz Hayim Street bustles with people in the morning. The roofed market is redolent with the smell of mint and onions. Butchers' knives, discarded by heavy hands, clang against the sides of iron scales. Hungry eyes devour the sight of a new, out-of-this-world food—chickens turning on a spit in an oven, exposed to the heat of Hell. Only one of the butchers had dared to buy that large, glass-doored oven, which attracted a constant stream of curious onlookers. Nella's shop is slightly beyond it, between the stationery store and the fruit store that was competing desperately with the market stands. A scrubbed and shiny window, a red carpet at the entrance, and a wine-red light fixture that colors the fabrics with somnolent warmth. Like a bordello, I said, laughing. Momma was shocked.

Do you know what a bordello is, she asked, the word sticking in her throat along with all the other words that taste of cinnamon and almond essence, and I suddenly didn't know whether I really did know, or whether the books that mention such places know what they're talking about, and I only knew that Nella did it, who would have thought she'd really do it. If we went back seven years, she would still be living with Arnold in the third house in the middle row, and this is how dreams become reality.

Arnold and Nella, Shimon and Esther. Their farms adjoining, hibiscus and oleander spilling over the barbed wire fence, creeping crab grass alongside yellow-flowered alfalfa. Esther cultivates her garden. A row of rosebushes along the entranceway, and beds of daisies and dahlias on the lawn. Twenty-five square meters of variegating colors, dominated by green, encircle her home, to which only recently a baby has been added. Nasturtiums in spring, geraniums in winter, and even a cluster of narcissi blossoming occasionally, as if unintentionally, during the rainy days of autumn.

So what does she really have to do, Yanek asks in his mother's name, during the pre-baby period. And with the help she gets, what's really left for her to do, Yanek's mother's continues, post-baby. Shimon pampers Esther, and Esther pampers the house. Two black braids encircle her rounded skull and the sounds of her singing pervade the yard from early morning.

Arnold's garden is limited to the purple flowers of a margosa tree that become pale green clusters of pellets in the fall. Nella doesn't sunbathe in the yard; nor does she bend over to tend flowers, lest they pale by comparison. Mutt and Jeff, Yanek's mother said, and Pini, who asked his parents, said that one was very tall and the other very short, meaning that those households were exact opposites. No one talked about the men. What is there to say about men? They were never at home during the day.

Nella had white skin and the kind of body birds sing in. While Esther weeds and rakes and plants, Nella moves back and forth from armchair to bed, from bed to armchair. The sunlight is blinding in this bare land, piercing the skin relentlessly until it reddens, pains, and peels, and Nella has pain enough without it. It's hard for her to chew, hard to swallow, there are stones everywhere. Heavy brocade drapes that do not move with the wind shade the dining room table which, although carved to seat six, is never used. Arnold comes home at night and grabs a few slices of bread from the kitchen, and Nella, who doesn't eat a thing but keeps getting fatter, loathes the shape of it. Nella's body, fat and soft, is concealed by the azure silk robe Arnold brought her from Tel Aviv. The pillows on their double bed are decorated with flowers, and the sheets are in solid, light colors. Nella twists and turns on the wide bed, straightening the wrinkles. She twists and turns, presses and straightens. What with the armchair and the bed, Nella works hard, and lunches without Arnold are unsatisfying. Only embroidering and crocheting relieve her exhaustion. Casting on stitches, tying, twisting, and loosening them. Nella crochets curtains, table-cloths, doilies, and blouses. White and turquoise and pink overlap, but never become entangled. Arnold admires Nella, her nimble white fingers, her nails that get a change of polish every other day, the smooth backs of her feet that never get muddied. Nella too loves her fingers. Olive oil, egg yolks, and honey at night, and hand lotion during the day. When Nella massages her hands, the gravel in her throat vanishes. A slow, easy current flows down through her trachea, spills over into her breasts, is swirled into her stomach with a gentle murmur.

Arnold works outside, in a world of sun, people, and the smell of sweat. You should get out, he tells her in the evening, sinking into an armchair adorned with crocheted and embroidered doilies. To a movie, a show. And Arnold isn't just a talker. Once every two weeks, they take a taxi to Habima National Theater, or Ohel Shem Auditorium, Nella decked out in a dress that reveals her smooth back and her cleavage, covered with a scarf woven from powder blue silk threads. Holding her elbow, Arnold walks beside her in places Esther and Shimon don't know exist.

That *schwartzer*, Nella says, she works and works and wastes herself. Even if she has help, that's still the only thing she knows how to do. Work. A work horse, she says to Arnold, who knows he is married to a princess, a queen, a high priestess who reigns over his household, gracing it with charming furniture and that white body he could have immersed himself in, if he weren't so tired, so troubled, so oppressed.

Shimon works on the farm. When he prunes the trees, his muscles ripple like they do in Lawrence's novels. Standing on the ladder, his biceps compete with his calf muscles and drops of sweat give his body a mahogany hue. Esther brings him a tall glass of cold lemonade and he takes it, sips and swallows, the cold freezing his throat, his glance searching for the right spot to saw a branch, then sliding over the brocade drapes and the vague shadows behind them. Esther has had her first child, and she is all milk and softness and saturated breasts. The lemonade tastes of sugar and freshly picked lemons still redolent with ether, but the darkness behind the drapes remains undeciphered, troubling.

They've all got the same hole, Shimon says to Marco as they walk side by side on their guard duty shift, and the Czech slaps his thigh. The spaces between streetlights are obscured by darkness and Marco, sensitive to undertones, is still insecure about his home and his wife. Women are just decoration for the hole, he laughs, excluding Toni, Esther, their mothers and sisters from this amusing generalization, and tapping his chest, he looks at Shimon. Give them kids, money for shopping, a nuzzle every once in a while, and everything's okay. Praise God!

There's one more thing, Shimon says pensively. Maybe we have to take them out. So they can take in the world.

And that's exactly how he found a good reason, the right reason, to knock on Nella's door one morning when day was barely breaking, and enter into the fragrant darkness of a doily-filled living room, notice the azure silk robe, and say, you know, "Five-Five" is playing now, and I want to take Esther, when are you going?

Everyone knows when Nella and Arnold go out in the evening. A taxi waits in front of their house, its headlights illuminating hard earth and a concrete wall interlaced with iron. Nella's heels clack against the stones of the entranceway, blocks of Jerusalem stone Arnold restored to the soil when they were just starting out, and a scarf wrapped around her back leaves flashes of white bosom visible to the driver, the neighbors, the passersby, and vies with the light of the interior lamp, which was switched off only when they reached Jabal al Kuds, so as not to attract the unnecessary, annoying attention of the backgammon players sitting at a street-side coffee house.

Maybe tomorrow, or the day after.

Do you mind if we go with you? And Shimon notices that the robe is tightly fastened, and the corner of the kitchen that he's able to see is spotless. I mean, if we share a taxi?

Nella, momentarily nauseated by the smell of sweat, sits down on the armchair, ignores the wide body opposite her, the arms, the belt that has fallen slightly below the waistline, the unfastened button and curly hairs caught in the button hole, the fastened buttons, the traces of moisture that . . . Talk to Arnold, she says, and the name hangs in the air, caroms off the walls, the Hungarian accent rounding it out, as if to conciliate, and it pierces Shimon with pricks of jealousy.

A different world, he would tell Marco what he couldn't tell Esther, but I'm still going to get inside her pants. What does she do in that dark house all day? And Marco, who loves walking with Shimon, agrees, and he pictures Arnold, who works away from home doing God knows what, and thinks about the baby his wife is about to have, and asks if it's hard to be with them after they give birth, you know what I mean, and Shimon, who watches Esther diapering, singing, cooking, walking back and forth, back and forth, knows that Marco doesn't mean to make him feel guilty, so he replies with restraint, it depends, it's not anything special, you know, it's not what it used to be. Wider. And he immediately thinks that Nella never had children, and she's probably narrow down there, the thought arousing anger and desire, causing his blood to flow.

Hidden in your room, you try to recapture the odor that had nauseated you, and you rush to the mirror to try on dresses for the approaching visit to the theater. Nella won't ask Arnold what he and Shimon had decided, and she won't tell him about Shimon's visit. She'll simply scrub the living room, maybe air it out, the hot sun penetrating the lacy round doilies, and we, walking along the road in front of the house, don't know what happened, what's happening, what will happen. Pillows and sheets lie on the window sill, Nella, so very tired, rests against them. When the drapes are drawn again, you'll stretch out on the double bed, twisting and turning, smoothing and straightening, and you'll know that, if you want him to, he'll fall at your feet, with all his sweat, and stench and muscles. But that's not what you want.

Excellent, we'll split it fifty-fifty, Arnold said. The tickets are expensive, and so is the trip. Now it'll be easier. Shimon is also pleased. Only Esther is angry. "Five-Five" or "Four-Five"—you can listen to songs on the radio, and none of the actresses on the stage have babies at home to love, to diaper, to inhale the smell of their breath.

Such a gem, your husband, Rosa asserts. Wants to take you to a show. And you? You get mad. Rocking the baby's cradle, holding a mug of coffee in one hand, patting his back briskly with the other, she pushes Esther with a third and fourth hand, the hands of women, towards the closet, the living room, even the kitchen, just so she'd get out of there. I'll stay with him, go, enjoy.

God bless you, Esther says, smiling on her way to the taxi. Its headlights illuminate pale roses and daisies hiding among their leaves. Nella is already in the taxi, sitting next to the driver, and she does not turn around in the glassy darkness. Shimon sits sideways and Arnold sits on the edge, so there's no need to open the folding seat in the center. Three in the back, two in the front, a clear night among the sorghum fields, and the sweet smell of perfume.

It was very nice, Nella says on the way back, and Esther dreamily hums melodies from the show. Shimon is bored, there's a big dent in his pocket, and the show, like all shows, was just a show, not life. It was very nice, Arnold repeats his wife's words, and his eyes close. Two in the front, three in the back, Esther leaning against Shimon, Nella sitting up straight, and Arnold calculating. An hour's ride back to the house. Half of it for sleeping.

The next morning arrives, like every other morning, after a night of unfulfilled promise. Shimon shoos Esther out of the yard into the kitchen. You, inside. Food, the baby, and some rest. Enough work, learn from her. And Esther laughs. Shimon is jumpy. He digs irrigation ditches around the trees, paints the trunks white with lime, and takes out his anger on the young shoots that had sprung up near the trunks, sprouting indifferently. Slashing and hacking, he tries to determine how resolute he really is. It is a little strange, he has to admit, at my age, but, when he notices the drapes moving, he decides in a flash. Esti, I'm going to the orchard. Through a hole in the fence, behind the field of peppers, he returns, as if flying, to his neighbor's door.

Knock. Get your breathing under control. Don't wait. There's no reason to wait, knock again, I won't wait, definitely not, what for? The trees in the orchard need to be sulfurized. Knock again, because she's obviously there, and knock again, until the door opens and now I'm here, and so is she, wearing a robe that isn't fastened, her hands give off the scent of lotion, her back convulses with laughter or tears, fear or desire, and Shimon is not embarrassed. I won't be embarrassed, God will help me. What's wrong, he asks, it's already clear that she's crying, and it seems to him that a delicate flower is falling into his arms, and with great compassion, he carries her to the bed, thanks his God, and perhaps it's a hunted deer, or a tigress.

What did Shimon see in her, what did he think he saw in her, and I say "he saw" as if I had seen.

It's a bunch of lies, he will say to Marco a week later, she's just like the other good women, what do they want from her? For after he had been with her, had savored her and continued to savor her, he could no longer speak of her. The world had changed. A faint yearning of perfume, Shimon thought, if such were his thoughts. Sweet sweat, he thinks, moisture, darkness, and rooms suffused with spending.

From then on, Arnold's meals were waiting for him in the oven when he came home from work in the evening. Covered in aluminum foil, they steamed until they cooled off, but their taste was preserved. Nella still scrubbed, her house sparkled, but shadows were already bursting through the drawn drapes, beating on the neighbors' doors and retreating. A dark alto, sometimes a soprano, a radio changing secret stations known to only a few.

There were fewer crocheted doilies, and less pain when she swallowed. If she had known how easy it was to be consoled, she would not have waited. Days are normally divided into clearly defined moments, small tasks, but when she lay with Shimon's hard, sweaty body, the hands of the clock raced with mad abandon. Even the sun had a new quality, tanning, with a promise of coolness. And the day seemed to ebb immediately after it began, every day, every day.

Nella is busy. If she weren't so miserly, I would have written happy. The birds feed their chicks in her body, tiny beaks twitter with hunger, and however much they receive, they still await more. Shimon is drunk. He drives out to the fields and returns secretly, pretending to be tending to the sick hens and chicks, repairing rusted machine parts, replacing fallen screws. Esther is happy to see him, and sometimes, she doesn't see. She thinks it's his love for the baby that brings him home, and she tells Mazal, Rosa, even Sima, when she runs into them on the way to the grocery, that a man changes when he becomes a father, an absolute puh-leasure. Everyone is satisfied, Arnold with his meals, Shimon with his women, Esther with her motherhood, and only Nella begins to feel new chasms gaping.

At the end of six months, her dresses are as beautiful as ever, her body is still white and no accident has rounded her belly. Anticipating Shimon's arrival gradually begins to be like waiting for Arnold, or for the evening, or the occasional show, all those things whose anticipation is more important than their reality.

Unsealed envelopes lie among the sheets in the brown wardrobe that lines the bedroom wall. At the beginning of every month, more blue-gray bills are added to the envelopes. Her mother's body may have risen skyward in smoke, but—her wisdom had remained in the house. When Arnold is immersed in the sweet sleep of evening, Nella searches his pockets. Arnold pays fifty percent less for the taxi than he did before, and Nella asks him for the difference. Clothes, she smiles, and he's relaxed, his wife is beautiful, her clothes are lovely, and anybody who's jealous can just eat their hearts out. Not only does Nella know how to crochet and embroider, but also how to sew and to alter. Her closet fills up with clothes, yet she's never short of money. The treasure lying between the sheets in the wardrobe increases, linens and lucre. If she had understood, she would have laughed. But Nella, like the rest of us, laughs only at others.

Nella counts the money in the early morning. Arnold is at work, strips of fearless light dare to penetrate the kitchen window, but the bedroom is in torpid darkness, refusing to awaken. In the light of the night table lamp, she empties envelopes, shifting the bills from one to another. Five years of saving, one with Shimon, and the last three months have been the most profitable of all. At first, Shimon blushed, embarrassment spreading across his face in shades of red and pink. He held the gold perfume atomizer he had bought her as a gift, shocked at the spoiled tone of her voice, no, money is better, really. I won't have to explain to Arnold, and the name spreads through the room, bent, ludicrous. It's hard for me to ask him for money, you know, especially now.

Shimon immediately pulls some bills out of his pocket, money he received the day before for some old layers he brought to the slaughter house, and puts them on the table, watching, and Nella doesn't take them, she merely looks at them. The next day she shows him a night-gown whose straps she has replaced, spinning around for him, her breasts swaying. This is from you, she smiles, seeing the satisfaction gathering in the fingers that desired to touch, to grab a handful, and from that moment on, life was easy and the envelopes swelled. Shimon was happy too. First a nightgown, then lipstick spread on her pink nipples, then lace panties. Every payment led to an erotic surprise or innovation, inviting more of the same. Esther, too, was pleased. Every night, she sprayed her throat and breast with the golden atomizer, Shimon watching her affectionately.

Shimon is supporting two women, works his land, his garden, and his home, and those who know, know. Exhaustion begins to drain into his arms and thighs, small drops of it entering his bloodstream. Sleep as heavy and smooth as granite overtakes him in the evening, and Esther begins to twist and turn in his bed. His self-satisfied snores drive her to the baby's room, the kitchen, the bathroom, the window facing their neighbor's house, and, noticing the light behind their curtains, her puzzlement at the late hour and the light grows, then vanishes instantly. What does she do all day, that one? Sleeps and gorges herself, and she suddenly feels a stab of pity for Arnold, those Ashkenazim, what women they have, poor things.

Nella sits in the armchair, her fingers hugging her body beneath the stole crocheted from soft white yarn, evaluating Shimon in terms of profit and loss. Profits are big, very big. For the last three months, the passing time has had a clear objective, and not a single day brings a loss. What should have taken many years would take only half the time. It was so easy. Nella is almost happy, and she turns off the light and gets into bed to wrap herself around Arnold. Warm and soft, a whiff of bad breath emanating from his mouth, he turns his back to her and bends his knees.

(1993)
—*Translated by Sondra Silverston*

Introduction to Leah Aini's
"The Fruit of Paradise"

Along with "Rest," Leah Aini's "The Fruit of Paradise" appeared in
Summer Heroes, a collection of short stories widely praised by Israeli
critics when it was published in 1991.[30]

Reviewer Roni Someck compared Aini's stories to the neorealist
films of Vittorio de Sica in their depiction of lives of cruel deprivation
momentarily illuminated by compassion and grace; for Hannah Herzig,
Aini's short stories are an "intermeshing of opposites—hardness and
softness, roughness and sophistication, realism and fantasy, violence and
charm, but above all a fusion of lyrical poetry and sharp intellect." They
are also expressions of social protest: Aini perceives Israeli society as
suffering from racism—particularly toward Arabs and Eastern, African,
and Eastern-European Jews—and from prejudice against "the weak."
"I'm committed to writing my 'truth,'" she says, "however piercing or
difficult, sometimes cruel, it may be."

Drawn from the impoverished, crowded, south Tel Aviv neigh-
borhood of her childhood, Aini's characters are the outcasts of main-
stream Israeli society. They live their broken, forlorn—but also

---

30. *Summer Heroes* has also been titled *The Sea Horses' Dance* or *The Sea Horses' Loop* in
English, for the name of the novella included in the collection. For a review of *Someone
Must Be Here,* see Haya Hoffman, "The Word Collector," *Modern Hebrew Literature* 17
(Fall/Winter 1996), 35–36.

dreaming, aspiring, and impassioned—lives on the social fringe. Her stories are populated by weary workers, the handicapped, mentally ill, developmentally disabled, poor apprentice hairdressers, sick and abused children, shopkeepers in cramped little stores, prostitutes, gamblers, drunks. And there are survivors of the Holocaust: "No one came out whole," says the butcher in Aini's story, "Until the Entire Guard Passes"; indeed, like the woman in "Rest," the survivors she portrays are tormented by their memories and unable ever to fully rebuild their lives. But from time to time there is also a wild beauty and tenderness among all this devastation: the passion between the couple in "Rest," the tenderness of the prostitute Estahore the opening lines of her short story "Micha," about a handicapped child who, though filled with hatred and envy, says: "At eleven I am outside, outside, outside. I look at the sun and cry. It burns my eyes and I am happy and I cry."

Leah Aini herself holds fast to her own memories. As she writes in "Shower," included in the poetry section, she keeps her memories "like a bitch/over a bone." Remembering both the grandmother who gave her a shower as a child, and the grandmother gassed in the "shower" at Auschwitz, she writes:

> . . . already a long time, a long time ago, I buried
> the bone of the murder
> and the bone of bathing
> in the garden of life.

That "garden of life" is a suggestive image for understanding Aini's work as a whole: her award-winning books of poetry (*Portrait*, 1988, and *The Empress of Imagined Fertility*, 1991); her collection of short stories, her children's books (*Call Me from Downstairs*, 1994, and *Mr. Rabbi's Job Hunt*, 1994), as well as her novels, *Sand Tide* (1992), focused on a young woman whose husband of two years is killed when he steps on a land mine during army maneuvers, and *Someone Must Be Here* (1996), which has been called "an Israeli version of Gorky's *Lower Depths* that is amazingly beautiful."

In *Someone Must Be Here*, a young woman with a passion for literature carries a notebook with her everywhere she goes, rescuing words that might otherwise be lost. Aini's own words seem like "rescuers" as well: of broken dreams, and moments of terror and of love as well as of violence and tenderness, that without her find no voice. Her poetry and prose cleave, as she writes in "One Girl's Dance,"

to a dream of the actual,
breathing touch
spinning the self
and the shadow.

When she was four, Leah Aini moved from south Tel Aviv (the "less beautiful" part of the city, as she says) to Bat Yam (whose name, "Daughter of the Sea," she adds, is strangely out of sync with its crowded reality). After elementary school, she chose to attend a chaotic religious high school in the north of the city, where most of her education transpired by witnessing the human dramas enacted in the court house nearby. The school closed, she dropped out, and after completing secondary school through extension courses, found herself at the Kibbutz Seminary, where she studied Hebrew Literature and Language. She worked as an editor for the newspaper *Al HaMishmar* for four years. She has won awards for her poetry from both Bar Ilan and Haifa Universities, a writing grant from the Tel Aviv Fund for Literature and Art, and the Prime Minister's Prize for Literature in 1994. Her fiction has appeared in both Italian and German. "Writing is not my 'love,'" says Aini. "It is *me*." She lives with her husband and young daughter in the Tel Aviv area.

The Fruit of Paradise

Leah Aini

Zisman awoke from his afternoon nap. It was still hot. His sticky chest-hairs curled through the holes in his undershirt. Pools of sweat collected on the rolls of his stomach and thighs. On the edge of a glass (of artificial fruit drink) which he had unthinkingly placed on the window ledge, a few bugs circled. He raised his heavy eyes and stared at the design that summer was painting with a buzzing brush on the cheap glass from the supermarket. Was it the bugs that had woken him up? Probably. Then a sudden wind drifted cold fingers across his sunken eyes and just for a moment his sweat cooled pleasantly. He looked at the clock. The digital numbers moved too fast for him to see. He was still half asleep. Slowly he realized: it was Saturday. The only thing he had on today (with a troublesome friend) had been cancelled. A movie? Maybe some beer later? Alone? He didn't feel like it. Better just to stay home (in his rented room-with-kitchen) and bury himself in the newspapers or in front of the TV. Maybe he could skim the singles ads with his eager pen. No, as far as he could recall, he didn't do that yesterday. He had no time. Why? He went to the market. Yes, he came back from the market only around late afternoon. He'd left the office late, but made it to the market.

Suddenly everything floated to the surface: a shopping bag full of summer fruits and in another bag—a watermelon. A whole watermelon. Just for him. He turned to the yellow saliva-stained pillow and shoved his face deep into it, burying his smile. What pleasure. How could he have forgotten the fruit!

71

The bag of fruit waited in the refrigerator and the watermelon sat heavy and tired by the gas plate. Only yesterday, late in the evening, had he remembered to put it in the fridge. His negligence ate at him.

Winter fruits didn't satisfy him. Apples, available all year long, had begun to bore him. He craved plums, peaches, pears, especially those juicy slices of watermelon and cantaloupe. He avoided the tropical fruits flooding the market these days. It wasn't easy for him to adopt new habits. Even the computers—the fruit of advanced technology—elicited his fears when they were installed in the insurance office where he worked. How do you peel those tropical creations?

Women, too, were out of his reach—exotic flowers either on a tree too high or a bush too low. He needed life to meet him at eye level, no higher than the counters of fruit.

"The apple?" one summer he heard a young man, working as an office temp, say. "The apple?" he went on, an earring dangling from his ear, "it's not even clear that that was the fruit the snake gave Eve. Open the book of Genesis. You'll see—there's no mention of what kind of fruit it was."

"So how did they decide on an apple?" asked the janitor Menashe, a *kippah* on his white hair, a light-hearted spirit tilting the broom that always accompanied him.

"Some fairy tale from the Far East that captured everyone's heart," said the young man. "So now go figure out which fruit he did give her, okay?" he persisted.

Zisman had had enough. He escaped to the restroom. Yes, he knew which fruit it was, but why should he tell? So they could laugh at him? He once dreamed it. No, actually he dreamed it twice. He knew very well what kind of fruit it was.

His legs pulled the sheet tensely and his fists grew hard. He didn't want to remember again, but discomfort overtook him and his stomach growled. How he longed for the red-orange-green sweating coldly in the refrigerator, waiting for his soft fingers to wash it under the faucet, waiting for the ceremony of purification. No. It was a dream, a twice-dreamt dream. But one can never tell. Nausea crept up his throat and he rolled over again in his bed of contradictions.

Yes. There was a woman, once, like a prostitute. Why a prostitute? He didn't know. He got her phone number. She seemed okay. They told him: she's divorced, mature, a secretary, a looker. He hated those words, intended to describe her, but he also craved them. They also told him: act nice, we said good things about you. Who knows what they said, but he was thrilled, so he went. He waited half an hour before knocking at her door. He waited for his organ to behave appropriately. How could he come in with a bulge in his pants? When he did go in, she was sitting on the balcony and asked him to come closer. She served him grapes and cold water and told him to feel at home. She didn't seem promiscuous. She was wearing this long shirt or was it a short housedress that hid her fat but smooth legs and heavy breasts. Chic sporty pockets covered her breasts—at least they tried to. He sat there like a fool, silent. Clearing his dry throat. Silent. Every grape was a stone in his throat. The woman laughed and chattered nonstop. She kept chattering. He realized that she was trying to get him to talk. She finally succeeded: he relaxed, broke out of his shyness, and began to ask her questions too.

He couldn't remember what his questions were about, but suddenly a conversation was taking place. It was a silly, kitschy, conversation—but a conversation nevertheless. Sometimes her hair did the talking in response to a breeze or a sudden movement of the body, his or hers. He can't remember now, but some words were involved, too. Shula (or Ge'ula? What difference does it make now, anyhow?) decided that he was a shy, inexperienced, overgrown boy. She was right, but his eyes denied it. He strove to look seductive, to catch her eye and send her a message: to seem like a man among men. That made her laugh even more until he found himself, with his balding head and his square jaw, lying in her lap. Suffocating in her warmth.

The woman began to cradle him. Pinch his ears, his cheeks. First he mumbled—what am I, her son? Then he hoped her strange maternality would turn into femininity: if only his hands would cooperate, caress her, the hesitation would disappear in her hips, her chest, her bra strap.

It all happened a long time ago. He had never before been with a woman. Everything she was willing to show him in her bed was like a first visit to the circus. She, the whole of her, was like fruit. Whenever he thought, imagined, daydreamed, about her, the image of fruit sprung up. Like when they touched: small and brown, heavy and pink, one big, juicy, fragrant, basket of fruit. For one long hour he rolled between the leaves of her pubic hair, her beauty marks climbing all over him like ants.

How beautiful this is, he thought, what pleasure! But what is the ultimate fruit, the concealed one? There, between the foliage of black leaves, curled and rustling like happy cellophane? Zisman pushed his head inside the lion's mouth. Odors of decay rose within him only for a moment, then his desire came back with its perfumes. He was like a drunk in an orchard. Inside, at the end of the curving path that came down from the treetop, where empty-headed birds twittered and flowers blossomed in unexpected places within the skin and above it and weeds were scattered, a bit here, a bit there, thin hairs and ornamental spots: inside, was the fruit.

Zisman pointed his head fearlessly, sticking out his tongue, eager to bite on that wild and well-hidden, quivering, all-knowing cherry. Nonsense poems tickled him. "A gardener grew a cherry in the garden." And the fruit, the fruit of paradise. Did Adam forget to create it? Perhaps had wanted to forget? And here the snake came crawling on its belly, handed him the fruit, said: "Bite!" Zisman already pulled out his undulating tongue to atone for that original disobedience, for the failure, the upripe fruit, but she bent towards him, a stem supple and perfumed, her sharp teeth deep in his neck.

Whose head was cut off he could not recall, but the scream, "Not there!" he would carry with him for weeks to come, in his ears, in his pockets, at the bottom of his stomach. He left a pair of good cotton socks there. More precisely: not really there, but with her. The "Not there!" kept him from returning and collecting what was his. His dignity, and his socks.

Zisman snored lightly, his mouth open. What a revolting dream, and he rots in it more and more. After all, apples bore him so much and cherries give him rashes. Cherries are the only fruit that give him rashes. Well, so many fruits wait in the refrigerator for him. Cool, heady, sweet as well-behaved children. Why not let them comfort him?

He got up slowly. Though his body was like lead, he still felt rested and relaxed. He decided to shower. Afterward, he'd sit with a big bowl of fruit and watch television. Screw it all, he'll eat to his heart's content. He shut the window heavily, placing his glass on the table. The bugs, which long ago abandoned the glass of juice, were waiting quietly now for him to turn on the lights. But he wouldn't turn them on. Let those blood-suckers die. He doesn't need light to take a shower.

He felt even more relaxed after the shower. Almost content. He didn't notice how his wet feet stuck to the dirty floor. Once in the kitchen, he finally turned on the light and approached the old refrigerator. Making a quick, crucial, decision, he skipped the fruits and grabbed a handful of the watermelon like a conqueror. He lifted it up, relishing its weight, and laid it in the sink like the severed head of some great general. He pulled a rusty old meat knife from the drawer and full of excitement lightly sharpened it. He met the edge of the knife with the tip of his tongue, satisfied. Armed with the knife, he stepped toward the silent watermelon, green, promising, shapeless. Zisman ignored the troop of flies ready to join this spectacular operation. Knife in hand, he lay a sharp blow on the watermelon's crude face and buried his own face at once in the dripping red sink.

His passion subsided slowly with the taste in his mouth: sour, mild. He looked, astonished, at the heap of pale pink and felt betrayed. The blurred face of the watermelon, cut in two, was laughing at him with tasteless revenge. Zisman's eyes were terribly dry, extremely thirsty, unbelieving. He turned off the light humiliated, and left the spoiled head of the watermelon to the indifferent flies. Exhausted, he carried himself to the chair on the balcony and sat in the dark.

It was still hot. The moon hung in the sky like spoiled peeled fruit and the street was quiet. He found a forgotten plate of shrunken pits on the window sill. With his rotting mouth he proceeded to crack them open, one by one. He spit the husks back onto the plate. A sharp pain pinched his stomach, then pinched again. Zisman doubled over. The pain came back and got hellish hold of him. You'd think it was caused by something he'd eaten. But what had he eaten? What?

(1991)

—*Translated by Gal Keidar with Miriyam Glazer*

Rest

Leah Aini

Even the ground itself was hard on you, hard and stubborn. The men from the Burial Society were doing the digging for you when they suddenly came across a sharp white stone lying in the ground. It looked at us like a kid screaming, "I was here first! I found this spot first!"

That must be a sign, I thought. We ought to leave. I'll take you home. Anyway, this is no place for you. The sand here is damaged, dirty, wet, and there's no ocean—and you are so white and clean. I'll take you home. But Dr. Katz was with me, his arm wrapped around mine. That needle, the one that so frightens me, the one that gets you in your behind, was right there in his pocket.

We were four: me, Dr. Katz, Estahore, and her client Azam from Gaza, who drove us here in his new Ford with the red seatcovers. He'd look nervously at his gold watch every five minutes. And I thought here I am, my life stopped at 12:35 P.M., and this guy is in a hurry to fuck and go home to his wife and kids.

When they lowered you, slightly on an angle, I wanted to jump in, just as I was, heavy and dizzy from the tranquilizers, and lay there in your place or underneath you, to make you warm and cozy. But, and I'm not sure why, I stayed where I was, like an idiot. Dr. Katz's words ran through my head a hundred times and more: "Ruthie passed away yesterday. A stroke. Tomorrow she will be laid to rest. The hospital arranged everything. You have to be strong. Do you understand?" And again . . . "Ruthie passed away yesterday, it was a stroke. Tomorrow. . . ."

76

The words lit up in my mind, on again then off again, one by one, like the theatre lights during previews at the Edison Cinema. I thought yesterday, tomorrow, today, right now, and that's it. Nothing more. Yesterday, yes; tomorrow, no. Like a children's game. One day she's here, the next, she's gone. She's here, she's not here. Is somebody making fun of me?

Later on, as they covered you with sand, I thought a lot about the phrase, "laid to rest." They all told me that it's good that you're resting at last, that it was time. I kept silent, but I told myself inside that they were all crazy. How can you rest with a mountain of sand on top of you, so you can't breathe? Besides, someone who knows you as well as I do knows that you weren't into resting. You hated resting. "Let the dead rest!" you always said when I wanted to rest instead of sleeping with you again for the fourth straight time.

I felt hot during your funeral. The sweat poured down my body like rain. Estahore cried a bit and kept pushing Azam's hand from her butt. He put it back, she pushed it away. The dark line circling her eyes dripped on her red cheeks like mud and the black dress hung loosely on her like a sack. Only the big silver belt helped hold up her waist and her chest. Suddenly she dug her hand into my pocket (I was wearing my khaki Sabbath shorts which you'd promised me for two weeks now) and she told me to wipe my face. I wiped it and left the handkerchief on my head, over the *kippa* made of cardboard, so it could dry off.

Dr. Katz said that the hospital arranged everything, but Estahore had to arrange for the obituaries. She asked Saul the "Gluer," the one who walks around the neighborhood like an angel of death mixing glue with water. She asked him to glue a few obituaries on the notice boards for her, but not too many. Whoever needs to know knows already. The rest will know without having to read about it. That's what she said. I think they copied the words from some other obituary that Saul keeps as an example. That's why it says, "To Our Dear Mother." I found it really funny. I kept saying, "That's not Ruthie, not in a million years. Ruthie didn't have children. She's sterile. I should know, because if she had kids I'd be their father."

When it was all over, Dr. Katz opened my fist and placed two more tranquilizers in it. I looked at him and he smiled and said, "Be strong. You hear me? Be strong." I smiled back and he left, not before whispering a few words to Estahore. She stopped wailing and began to shake her head vigorously, pushing Azam away from her.

We came back home. Estahore opened the door for me, led me to the bed and took off my sandals. Then she cooled down my face with a wet towel. She said I was red as a beet. As she was taking off my shirt, she asked if I understood what happened to you. I didn't know how to respond so I said, "Yes." She said, "Good. In that case, everything's fine. You rest now and when I'm done with Azam, I'll come to you and we'll sleep together. You took your pill?"

She didn't wait for my answer. Just like Dr. Katz, she opened my fist and took the two tranquilizers that were smeared all over my hand and brought me a glass of water. I pretended to swallow, just like you taught me, and lay down on my side. Estahore kept watching me until Azam peeked in, hungry as a horse, and threatened to leave if she didn't join him. She left only after she leaned over and kissed my forehead. I could hear them laughing all the way to the shack. Jimmy was kicked out of the shack, right into the *khamsin*, and he was crying. But soon I could hear him noisily squeezing underneath the yard chair and going back to sleep, dreaming dog's dreams.

Getting out of bed made me dizzy, so I leaned on the wall like a broom until the dizziness subsided. Finally, I went to the closet and opened it. Your half was full, as if you were never laid to rest, as if tomorrow was Friday and you'd be coming home from the hospital for the weekend. I picked out one of your dresses, my favorite, the one with the shells and the yellow flowers. I took it out of the closet. I pulled it toward me just like you were in it and your fragrance filled me up all over again. I was filled with hunger a little like Azam and I felt as if I needed to touch you for real. Suddenly I spotted the mirror across the room, and on the shelf under the mirror, there was your hair-brush. Clumsy and barefooted, with the dress clinging to my body, I ran to the brush and embraced it too. Sitting on the floor, with my chin clutching the collar of the dress close to my neck, I pulled out most of the hairs in the brush. Slowly, I made them into a curl for myself, your curl, light brown and smooth. I twirled it around and around my finger, the dress still clinging to me. My saliva dripped on the dress and the curl with love.

I fell asleep on the floor. When I woke up, it was already evening. Through the window I saw Estahore with a new client, sharing a watermelon. He was licking the watermelon juice on her hands. He was an Arab too. You know how Estahore always says, "Only with Arabs. They're clean and honest and pay up front. When they come, they sigh like the songs of Farid and they take me home to Casablanca." She was blunt. Without shame.

When we first came to live here and you were still at home all week, even Estahore resented us. I haven't forgotten. There's the crazy couple, they said in the neighborhood, pointing with the knife they used for cutting apples or with the jackknife they used for their fingernails. There's the holy couple, they used to say, the mental case and the cripple, dancing the tango in bed together all day. But I told you to shut your ears, pay no attention. The problem was when you had to listen only to the voices in your own head. Then all the demons came out, skinny and burned, and everyone heard the screams.

I never really completely understood what you were talking about and Estahore couldn't explain either. Dr. Katz tried, but I didn't get it. I thought he was pulling my leg when he said that you lost your whole family in Germany and that you'd been in the camps, in experiments. Remember how you'd joke around? "I was a mouse," you'd say, and show me for the thousandth time the scars on your hands, legs, and back, and the green number. Sometimes you'd really act crazy and try to scrub off the number with a piece of soap. You'd rub till the skin came off but the number didn't and I'd call Estahore for help because I couldn't stand to see the blood.

I really didn't understand, only that you had a hard time and that's why you'd sometimes flip out and cry and laugh hysterically and drag me with you to a laughter that was too big, too intense. So after two years they hospitalized you for the whole week except Friday and Saturday, so you could rest and relax there in the hospital and make colorful raffia baskets for religious kindergartens in Jerusalem.

But Saturdays were still nice when we sat in the yard. With our fingers all sticky from our sunflower seed cracking competition, we touched one another in all the good places, the ones that bring pleasure, and then we'd go to the ocean, go wild in the water, pee, and make love. You'd fill a jar with seawater for decoration. The water was gray and not too clear and the salt patiently sank to the bottom. Then you'd turn the jar over, spill out the water, and start all over again.

Sometimes, instead of going to the ocean, we'd go to the movies. We'd both laugh when everyone else cried, and cry when everyone else laughed. When we didn't understand the ending, Estahore would go by herself in the middle of the week and see the afternoon show and then she'd come back with an explanation we hadn't thought of. When Saturday was over, I'd pack up some clean clothes for you and put in the jar of seawater too. I'd walk you to the bus station, buy you a lemon ice. It was so hard to say goodbye to you. It was so hard.

Now I'm here with Estahore. We went to sleep. I swear we didn't do anything, just undressed and crawled under the blankets. Estahore hugged me like I was the big teddy bear she had had in Casablanca. She asked me a few times if I understood what happened to you until she fell asleep with her mouth open.

I can't sleep. It's terribly hot and some mosquito is buzzing around. Once it even landed on my leg, but I scared it away. You know I don't like smashing them. Disgusting black juice comes out of them and besides I feel sorry for them. Tomorrow is Friday. I think I'll clean my room in the morning and then go to Leon, the guy who sells nuts and sometimes cheats me out of my change, and buy half a pound of sunflower seeds, white and fat, and a quarter of a pound of salty almonds. Before Estahore fell asleep, she said I don't have to go to work tomorrow and not on Sunday either. And no permission from the doctor is necessary, nothing—they'll understand. All I need, she said, is to understand too and to rest. Only understand and rest.

It's easy for me to rest. And I want to. Besides, like Dr. Katz was saying, you're finally at rest and actually it's like we were resting together. It's still kind of strange to me that Estahore is resting next to me now, in your place, long, naked, olive-skinned, her braid unwound and smelling like cumin. I'm afraid that if I sneeze I'll wake her. Still, tomorrow is Friday and you're coming home, cheerful, relaxed, full of stories and nonsense that I'll try hard to grasp. Then we'll go to bed, we'll kiss and make love all night, all night, without resting for a minute. You're coming home tomorrow. What more is there to understand?

(1991)

—*Translated by Gal Keidar with Miriyam Glazer*

Introduction to Savyon Liebrecht's
" 'It's Greek to You,' She Said to Him"

"The silence in the homes of Holocaust survivors is unique," Savyon Liebrecht has written. It is a silence, she says,

> that covers pain and dark secrets, and it takes time until the child who grows up in such a home understands that this secret is not a personal one but a national, or even a universal, one. . . . [Parents] don't speak about the past; they don't speak about their thoughts; they don't speak about their feelings. In a way, the children in such homes are compelled to develop alternative ways of expression.
>
> If you see art as a form of communication, the silence in their homes is the key to the children becoming, one day, artists . . . . When I write a story today and have to enter into a character's mind and observe the world through his eyes, it comes naturally to me. I spent years in my childhood doing exactly this.
>
> —Savyon Liebrecht, "The Influence of the
> Holocaust on My Work"[31]

---

31. In Leon Yudkin, *Hebrew Literature in the Wake of the Holocaust* (Rutherford: Fairleigh Dickinson University Press, 1993), p. 126.

81

At the heart of Savyon Liebrecht's "It's Greek to You," is an excruciating silence: the never identified, never named, source of the lost mother's woundedness with which the now adult daughter in the story has been long obsessed. In Almog's "Invisible Mending," only in an allusion to the grandmother's plight as a housekeeper does one sense the background of the Holocaust. Similarly, in "It's Greek to You," from Liebrecht's eponymous collection, there is only a fleeting image of the parents having been "bound together by war" before the daughter's birth, as well as the daughter's recollection of her father's words: "Even after the war, when sometimes I couldn't tell a woman from a man, only she. . . ." Yet the past of the parents remains elusive, even as the story maps the daughter's determined attempt to unravel the knotted connectedness she feels with her dead mother and thus to grasp the pain of her own past.

Women's connectedness with one another is central to many of Liebrecht's stories: as mothers and daughters, grandmothers and granddaughters, mothers and daughters-in-law, sisters, friends. The Holocaust lurks in the background of earlier stories such as "Cutting," in which a grandmother living in Israel is suddenly overcome by memories that drive her to cut away her granddaughter's hair in a brutal way, and "Sonia Muskat," in which a young woman is exploited and victimized both as a Jew and as a woman by a cousin who should protect her. In more recent stories such as the highly disturbing "Mercy," Liebrecht links the suffering of Jewish women survivors of the Holocaust with that of Arab women in the latters' strongly patriarchal society.

Liebrecht was born in Germany and came to Israel with her parents as an infant. She studied Philosophy and Literature at Tel Aviv University, and has written for Israeli television. She received the Prime Minister's Prize for Literature, and has published three books of short stories, *Apples from the Desert* (1986), *Horses on the Highway* (1988), and *It's Greek to You* (1992). *Apples from the Desert,* a collection of her short stories, appeared in English in 1998. She lives in Holon.

"It's Greek to You," She Said to Him

Savyon Liebrecht

Real Estate Agent Eliyahu Yitzhakov assumed his professional smile of welcome for the woman; she had attracted his attention from the moment she got out of her car, scanned the signs on top of the building, and made her way to his office. His mind immediately conjured up a picture: black marble floor, wide staircase leading all the way to the roof, French windows in the front room. Closing the door quietly behind her, the woman walked in, bid him "Good Morning" in a pleasant voice, peeled off her gloves, and looked around the walls of the office. Eliyahu Yitzhakov eyed her with pleasure as she quickly took in the photographs that contractors had given him to hang in his office: of unfinished structures surrounded by scaffolding, of completed buildings, and one of a house undergoing renovation—draped in purple plastic sheets, like a gigantic gift-wrapped birthday present—that he himself had taken somewhere in Germany. It did not escape him how her eyes lingered on an enlarged newspaper photograph of him and the mayor shaking hands at the Awards ceremony for "Business of the Year."

When she sat down facing him and turned her eyes on him, he shot a quick look like a seasoned hunter at how her fingers trailed the gloves across the desk, and he said hurriedly, "I have something just for you, ma'am, an agency exclusive. A penthouse not far from the beach. Imported tiles, black marble floor, completely furnished, leather in the living room, a watering system for the roof plants, super deluxe!"

The brim of her hat shaded her eyes a little when she politely turned her head and smiled furtively, a smile that made him uneasy, as if she were enjoying a private joke. A slight hostility toward her arose in him, but he allowed her pleasant voice to seduce him.

"I'm interested in the flat at Thirty-four Ha-mered Street."

He sat back in his executive chair made of perfect imitation leather, his face looking insulted, his mouth contorted with affected disgust that left no doubt about his reaction. "Ha-mered! It's just a dump next to the junkies' park."

"I saw your agency's sign in the window."

"Thirty-four Ha-mered Street." He sensed the determination in her voice and tried one of his other tactics. He leaned forward with a gesture that insinuated intimacy and persisted in a smooth voice, "Thirty four Ha-mered Street is not a place for a woman of your class."

"Why not?" The furtive grin was back on her face.

"I have a feel for people," he explained ingenuously, ignoring the amused smile lingering in her eyes. "Just like a good matchmaker knows how to introduce the right people, so I set my eyes on someone and know immediately the apartment that suits them. I once saw a woman's back. She was standing here, looking in the window of a jewelry store. Right away I knew I had the apartment for her. I went out and asked her if, by any chance, she needed an apartment. To this day, whenever she's passing by, she comes in and thanks me for the apartment I found her. Just by looking at a back, I can find someone the right apartment. I can tell by your face—the Mered apartment is not for you. Look—" he spread his open palms in front of her, as if to underscore his utter candor, "I'll tell you the truth. The owner of the apartment on Ha-mered came to me and says he had this apartment on Ha-mered Street. The minute I heard 'Ha-mered' I said I don't want it. List it with some other broker. But he insists and gives me an exclusive. So I told him I'm not committing myself. I once had an apartment for sale on Ha-mered— I told him—and couldn't get rid of it for half a year. Finally a couple of blind people came by and took it. But for you—it's a waste of your time going there. Better let me show you the penthouse."

Twenty minutes later he stood in front of the ground floor apartment, struggling with the old lock, leaning his weight against the door trying to force it open. The door gave suddenly, and he was thrust inside, immediately assaulted by its overpoweringly musty smell. He rushed to a window, fiddled with the rusty handle, and opened the shutter.

Only then did he turn to invite her in, but she was already inside, standing at the entrance to the room next to the kitchen, her gloved hand still on the doorknob, her head tilted upward to look at the ceiling.

Even before he knew her motive there, his senses told him that things did not bode well. "Let's start with the living room," he suggested, trying to steer her toward the best room in the apartment, but she didn't respond. She just stood there, stretching her neck upward, concentrating. And without moving her head, she took off her hat with her free hand, and the blond hair that had been trapped under her hat fell straight down to her shoulders, like plastic fibers, the strands down the middle of her back looking very long because her head was tilted back. He wondered what drew her to look up like that, so he came closer, peeked, and immediately realized where the musty smell was coming from. He also knew he would have to lower the price of the apartment.

"It doesn't look good, but it's only a minor plumbing job. Nothing serious. It wasn't here a month ago." The fragance of her hair hit his nostrils when he craned his head over hers.

She grimaced, remembering when she had first seen those stains.

"Just a month?" she said, unable to contain her scorn.

"A month and an hour." He tried to impress her with an old joke that had worked for him before.

She did not respond; her memory became clearer and sharper, carrying her back to the moment that had haunted her for so many years: the morning after that awful sleepless night. Right after her parents had left the house she leapt out of bed and snuck into their bedroom like a thief, searching for the stains her mother had spoken of as she sobbed. There were two gray spots in the corner of the ceiling, like two unmatched eyes with pale pupils, as if the result of a shoddy painting job.

She now noticed some black sooty squiggles across the ceiling, surrounded by flecks of all shades of gray, like a batch of x-ray pictures laid side by side.

"This looks more than a month old," she said in a broken voice, empty of argumentativeness, her neck still craned. She wondered how her mother knew how to predict how long those stains would last as she wept on that terrible night, long after midnight. "How can you say they'll disappear? They'll be here long after I croak."

"Trust me, ma'am. I have experience in things like this happened a month ago—two months tops."

"More like twenty years ago," she chuckled, her head still tilted toward the ceiling.

He stood behind her, feeling his anger well up at her persistent examination of the stains. It suddenly occurred to him that she was lingering there solely for the purpose of bringing down the already low price of the apartment.

"Listen," he shouted in her ear, "I'm going to see a house a block away. I have some business there, I'll be back in half an hour. Look around as much as you want till I get back."

At the door he heard her say, "What, you're leaving me here alone?" Before he slammed the door he retorted, "I have a good eye for clients. You'll end up buying the penthouse. But if you like looking at stains on the wall, be my guest."

As soon as he was gone, a strange sensation overcame her. Now that she was alone in the empty apartment, the silence suddenly became overwhelming, like the silence she remembered from nights at summer camp when she used to lie on a mattress she never got used to—not even by her last night there—an ominous silence, as if beasts lurked in the quiet dark, moving swiftly, voicelessly, on padded paws, knowing a short-cut toward the innocent prey that, suspecting nothing, smiled in its dreams. Now she found herself walking gingerly around the apartment, feeling her way, absentmindedly caressing the walls, the panels, the bath-room tiles, searching for old clues, for regards from the girl who lived here years ago, who dreamt so much, who imagined her future in secret, still not knowing that the future she imagined was waiting for her in the bosom of coming years, not realizing that one day—like a visitor from another planet—the heels of her boots would click on this floor that she used to wash every Friday after school, and she would recognize the exact spot where the water had always stubbornly collected in the dinette in the crooked tiles, and she would look in vain for the pale squares left on her bedroom wall by her kindergarten and elementary school pic-tures, for marks left by hooks that supported shelves laden with her textbooks and the Junior Encyclopedia that her father had bought sec-ondhand. Only the stains that her mother mentioned in the midst of her tears were left. She went back to the old bedroom and stared at the ceiling.

Had she not asked for a reading lamp for her fifteenth birthday, she would never have heard the crying. But she did ask for a reading lamp. The light socket, they realized after they bought the brightly wrapped lamp, was hidden behind the wardrobe closet. Her mother immediately declared in her sarcastic voice, "Chelm. It's like Chelm. First they buy a pig, then they find out it isn't kosher."[32]

---

32. *Chelm:* The traditional land of fools in Jewish folklore.

Even before her face registered her disappointment, her father rushed in with, "Actually, it's time we moved the wardrobe. I always thought it was standing in the wrong place."

She emptied the shelves and the drawers of the wardrobe, and her father struggled, his face all flushed, to turn the wardrobe around and push it against the opposite wall. The light from the window hidden behind the wardrobe for years burst out, filling the room. Afterward, the two of them easily moved the bed to the wall where the wardrobe had left a pale square. Her father plugged in the new reading lamp and turned it on. As if witnessing a magic trick, they admired the bright beam of light falling on the sheet.

She spent all that afternoon replacing her belongings one by one in the wardrobe, in a meticulous new order: a drawer for socks, a drawer for stockings, a drawer for underwear, a drawer for handkerchiefs and her white scarf, a shelf for school blouses, a shelf for everyday blouses, and a shelf for her two dressy blouses. Then she got down on her knees and diligently polished the floor tiles, placed a small rug next to the bed, smoothed its ruffles, laid her slippers precisely in the middle of the arches in its pattern, shampooed her hair, combed it till the strands looked like stalks of flax, then snuggled under her blanket and lay in bed reading until late at night, her face turned to the window, her eyes over the book watching the drapes puffed up by the wind, like a pregnant belly.

At midnight the voices started coming through the wall; she reread the last line on the page and her heart sank at the thought that the neighbors might be turning up the volume on their radio, as they had been doing since their last quarrel with her mother. But soon she recognized her mother's voice, and then her father's, and even before she caught the words, she was horrified by the realization that all those years the wardrobe had served as a buffer between her and them, absorbing their voices, and from now on she was doomed to hear them.

"I need it, Marilla," her father was saying.

"I can't tonight." Her mother's voice sounded sharp and metallic.

"That's what you said last week, too."

"I've told you before and I'm not going to repeat myself like a parrot."

"You won't even have to take off your nightgown."

"No."

"Do it tonight and I won't ask again until next week."

"Cut it out."

"I'm begging you, Marilla."

"No. Period."

Even before she pieced the words together, even before she under-
stood the exchange between his drooping voice and her relentless voice,
she knew what they were talking about. But part of her kept on reading,
pretending, clinging to the letters sliding down the page. When she got
to the last line on the page, she realized she had not understood any-
thing: and she started all over, struggling hard to be engrossed by the
story, terrified by the voices rising anew on the other side of the wall.

She shrank into the bed and turned off the reading lamp, as if the
power of darkness would drive away the sounds, but the voices only got
louder and stronger.

"I don't know what to do anymore. I can't hold back any longer."

"Then don't. I can't stand the pain."

"You promised to see the doctor."

"It won't help. No one goes to a doctor for something like this. It's
a question of age. We should quit doing it. Period."

"I had a minor accident with the new machine today."

"'That's my fault too?"

"I've been edgy a whole week."

"You're edgy? Well, I'm edgy too! You think I should do things for
you—and you don't do anything for me. I can't stand these stains. I told
you a month ago."

"What stains? There are no stains here. It's something in the
plaster."

"The painter must have done a bad job."

"I must be speaking Greek to you."

She tried to force herself to fall asleep, conjuring up the image that
always brought her calm before slumber: she is swimming in placid water
with measured motions, gliding like a dolphin on the smooth, shimmer-
ing face of the water over a murky bottom, and then sinking, sinking
into the blue, beckoning her on, forever deepening and darkening.

She was abruptly aroused from the deep, wide awake, all her senses
alert. For the first time in her life she heard her mother crying, and
immediately recognized the voice she had often heard. In the dark she
saw the curtain sweep into the room and she heard her mother's sobs
and her father's words. "Now it's the stains. A month ago it was the
faucet in the bathroom."

An unidentifiable sound came from the other side of the wall, like
people wallowing in rustling sheets unrolled from huge bolts of cloth.
Her mother's voice spoke, harsh and tearless. "And paint the ceiling, for
God's sake. You can already see these stains in the dark."

She got up quietly, went into the bathroom, locked the door, and filled the tub, muffling the faucet with a towel, undressed, and submerged herself in the water. She washed her hair, dived and surfaced, rubbed her ears, the nape of her neck and her temples, scrubbed her skin so raw it looked infected. She combed her wet hair again and tiptoed back to her bedroom, wrapped herself in the blanket and pulled it over her head. She lay that way for several hours, waiting fearfully for the voices behind the wall, but there was nothing and she fell asleep only to wake up in alarm and see her window getting lighter and brighter. In the morning, when her father came to wake her, he found her lying in bed with her eyes open, red, and he said immediately, "I can tell by your eyes that you read all night. So what's going to happen with the new lamp? You'll just read on and on and on?"

"I want to put the bed back the way it used to be," she said, and sensed that her voice was sick.

"Now, when the wardrobe is finally standing where it should be?"

"I want to sleep on that side." Her voice, high pitched, sounded foreign in her own ears.

He tried logic. "But there's no socket there for the lamp."

"Then I won't read!" she protested.

"You must read a lot," he said softly, lovingly, caressing her hot forehead. "There are still so many things you have to learn."

In the mornings after her recovery she would sit with her parents in the kitchen, the three of them eating silently, elbows touching, her eyes focusing on the bread, the butter, the serrated knife, not daring to look her parents in the eye.

Breakfast on Saturdays was hardest for her, but as she sat hunched over her slice of bread, studiously spreading the margarine, she was surprised to hear them discussing everyday matters in an ordinary tone of voice.

"'This notice from the post office about a parcel has been lying here for two days. You've got to go to the post office."

"Maybe it's not a parcel. Maybe it's Internal Revenue again."

"We just got a letter from Internal Revenue last month."

"So maybe it is a parcel."

"They have nothing better to do at Internal Revenue than to write to us? They must have a special clerk just for us."

Her knife stopped spreading the margarine and she froze, as if she expected last night's conversation to continue in front of her, with her father saying as he said at night, "Just once." And her mother immediately shooting back, "That's what you said on Monday. It took you half an hour."

"Maybe now you'll see the doctor?"

"I should see the doctor? Greek. I must be speaking Greek."

The door to the kitchen porch, exposed to the rain year after year, was peeling and its pane was cracked. She tried to open the shutter, pulling hard on the frayed cotton rope, but the shutter refused to budge and stayed stuck and crooked in its rusty casement. She peeked through a gap in the slats and saw the back of the neighbor's house, a patchwork of peeling plaster; her eyes were drawn to a line of striped kitchen towels hanging out to dry on the ground floor balcony.

Sometimes she remembered the young couple who used to live in that apartment. Their window faced her bedroom window. She remembered the laughter that came from there sending strange shivers down her body, from her throat to her toes. Sometimes, in the morning, on her way to school, she deliberately stopped to wait for them to get on their motorcycle, which was always parked in the same spot, leaning against a pole. She pretended to busy herself with the lock on her bookbag, watching them from the corner of her eye as they climbed on the bike, the woman hugging the man from behind, clasping her hands over his fly of his pants, the two of them fusing like characters in a movie getting ready for the final scene when a helicopter would rescue them from a jungle thicket. Many years later she would talk about them to her lovers, always whispering, always with the longing that accompanies a belated realization.

The first time she heard their laughter, she was sitting with her mother in the kitchen: she was peeling cloves of garlic while her mother was furiously chopping cabbage for pickling, her hand holding the big knife firmly, pounding the sharp blade very close to her fingers. Suddenly there was a peal of laughter sounding fresh and surprised. The two of them fell silent at once. Her mother stopped in mid-motion, pricking her ears as if she had heard a declaration of war. She stood still for a moment, then braced herself and said to her daughter, "Don't go out." She burst out of the kitchen onto the adjacent porch.

"'There are small children here," she heard her mother's voice outside, and she peeled the garlic more quickly. "You should be ashamed of yourselves!"

When her mother came back into the kitchen her eyes glared and her face flushed with fury.

"Who were you talking to?" her daughter asked.

"Talking? Can you talk to them? Animals!"

"Why did you tell them to be ashamed of themselves?"

"They know very well why."

Outside a young voice called derisively, "Lady, we're terribly ashamed!" Blood rushed to her mother's face.

There was another peal of laughter and her mother rushed outside to the porch, brandishing the knife in her hand. The girl got up, garlic peel in her palm, gingerly walked to the door and peered out. On the balcony next door she saw the man and the woman, looking like a pair of high school kids. The woman was hanging laundry, bending toward the taut washlines, intoxicated with laughter, her curls cascading to her neck. The man stood behind her, bent over, hanging the laundry above her head.

The girl stood, half hidden, smiling at the sight of the handsome couple hanging laundry together, like a four-armed creature: two arms placing a blue T-shirt on the line, two arms clipping clothes-pins on it, moving in unison, like synchronized rowers.

"Pigs!" her mother shouted at the top of her voice, flailing the knife; the girl recoiled and went back to her chair in the kitchen. "Only pigs carry on like that!" Her mother slammed the door, eyes bulging.

Years later, while she was shaking out a rug over the balcony railing, her husband came behind her, lifted her skirt and pressed against her bent body, whispering in her ear, "We're like Napoleon, we can do a few things at the same time." In that instant, the scene flashed through her mind, as if on a giant screen, and for the first time she realized why the skirt had flown over the young woman's back and why the laughter had burst from behind her curls. "What's the matter with you, lady? Come over and look. All we're doing is hanging the wash together, so we don't waste our precious time."

The bottom cabinets and the marble counter in the kitchen had already been replaced by other tenants, but the upper cabinets, ordered by her mother a few years before they left the apartment, were still in place. She opened the cupboards, one by one, finding them empty, and remembered the flowery lining paper her mother used to replace every spring and the pretty muslin ribbons she used to attach to the middle shelf behind the glass door where the beautiful crystal goblets were displayed. During Passover holidays, she used to help her mother in the kitchen, polishing the silver candlesticks, peeling the old wax paper lining off the shelves, scraping the hardened glue with a knife, scrubbing the shelves with a wooden brush and laying them on the floor to dry. During the hours they spent together, her mother worked diligently and efficiently, her lips pursed, constantly carping about the glue that dried too slowly, about the inferior paper that could not be cut straight, about the dishonest merchant who sold her defective lace ribbons. Bitter and cantankerous, she would settle accounts with the greengrocer who snuck a rotten eggplant into her bag; with the neighbor who saw a sheet blow by his car but did not bother to pick it out of a puddle; with the insolent couple, the new neighbors who had no shame: day and night you could always tell when they were at home, carrying on loudly; with father who would not lift a finger around the house, and look at the grimy door frames that he claims are perfectly clean.

When her father's name was mentioned, she lowered herself further over the shelf and worked more industriously, shrinking as if to protect herself, listening to her mother fuming. "He doesn't understand anything; it's like I'm speaking to him in Greek."

Now, standing in front of the empty cabinets, she felt sorry for her mother, for the free-floating bitterness she had injected into her life, for the poison she had accumulated in her heart all those years, letting it fester and bubble like boiling lava, bolting her heart against even rare moments of sweetness. Suddenly she remembered one Saturday night her father had come out of the shower, clean and fresh, a towel around his shoulders, looking like a poster advertising a summer vacation. His face was so happy and he looked so handsome with his hair brushed back, his hands stretched out at his sides, singing an aria from an opera loudly and terribly off-key. He approached her mother, and hugged her from behind, but her mother drew back from him crossly, wiped her neck where he had dripped on her, smoothed the blouse he had wrinkled, and snapped, "Why are you shouting in my ears?"

Even in old age, her father never ceased wooing her mother, always bringing her flowers and small gifts, never begrudging her refusals, and all the years trying to reconcile his daughter's heart to her, telling her, his voice full of love, "You have no idea how beautiful your mother was. Even after the war, when sometimes I couldn't tell a woman from a man, only she, with her grey eyes—like a butterfly."

So why does she cry at night? The question tore out of her but stopped at her twisted mouth and in its place another line came out, with a smile that replaced the twisted lips: "You can't mean 'butterfly,' you can't."

"But it's hard to love her," her father went on with his train of thought. "So don't be angry if at the end she won't let you have a party here. She doesn't know how to give of herself."

In her parents' bedroom, her eyes still fixed on the ceiling, she heard the key turn. The real estate agent stood in the doorway.

"You're still looking up?" His eyes opened wide with amazement. She stared at him and suddenly burst out laughing, the kind of carefree, light-hearted laugh she used to let out when her children were small and surprised her with newly invented words or with a clever unexpected act. It was the first time he saw her shed her sardonic grin, and he joined her mirth.

"At this rate, it'll take you a month to inspect the apartment," he said, glad to hear her expansive laughter.

"And maybe six months to inspect the penthouse." He was encouraged by the laughter, which had turned compulsive. His anger disappeared and he was filled with kindness. "Now my time is yours. I'll show you the apartment tile by tile. I can see that you like ceilings, so I'll show you ceiling after ceiling."

"There's something I really want you to show me," she said, her laughter subsiding. She leaned forward, raised her right leg, and standing on one leg, chin-to-knee, started to untie the laces of the boots. Her long fur coat hid her hands, and he could see the golden curtain of her hair divide, exposing its dark roots.

"Is everything all right, ma'am?" he asked, perplexed, trying to fathom her actions.

"Perfectly all right." She did not raise her head to him. She looked like a big polar bear hugging its raised knee, as her laces showed longer and longer under the hem of her fur coat. Suddenly one boot was in her hand, and she put it on the floor next to her leg in its sheer nylon stocking. She raised her left foot and bent down again to unlace the other boot.

"I was thinking about the stain in the ceiling," he said, ill at ease, trying to divert his attention from the woman who was acting so bizarrely and with such determined motions. His eyes, followed the laces dangling from under her coat. "Something in your boots pinching you, ma'am?"

She raised her head, a surprised smile brightening her face. "You could say something's pinching," she agreed pleasantly.

"About the stain," he reached for something familiar, trying to extricate himself from the confusion she caused him, "it can't be dampness, because in the apartment upstairs, the bathroom and the kitchen are on the other side."

"You're selling the apartment upstairs, too?" She stood the second boot next to the first.

"No . . . I just looked . . . from outside . . . judging by . . . " He followed her motions with burning eyes as she stood in her stocking feet, took off her coat and lay it down, its white lining facing the dirty floor that had not been washed for many months.

"Judging by the windows . . . Isn't it a pity to ruin your coat like that?"

"There's no choice," she said.

"I could hold it for you," he offered.

"You'll see in a minute that it's not that simple," she smiled, stood on the coat, bent her knees, and again, standing on one foot, started taking off her stocking. He stood there, his eyes mesmerized by the thighs momentarily exposed under her skirt as she lifted her leg to take off the stocking held up by a thick lace garter. Her stockings rolled down one after the other, and she unzipped her skirt, letting it fall at her feet on the white fur.

"Ma'am," his eyes were riveted to her short muslin slip, "are you okay?" His eyes followed the skirt that now lay near the boots, followed by the delicate slip that joined them.

"We'll soon see. It depends on you." She looked at him amused, and saw a need to intensify his embarrassment by explaining, "I usually start undressing from the top." She watched his eyes roll in his face.

"What are you doing, ma'am?" he muttered confusedly, fearing her, and fearing even more that the magical sight would disappear before his eyes. "Is the door locked?" she asked.

At that moment what she wanted dawned on him and he rushed to the door, his hands already reaching down to undo his pants' belt. By the time he came back, he had managed to undo his belt, his fingers struggling with the loops and with the buckle—she was already lying on her white fur coat, naked, her legs stretched straight out, one foot on the other, her hand supporting her head, watching him as he hurriedly undressed. His pants dropped to the floor and revealed a small belly, surprisingly tanned legs, and dark purple boxer shorts, the color of a velvet dress she once wore on Purim when she dressed as a gypsy. He dropped his shorts to the floor quickly, but when he noticed her eyes following him, he thought better of it, picked them up, and folded them neatly together with his pants. As he bent down she saw a tiny, spider-like flower tattooed on his shoulder in pink and turquoise. The sight made her laugh, a pleasant, surprised laugh, as if she were making a mental note: a man with a tattoo—that's a first for me.

To her surprise, she felt neither awkward nor strange. She watched him as he lay his pile of clothes next to hers, and, naked, stretched out alongside her on the fur that her husband had bought for their tenth anniversary. The fur now lay face down on the gray pavement-like floor, in the exact spot on which her parents' double bed used to stand. The touch of his body, she noticed, felt familiar, and her palm stroked the inside of his arm as if she had done it many times before, and the scent of his aftershave smelled familiar too, and so was the way he slid his hand from her waist to her shoulder and bent his head searching for her mouth. She jerked her head sharply and he found his face buried in her neck. With his sharp businessman's sense, he grasped what it was she was trying to convey, and immediately he heaved himself up and penetrated her. She received him without protest.

Eyes closed, she drew inward, ignoring the hard floor under her and the man above her. Water, clear and cool, swirled around her and she swam across it in a straight line, her arms outspread, then palm to palm, swimming forward, in long, even motions, cutting through the encompassing azure that glimmered like silk. She was engulfed by a sense of well-being, infusing her body like a stream. And all the while—even as the blue light receded from the water, like neon, and she started to dive away from it, further and further—she remembered the man crouched on top of her, and a faint voice, like a distant call rose within her: "Mommy, mommy," not in panic, or desperation, or supplication, or demand; "Mommy, mommy," came out of her with love, like a person of experience conveying important knowledge to someone young and very dear, "Mommy, mommy, it couldn't have been that terrible with a man who really loved you, who even in old age remembered you as he had first seen you, the two of you bound together by war. Here I am, mommy, with a strange man I met by chance, a man without merit or distinction, and he is pinning my head to the exact spot where your head used to lie, my eyes face the stains that give off a terrible musty smell, and I wonder why you never accepted the consolation of the body, why you never taught me this great conciliatory gift, this immeasurable pleasure, I had to learn all this by myself, as if I were a pioneer. I always remember your voice rasping 'Greek, I must be speaking to you in Greek.' What were you crying about all those nights, always bitter and sullen, so harsh and cruel to your loved ones, without a drop of lovingkindness for yourself or anyone else?"

She opened her eyes and saw the agent's face close to hers, his eyes shut. He crouched over her without pressure, supporting his weight on his elbows on either side of her body and all the while—she suddenly noticed—whispering in her ear sweet words he must have heard in movies and imagined that a woman like her was used to hearing at moments like this. She felt a wave of warmth toward him, for his naivete, for the words he whispered to her neck, for the lightness of his chest against her. She smiled, grateful, realizing how tender his actions were, how unexpected for a man whose tattooed spider went up and down before her eyes, as if about to pounce, then regretting it, drawing back.

Above his bouncing head she suddenly noticed the ceiling with two stains shaped like butterflies: one huge and gray with yellow specks on its outstretched wings covering half the ceiling, hiding another butterfly, small and slightly lighter in color. Both butterflies were flying away from the corner toward the window, as if trying to extricate themselves from the plaster, take on bright colors, and fly out. Her eyes wide open, she followed the man's face in front of her as he groaned, shook, and then relaxed, still hovering over her, supported on his elbows, opening his eyes.

"Next time we go to the penthouse," he panted, "there's a bed and a jacuzzi in the bedroom there."

Greek, she told him softly in her heart. "Who needs a jacuzzi? Does the penthouse have butterflies on the ceiling?" Her voice was derisive.

"Who needs butterflies when you have a penthouse?" he answered seriously.

She smiled at him with affection, with the kindness of someone to whom a secret has been revealed, and she thought: You don't even know, Mr. Eliyahu Yitzhakov, what pearls of wisdom are coming from your mouth.

"I'm the only one who has the key to that apartment," he smiled in return, "if you want, I'll draw you butterflies on the ceiling."

Without warning, tears rose in her throat and gathered at the corners of her eyes despite herself, and she thought: You'll also never know that you were the first man to see me cry naked. It's this uncanny tenderness of yours, your warmth. Things one is unused to break one's resistance easily. She felt the tears streaming down her face.

"Lady." He raised himself on his hands, alarmed. "What's the matter? Why are you crying?"

She covered her face with her fingers, smoothing it and taking the hair off her face.

"Something wrong?" His tone was like that of a man used to being of service.

"You were very good." She heard herself giving him a grade, like a teacher to a student. Supporting herself on two straight arms, she lifted herself to a sitting position, face to face with him, leaned against the wall, and wiped her eyes with the back of her hand, fingers straight as if in salute.

"Lady," his voice sounded hurt and his eyes narrowed, "You wanted it. Don't tell me you didn't. A friend of mine was once tricked like this. A woman seduced him and then went to the police and accused him. His name was in the papers."

"Don't worry." She reached for her panties. "I won't go to the police."

His face reddened at the sight of the sudden, cold, aloof, expression on her face. "You dragged me here," he fumed, humiliated. "The minute I saw you get out of the car, with your blond hair and all your rings, I knew something wasn't okay."

She rose to her feet, stockings in hand, all matter-of-fact, her eyes dry. She peered at him and saw the big shoulders contracting their muscles, extending the turquoise spider's legs. All at once she realized that he was offended because the rules had been reversed and he couldn't accept it. As she put on her stocking, stretching her toes all the way down, she glanced at the rings on her fingers and at the white fur spread on the floor, and for the first time genuine fear gripped her. You can never tell, her alert senses told her, how a man like him will react when crossed. She smoothed the stocking and adjusted the lace garter on the top of her thigh, then saw him approach her on his knees, naked.

"And when you walked in my office and told me Ha-mered Street," he raged, "I had a feeling about you. From the beginning you wanted to drive me nuts!"

His eyes were glazed over, as if hypnotized, and she glanced nervously at the door, calculating fast: if she grabbed her blouse and skirt and dashed to the door, he wouldn't run after her naked. But he seemed to have read her mind and grabbed her arm. He noticed her free hand reaching for her blouse and clamped his other hand on her outstretched arm. With her arms imprisoned, she gazed into his eyes, admitting to herself that she couldn't decipher his look. She searched his face for clues, but its language, too, was foreign to her.

She decided to gamble, knowing his reactions were slower than hers, and the sooner she acted, the better her chances to win the battle they were waging and whose rules she didn't know. She moved her arm gently, letting the pain climb up from her wrist to her shoulder, and seemed to feel his grip loosen. She kept shaking her arm, till she realized that her hand was free, wondering at the ease with which she had done it and knowing that now she had to calculate her moves cleverly, so one by one, she lifted his fingers from her other wrist. With both hands free, she picked up her blouse, straightened up, and with knees aching from the strain, she stood over him and put her arms through the sleeves, afraid all the while that he might toy with her a little more, and pounce on her in a minute and nail her down again.

But then she saw his eyes.

His eyes, she noticed, looking down on him as he stood on his knees, naked, were sad—and her fear dissipated at once. She bent down facing him, without her skirt, her blouse still unbuttoned, and took his face in both her hands, the way she used to hold her children when they got bruised and broke out in tears. Like them, he let her close her hands around his large, stubbly, cheeks, and he stayed there, quiet and obedient, as she bent her face toward him, kissed him on the cheek, and said, "Don't be angry, I don't want you to be angry at me. I'll always remember you with great affection."

He seemed confused, wavering between his anger and the realization that those were parting words. The hurt was still in his eyes, his cheeks were still flushed, but his face already showed resignation and wore a childish expression. "You women just drive us nuts, that's all," he said, distancing himself from his present predicament, as if this wasn't something that had happened between a particular man and woman, but a conspiracy of all women against all men.

She laughed with a great sense of release, buttoned up the delicate pearl buttons on her blouse, gathered up her skirt, and said, relieved, as she watched his eyelashes blink rapidly, "You'll find tenants easily. This is a very good apartment. Just make sure you paint the ceiling—then everything will be fine."

(1993)

—*Translated by Marganit Weinberger-Rotman*

Introduction to Nava Semel's "Hunger"

Although Nava Semel's collection *A Hat of Glass*, which includes the story "Hunger," was first published in 1985, it took nearly a decade before the Israeli literary world regarded the book as, in Semel's word, "legitimate." Until then the question art critic, journalist, playwright, and fiction writer Semel repeatedly faced was, "Why is a Sabra, a native-born Israeli, like you, writing about the Holocaust? Are you out of your mind?" The publishers worried that writing about the Holocaust would ruin Semel's career. Nava Semel herself had a different anxiety: "I asked myself: 'Will I hurt my parents again? Will I be responsible for opening their wounds?' "

Semel's experience as the child of Holocaust survivors echoes that of Liebrecht.

" 'Auschwitz' was the code word for ultimate evil never spoken directly in my house," Semel has said. "There was a silent agreement: the children wouldn't ask anything and the parents wouldn't say anything. Silence was the bottom line. Instead, we Israelis were brought up to remake the old Jewish stereotypes. We were told that we had to build a new identity with no connection to the Jews of eastern Europe. We were a blank page, born out of nowhere.

"It wasn't just a question of identity—it was a question of life and death. If we were a blank page, a totally new model, we could become strong, tough, Jews with the best army. We would never again be the 'sheep going to the slaughter' that we had been in eastern Europe. Our parents made a tremendous effort to speak Hebrew, which was not their language, and to raise their children in a culture they had not experienced.

"We children of survivors grew up with the feeling that it would have been much better to have been born to a parent who had been a member of the Palmach, the elite fighting unit of the pre-State days, and if you had been born to a survivor it was better to have been born to a partisan. But my mother was not a partisan. She was among those who stood naked on their way to the gas chambers, and with such an identity it's necessary to revise every concept of heroism we ever had."[33]

The compelling center of "Hunger," as in the collection *A Hat of Glass* in general, is the subterranean but persistently powerful role the never-acknowledged Holocaust continues to play from generation to generation. In all the stories, as in "It's Greek to You," the second generation, subtly but inevitably, continues to bear the pain of the parents' past, the unhealed wounds, the scars. Like "It's Greek to You," as well, "Hunger" probes a knotted and tragic relationship of mother and daughter; here the mother starves herself to death and her daughter, a "modern" Israeli woman, becomes entrapped in that deterioration.

Nava Semel was born in Tel Aviv in 1954, and earned her B.A. and M.A. in Art History at Tel Aviv University. She has written fiction, plays, scripts, and librettos, including *Becoming Gershona*, a young adult book (New York: Viking, 1990) and *Flying Lessons* (New York: Simon & Schuster Books for Young Readers, 1995), "An Old Lady," a one-woman award-winning play produced at the Haifa Municipal Theatre, "The Child Behind the Eyes," about a Down Syndrome child, which was produced throughout Europe, and as a reading at the Dortort Writers Institute and Jewish Women's Theatre Project's Festival of Israeli Women Playwrights at the University of Judaism in Los Angeles co-sponsored by the Consulate General Israel; the novels *Nightgames* (1994), about forty-something Israelis, and *Bride on Paper* (1995), which takes place in Palestine during the 1930s. Among the many honors she has received for her work are The National Jewish Book Award (USA, 1991), the Women Writers of the Mediterranean Short Story Award (France, 1994), and the Institute for Holocaust Studies Award for *A Hat of Glass*. She lives in Ramat Gan, near Tel Aviv.

---

33. Personal correspondence, and the following articles: "The Dybbuk [Genie] Comes out of the Bottle," *Maariv*, May 27, 1985 [in Hebrew]; "A Crumbling Life" [HaChayim B'bisqvitim], *Kolbo*, May 17, 1985 [in Hebrew]; "Coming of Age in a Young Country," *Forward*, September 21, 1990; and "She Broke New Ground Writing About Children of Holocaust Survivors," *Jewish Advocate*, January 26, 1989.

Hunger

Nava Semel

Medical file number 1748.

First the blank page, painless, as though under general anesthetic. Patient's name: Paula Zimmermann. I filled in the blank form, running the letters to the very end of each line. Age: 62. Initial diagnosis: severe depression. Physical condition very poor. Principal symptom anorexia, self-starvation. Admitted at 10:15 A.M., by her daughter Naomi.

I signed my name at the bottom: Dr. Gideon Adar. That would do. The duty nurse knocked at the door to inform me that the new patient was in room nine. I thanked her, but didn't go in. The room was stifling. It was late summer with not so much as the faintest breeze coming through the open windows. As I fanned myself with the medical file to keep from falling asleep, their names kept leaping up frenetically: Paula Zimmermann and her daughter Naomi.

Naomi didn't know if there had been any warning signs. But the more she thought about it, the more it seemed that some signs had been there, flickering, ever since they were small children, when her mother used to prod them to eat, or in the way she used to sit tensely by the window waiting for them to get home from a scout meeting or a class party. They'd spot her silhouette against the glass on even the most ordinary days. Still, there was something dark and bizarre going on. Once afternoon, as Naomi opened the door with her own key the way she always did, she found her mother napping in the armchair that faced the TV. Not wanting to wake her, she decided to get herself a cup of warm milk, and opened the pantry door. The sight of all those cans piled one on top of the other in such meticulous order left her speechless. They were arranged by their contents, and filled the cupboard to capacity. And not only cans. There were two small bags of sugar too, and bottles of oil, and bread in tightly sealed nylon bags, one loaf on top of the other, like a display of organs in a science exhibition.

"Mother," she said softly when she dared touch the sagging shoulder. "Are you stocking up for a siege?"

And though she tried to sound light-hearted, she could feel the chill snake its way to her very marrow. Furiously, her mother sprang out of the chair and rushed to the pantry, slamming it shut, then leaned against it and crossed her arms as though to protect it.

"Don't touch it Naomi," she said, her gaze far away. "Haven't I told you there's going to be a famine!"

Then she drove the sight out of her mind—of her mother the lioness blocking the pantry with her own body. And as her mother got thinner and thinner, she thought of it only as a bridge to the next biological phase, when the body rids itself of all those surpluses created by self-indulgence, and makes do with simply satisfying its own modest needs.

Only many months later did the doctor ask her pointedly how she could have failed to do anything about her mother's sudden emaciation. It was because she saw her every day that she didn't notice the change, she explained. Come to think of it, she did remember that one of their distant cousins, who used to visit her mother only twice a year, had squinted suspiciously and commented, "Your mother's been losing weight, Naomi. You'd better take her for a check-up." Which was when she began keeping an eye on her and checking her plate.

It was then that she noticed how her mother would hold the fork like a little wand, moving the food to the sloping sides of the bowl until there was nothing left in the middle but a hollow well surrounded by a full circle. Or else, when Naomi prodded, her mother would reply, "I ate already, just before you came." But when it came to Naomi's own meals, her mother would goad her: "Eat! Eat!" and stand guard over her, taut as a string. And even when the plate had been cleaned, she would stare despondently at the inevitable scraps. On one occasion, Naomi heard her mutter, "You've got to build up your strength for what's coming."

There were other signs of descending darkness. She'd spend hours staring at the square TV screen. Even when the programs were over for the night, she would sit there across from the piercing beep, not budging from her chair to turn off the TV. People wanted to see her, but she'd make all sorts of excuses to avoid them. It reached a point where days would go by without her leaving the house. Her hair grew long and dishevelled, and the white showed through like weeds in an untended field. She stopped dyeing it, and one day, when Naomi came to visit, she saw an old woman, the light gone out of her eyes.

She tried to get her to see a doctor, but the silences got heavier and longer. The plates were the only thing she held on to. She would carry them to the table, in what seemed a vestige of nimbleness. Once she brought in a plate with nothing on it but chunks of bread, and when Naomi refused to take any, she burst into a tirade. It began softly, then grew as loud as she could go, though even that suddenly sounded feeble, as though coming from the throat of a chicken about to be slaughtered. "You have to eat. I'm collecting it all for you. How dare you leave any!"

Naomi told herself that something had to be done. She mustered the courage to phone her brother in Canada. "Mother's getting old," she said. "She's taking menopause very hard." To which he replied, "For that you call me? It's natural. There's nothing you can do about it. People get old. It'll happen to us too some day. Take her to a doctor and get him to prescribe something."

It was morning, the middle of second period, when the principal came into her class and called her out.

"There's an urgent phone call for you," he said.

"Naomi Zimmermann?" the neighbor asked over the phone. "I"m terribly sorry to bother you at school, but we thought you'd better come. It's your mother . . . "

"Something's happened to her?" Naomi shrieked into the receiver.

"No, not an accident or anything, but I think you'd better come right away."

She left her class with a substitute and ran all the way from the bus stop. The neighbors were there waiting for her in the entrance hall but their reports were so choppy that it took her a while to piece together the fact that her mother was all right. Apparently, she'd come out of her apartment and begun banging on people's doors, screaming, "My children are starving! We've got to find food for them. Yigal is out in a street somewhere dying of hunger, and soon there'll be nothing left of Naomi either. Can't you see the way she looks? That's the only reason she hasn't found herself a husband. She keeps getting thinner and thinner. Doesn't eat a thing. We have to stock up!"

She went from door to door, using whatever strength she still had to keep banging. In front of the locked door of a neighbor who was away from home, she declaimed her entire speech, down to the last word. When they tried to calm her, she locked herself in her own apartment again and refused to answer.

One neighbor put his ear to the door and said, "I can hear something. She's in there." Naomi's hands were shaking so badly she couldn't get the door open. When she finally did, she found her mother sitting in the kitchen, surrounded by piles of food from the pantry. She looked up and said, "I told them. They all know now."

Naomi hadn't left her alone for more than a minute. Just to put the kettle on. But when she turned around, she saw her lying on the floor, the color drained from her face, unconscious. The bag of sugar had toppled along with her and as Naomi bent over her, the white crystals crackled underfoot as though worms had crawled out of the earth for some easy prey.

"Mrs. Zimmermann," I turned to her, my voice very low.

She was sitting there transfixed, right under the window, but with the shutters sealed. A ray of light caught a few strands of hair, granting her a moment of reprieve but you could see the protruding bones of her forehead, and the shadows nesting securely in the hollows of her emaciation.

Her hands were gathered in her lap, perhaps to conceal the look of those bony fingers and twisted fingernails.

"I've brought you a cup of tea. With plenty of lemon. Your daughter tells me you like it that way."

I put the cup down on the table next to her, added two teaspoons of sugar and stirred, making a point of banging the spoon against the sides of the cup to draw out those ghosts inside her. But she didn't bother looking in my direction, didn't so much as twitch. There was no way of hearing whether my patient was even breathing. I pulled my chair over across from hers, and tried to catch her irises, but even the catapults of my gaze were powerless against that thick wall of hers. I studied the expression on her face closely. Not even the shadow of a cloud passed across it. Over her muteness, I spoke again.

"Your daughter Naomi told me about you. You're a sensible woman. You've always been so careful about your appearance. The beauty parlor and attractive clothes. And you have so many friends. You have a subscription to the Philharmonic, don't you? I like music too, especially first-rate instrumentalists. Do you think you'd like to listen to some music while you're here? Tell me who your favorite composers are and I'll make sure you get a phonograph and records. How about the Third Brandenburg Concerto? We could listen to it together."

My patient showed no signs of reacting and when I pulled her hands out of her lap, they were as slack as a cadaver's. I checked her pulse while I was at it, it was slow and fluttery like the heartbeat of a bird. I had to wrap her fingers round the steaming cup of tea to keep her from dropping it on my knees.

"Yigal called," I told her. "He asked about you. Do you want him to come see you? It's been a long time. Your daughter told me he left eight years ago. He promises to come for Rosh Hashanah[34] or maybe even a few weeks earlier. She says he's doing very well over there. I hear he's got a nice girl too. You must be proud of him. You have two children who've done very well for themselves, Mrs. Zimmermann, and you really ought to take care of yourself."

Her animosity towards me was embodied in her total indifference.

I walked over to the window, so that her body was behind me. The tips of her hair kept stabbing at my back. Slowly I opened the slats, and the light eased its way in. I had all the time in the world.

"Come," I coaxed her. "Come over to the window. Just look how beautiful it is out there. Let's look together. Your daughter teaches nature, so she tells me. Collects all kinds of plants and teaches the children how to tell when the seasons are changing."

When I leaned over and touched her shoulder, I could feel the bones jabbing into my fingertips, stiff as two axles of an old carriage.

To get her to the window, I had to support her like a puppet. Her sealed mask showed no sign of cracking, but the nostrils were fluttering, almost invisibly.

"It's a beautiful day," I said. "When I was little, we used to head for the citrus groves on days like this, just to smell the first tangerines. My father had a big orchard. Our shoes would be caked with mud and my mother would scrape the soles clean with a knife so I didn't get the floor dirty. Where you come from, it must have been snowing. I wonder what it's like to grow up surrounded by mounds of whiteness."

I kept chattering away at her and pouring more tea as I went along. I had to serve it to her lips.

"Drink up," I told her. "It's nice and hot."

Since she didn't budge, I lifted the cup myself and tried to get her to drink, but my hand was very soft.

The gateway to her lips wouldn't yield and the hot trickle scalded my hand. I hoped she wouldn't notice as I wiped my hands against the side of my trousers, but the burn throbbed.

"You're like a little girl," I scolded her. "You've got to eat and drink to put the color back into your hair. Don't you remember what they

---

34. *Rosh Hashanah:* The Jewish New Year, beginning of the "Days of Awe" culminating in Yom Kippur, Day of Atonement, a fast day.

used to say about you? How nicely you look after yourself, always so well-groomed. The neighbors never even saw you in a house-robe."

In an effort to woo her, I touched her mass of prickly hair, trying to give it some shape.

"Don't touch me. Can't you see it's all rotten. If you touch, it'll stick to you too!" Those first words were labored. They rattled deject-edly, as though something had snapped inside, leaving her eager to spit it out. But there wasn't a drop of moisture in her jaw, and when I stole a glance, I saw her lips all parched and cracked.

I called the nurse, and together we put an infusion into a vein in my patient's arm.

In those long dank corridors, Naomi compared herself to a worm. Like a schoolgirl, she slithered along the covered tunnels, studying the lettering over the closed doors. What dark secrets lurked behind them, things that boggled the mind, she thought to herself. Behind each door was another human being, and the names of those doctors and nurses were so strange. Like the head nurse, Ofra Betuel, whose surname was so reminiscent of the word *betulah,* virgin. Young and attractive, no doubt, but why "Betuel"? Perhaps because she never once went astray. The kind of woman who never knew a moment of weakness.

Even if she wasn't a Bible teacher Naomi knew enough to remember that Betuel was Rachel's grandfather. A disillusioned biblical elder with a sneaky and underhanded son and two granddaughters—one of them just as conniving as her father, the other an artless heartbreaker.

"I'm here to see Doctor Adar."

"Fourth door down the hall, half a floor up."

What an efficient reply. Didn't even pause to wonder why she was looking for him. Maybe a relative of his, or a close friend, or his secret mistress. Or simply a new patient. The sound of the head nurse's brisk footsteps disappeared down the hall.

Naomi proceeded gingerly, beginning to feel as if the light were polluted, as if it were soiling her. Once she found the sign with his name on it, she took a seat on the bench outside and waited.

What seemed at first like a quiet tunnel was beginning to reverberate with clattering dishes, a mixture of metal and plastic. Turning in the direc-tion of the noise, she discovered that she was right next to the kitchen. The door was ajar, and the nurses, like a swarm of bees in their white robes, were performing the lunchtime dinner dances. She could see a heavy-set body with a white cloth stretched across its back bending over a metal cart and loading it with blue dishes. An orange mound of grated carrots was piled onto each of the plates. The experienced nurses were careful not to short-change anyone; those orange mounds were meticulously uniform.

Mother didn't like that kind of food. She wouldn't eat it. Just lots of bread and potatoes, cooked or boiled, and golden-poached chicken-wings. As a child, when Naomi used to push away her plate and say, "It's disgusting," her mother would shudder. "You can't talk about it that way. You should say, 'I don't like the taste' or 'It isn't the way I like it' or better yet 'I'm not hungry right now.' Stick to words that slide by, nothing that can sound insulting. Never ever make fun of it, because bread never forgets an insult. It holds a grudge." To this very day, she didn't dare throw out old bread. It just lay there in its drawer getting mouldy, with green fungi sprouting all over its stomach.

"What do you feel when you throw bread away?" Dr. Adar would ask. If I'd been a Christian, I'd have crossed my heart. I'd have tried to give it another chance. Maybe I could scrape off the mould, force it to take a new hold on life. Make toast, for example. I put off the final verdict, because when I did throw out that chunk of bread, I'd be throwing myself out too.

In the chronicles of bread there was one dark chapter, five years that Paula Zimmermann had rubbed out of her life—those years between ages nineteen and twenty-four. She'd never lift the cover off again, she'd never reveal what was lurking beneath. Just one detail had seeped through and Naomi shuddered at the recollection.

Alice and her sixteen-year-old daughter were her block-mates. The prisoners would pick at each other's plates to see if any of the others had been lucky enough to wind up with one of those dark pieces of apple peel. The mother and her daughter wouldn't share with each other. Instead, the daughter would peer harshly into her mother's plate, to make sure she hadn't been indulged by some wild stroke of good fortune. The daughter might have been forgiven, but as for the mother, she had turned into a black widow, begrudging her own flesh and blood, prepared to rip her apart for a stray string of meat.

Apart from this there was nothing Naomi could tell Dr. Adar to shed any light on that passageway of missing time.

Paula Zimmermann was lying in bed now, a tube running along her arm. One end was attached to that transparent bag of nutrition, swaying on its pole like a weather vane on a rooftop.

Her grey face had taken on a semblance of tranquility. To tell the truth, she was relieved to be able to starve herself openly. From under the blanket, her two legs looked like outstretched stilts, with only the knees giving any sign of movement. Her file had no record of any outburst.

"A very quiet patient," one of the junior nurses in the ward said. "Well-behaved, you might say."

"What do you mean, 'well-behaved'?" I asked, taken aback. "She refuses to open her mouth. There's no change as far as that's concerned."

I didn't say it, but I couldn't help thinking how determined she was to run this race to the finish. And I was the one who had to jump the train as it rushed by, to grab the engineer and toss him out—either by screaming and kicking or by sweet-talking and cajoling. Then it would be up to me to latch onto the wheel with both hands, apply my foot slowly to the brakes, and ring the train carefully to a halt.

"How are you today?"

The sockets of her eyes had turned much darker, like the twin mouths of a volcano storing up energy to pounce.

"The holiday's coming. A new year. You'll celebrate here with us this year, and next year you'll be back with Naomi. Yigal will come too, maybe even with his wife."

There was a glimmer in her eye as she tried to mumble something. I pulled up closer, thirstily, unable to contain my eagerness.

"Is there something you'd like to tell me?"

She signalled something with her free hand, counting five fingers and then another five. I didn't understand.

"In ten days," she whispered, like someone just learning how to talk. "What's going to happen in ten days?" I asked eagerly.

"Yom Kippur, the Fast of Atonement. Then you'll let me, won't you, Doctor?"

I turned away abruptly to keep her from observing her mentor in a moment of weakness.

"You don't have any sins to atone for. God forgave you a long time ago."

"You don't understand, young man. I've gone through forty Days of Atonement, and I'm still unclean."

Quickly I summoned the all-knowing look.

"I'm your friend. I'm here to help you. Maybe because I'm a complete stranger, you'll agree to trust me. There's no reason to torture yourself. Open your eyes, Paula. None of it makes any sense. Your self-denial is pointless."

She let out a shriek of laughter.

"Once I'm finished, it will be the end of the horror too. And of the terrible stench . . . "

She sniffed her free arm.

"Why, you're liable to suffocate in here. I'm not just one corpse but a whole pile. Maybe you know the kind I mean? Elegant and wrapped in nylon bags, inside your refrigerators, like loaves of bread. But we're different. Lying in the ditches, getting bloated. How can you stand to be near us? Then again, you're a doctor and you've got your Hippocratic Oath, even when it comes to filthy bodies that contaminate everything around them. Someone has to be brave. To sweep up and do the disinfecting. To finish the job once and for all. Someone simply has to finish me off. Forty years too late. Another Yom Kippur is coming now. In our blocks back then they brought pots full of real soup for us on the fast day and we didn't taste it. Even when they whipped us. Now I don't have to fight over every crumb any more. I kept putting it off, but I knew it would happen. Yigal is gone already, and Naomi hasn't found a man. She sleeps quietly like a mouse, thinks I don't notice. For forty years, I tried as hard as I could not to see any of it. I had to scrounge for every scrap. Just for them. It's my duty after all. I have to make it up to them. The boy will need a slice for emergencies too. I'm getting it all ready for them. I'll steal away quietly. They won't even notice I'm gone. Think how relieved they'll be. I was a nuisance. A threat to their wellbeing. They'll finally be able to start living again. You've been the only thing in my way, Doctor Adar, tying me down with your handcuffs, even if they are transparent. If you think I'm just a dog you can tie down with a leash, you're probably right. You're not very original either. Others had the same idea, but I figured out a way out of prison. From my own private camp. I'm appealing to your sense of reason, as a doctor who spent seven years studying a respectable profession. I'm begging you to find compassion within yourself for a creature who's been damned. I'm running out of strength. Why don't you just let me finish myself off in peace, and stop interfering?"

She was utterly drained. As though she'd been standing on top of a tall mountain, yelling out over the entire desert. Beads of perspiration formed on her forehead, trickled down and merged with the saliva at the corners of her mouth. I took the sponge from the table and wiped her face. The bones protruded at the front of her skull and the flesh was so transparent and thin that I was afraid it would tear away at the stroke of my hand. A warm knot burst inside me. As I kept wiping and wiping, she went along with it, lying there underneath my hand and dreaming how they would prepare her body to be laid to rest.

Naomi worked her way ploddingly between the desks. Dozens of eyes hung on her like tiny sacks depleting her. By the end of the day, there would be many more eyes piercing her. She took the damp sponge and wiped the board. As she rubbed it painstakingly, streak by streak, it turned into a smooth and sparkling field. Then she took a step back and squinted to examine the vast dark green rectangle. A tiny area she had missed looked like a dusty island in the heart of the board.

"Just a minute," she told her pupils and headed for the door. The hum of children taking advantage of a flash of freedom rose behind her.

In the bathroom sink, she rinsed the sponge thoroughly and squeezed it so hard that her wrists hurt, then returned to her class. But when she tried to find that dusty island in the heart of the board, it was gone. A separate rage mounted within Naomi and she lunged at the board, cleaning it with a vengeance until it met her satisfaction.

"Where did we end the last lesson?" she asked the class. Taking a piece of chalk, she wrote on the clean board: "The Insect Families," then drew a crooked line and added underneath: "The Honeybee."

"The bee is a social creature if ever there was one," Naomi said. "It lives its life tied to a hive, in an organized, highly developed society."

An early breeze skimmed the windowsill and brushed across her face. With a frail line she traced the honeybees' dance. "It's a language that provides information about where to find food—its direction and distance from the hive," she explained to her students.

"Does she always tell the other workers when she finds flowers?" one of the boys asked.

"She's a very loyal Lady Insect," another girl remarked.

"As for the one who never leaves the hive, the royal prisoner, smothered in devotion and in the nectar that the other bees bring to please her, she does her duty by producing a new generation at regular intervals. She has no use for the father's love or the young ones' longing. Nestled in her bed of comforts, she grows a belly. She might see the others join the circle dance which means that there's food not far away—and might even long to join them. But just for an instant. A bee's sense of timing does not depend on any outside factors," Naomi, the teacher, explained. And from the corner of her eye she suddenly spotted that elusive island floating on the board.

The miraculous clock was beating silently inside her. Her mother used to warn her, "Naomi, if you don't do what I say I'll die and you'll be to blame!"

Those words evoked caustic memories. At night Naomi used to curl up under the blanket like a baby in the womb, thinking about the power she had—the power to kill her mother. Sometimes Mother would adore them, sometimes they'd be like sworn enemies. And always there was the veil of fear. Fear that she'd fall apart.

"Doctor Adar," Naomi wanted to shout. "Help the Queen Bee. She's being lured by the workers. Something has gone wrong with her miraculous sense of timing."

People used to point her out, "That teacher is Naomi." At meetings with parents she was always beautifully poised. Filling in those grade sheets without hesitation, she was like a doctor following the progress of a disease. She had her fill of pages and students, but her love life was empty. Over and over again, she kept losing that dusty island in the heart of the board.

Ever since she let me wipe her face, she'd shed another leaf. It was still fluttering around in the room, invisible but unsavory to the smell.

She began letting me puff up her quilt, and though I knew that the duty nurse did a better job of it, still I made a point of smoothing the blanket and stretching the sheet. I checked the infusion and allowed myself the liberty of a quip like: "What a banquet you're having today, a regular five-star restaurant."

Her face contorted into something like a smile, sending a chill down my back, as though I'd looked into an open grave and couldn't stop looking.

The intravenous tube was like a flimsy rope binding her to me, and I, for one, knew just how tenuous that line between being and not being was for her. She seemed to have made a choice, but it wasn't the real one.

Sometimes I couldn't help feeling bitter. The burden of life was weighing too heavily on her, but she wouldn't go all the way through to the final nothingness either. So she just hung there in the balance, refusing to accept either possibility. At times, I was convinced she was taunting me. She was obviously out to dump the responsibility for her choice on my shoulders, but that was one role I categorically refused to accept.

The surge of anger didn't last long though. When I saw the shrivelled body, bereft of every superfluity so that nothing but essence was left, I lifted her frail, feathery hand and stroked it, as if to infuse it with some of my own thin fluids.

"You're tired, Doctor Adar," she remarked softly. I believe that was the first time she'd actually noticed me.

"A hard day," I told her. "And how are you feeling? Want me to turn on the radio?"

"No, not now," she whispered and a fire stole into the corners of her eyes. "I have other sounds to listen to, you know," she confided in me. "I can hear the drops going straight into my bloodstream at a steady rate. It's only at night that their rhythm is upset and they grate on my ears. I'll let you listen too. You're a nice man actually. Put your ear right here, where the tube touches my arm."

I put my ear there. The bluish veins wound their way under the outer layer of her skin, like the map of a remote star.

"Can you hear it?"

I nodded. "It sounds like the last drops of melting snow."

"That's right," she confirmed. "I'm so happy that someone else hears it too. I'm very lucky to have found myself a doctor with a musical ear. There's something I won't tell anyone but you. All those years, while I was raising that food at home, I watched over it the way you watch over a baby. One day I heard the bread talking, and the grains of rice whispering to each another. They were saying how they were taking care of themselves for my sake or for anyone I chose.

" 'My Fuehrer, Fuehrer. I thank you for the meal and for the food. The young lad stands guard—faithful companion to the old. You assuage all my cares, peace reigns in my heart. My soul is in Your keeping day and night. My Fuehrer, there can be no other. Heil, my Fuehrer, Heil.' That was what they sang. I can still remember every word of that hymn of thanksgiving."

I recoiled.

"Don't be afraid," she said. "It's an after-dinner prayer out of their prayer book. Look, I clasp my hands like a good girl. You see, I haven't forgotten the hymn. Those grains of rice kept reciting it for me. I was like any decent German girl back then in Koeln. Still, they deported me. A neighbor snitched." Her eyes burned with a strange fervor.

"That's why I learned how to set a table. They're not about to burst in on me and catch me off-guard again. You'd better be ready too. I'm warning you. You may be a doctor, but you're a bigger fool than I thought."

I could feel the enormous iceberg I'd been walking on split open with an ear-shattering crash.

Paula Zimmermann was breathing easier. But no sooner did I detect a hint of *joie de vivre* than I had to remind myself that it was actually a *joie de mort*.

"What a wonderful feeling. My jaws are at rest now after years of pointless chewing. My body's light. I feel as though I can try to take off already. Except for that damned tube of yours tying me down. Come on and cut it away, Gideon! Now! Now! It's the right time!"

A strange woman was inciting me. My foot was lodged in the ever-widening crack and I struggled to pull it free. Once, as I child, I lost my way in the countryside and a pickup truck full of Arab workers passed by and they took me home.

"Come, Gideon! Do it right away! Forty years I've been waiting, and time is so tiring. I kept away from the fence back then, you know.[35]

---

35. The electrified fence of the concentration camp.

But you can hear them whispering, can't you? Doctors know the truth, even if they won't admit it. I let you listen to the drops. I sang you the hymn. The drops of that damned liquid of yours tell me that you're the one who's been forcing them into my vein. Don't punish them, Gideon. Even a heart of stone would melt from their tears. They keep yelling: Stop it! Stop the excruciating flow!"

She had me hypnotized with the dark sockets of her eyes. I sat there alone in the orchard, and the leaves kept swaying all night long. I could see the grapefruit turning yellow like so many moons between heaven and earth. I knew enough by then to realize that medicine was like a taxonomical list. It leaves the burden of choice to the doctor and crushes him without pity.

"Paula," I sighed, my resistance was running low. "That's impossible."

The drops rolled out of her eyes, running down the blanket in utter silence, spreading in dark stains over her white collar. I took the old woman-baby in my arms and cradled her. The damp warmth soaked into my shirt, and I was careful not to sever the transparent tube dangling between us.

Once there was a man she loved very much. She doted on him like a foolish kitten for several months before he told her in so many words that he wasn't interested. For the first few days she was totally numb. Only later did the first stabs of pain begin to dart through her at the strangest times. In the teachers' room of all places, during the tea break, she thought back over the only weekend she ever spent with him, one body joined to another, while her soul dissolved with longing. He was a very efficient lover. The kind who waited for her to take off all her clothes herself and come to him all ready. Feeling his way around in her a bit just till the warm fluids dripped down her thighs, then in and out, heaving a few stifled moans into her shoulders for a finish. And falling asleep immediately.

If that's all there is, Naomi told herself, maybe it's just as well to do without.

Now she was living in welcome torpor. Her daily routine was as compartmentalized as an office form.

Until the high tide came along and upset everything.

She maneuvered through the scrambled hours of her day and rushed to the hospital. She even skipped a few extra seminars. Every day during recess, the other teachers would ask: "How's your mother? When are they letting her out?" And she would answer mechanically, "She's better. The doctor says she's on the mend." Only the principal, a nosy person by nature, asked suspiciously, "What happened in that house of yours?" He even tried to pit her against Yigal: "Why doesn't he come back to share the load with you? It's all on your shoulders, isn't it?" The gym teacher had a secret to share with her: "It's tough with old parents. Till you figure out a solution. I know. I have a father in a nursing home. I know it's not quite the same as a psychiatric ward, but the embarrassment. . . ."

"How could you let it get this bad?" Yigal rebuked her on the transatlantic phone call, and his question echoed back to her.

Naomi didn't know what to say. "No, you don't have to come if it's too difficult. I'll let you know if it gets any worse." She even forgot the anniversary of their father's death.

She put the receiver back gently. Ever since he left, the rift between them had been growing more and more oppressive. It was early morning where he was, maybe even the middle of the night. She hadn't thought about that. Maybe that was why he sounded so annoyed. Dr. Adar deluged her with questions about him. He even told her to insist that her brother come back. What would she tell him now? Once again she had to admit her inability to make demands. It seemed as though Dr. Adar was pointing an accusing finger at her too.

What could Naomi have done? She'd never asked and her mother had never told them. How she met Father, for example. All she said was, "We met after the war. . . ." There were no snapshots at home, no albums. Nothing to show what Mother looked like as a child, either. Mother as a young girl, as a beloved wife. No wedding dress. No object in the house brought along with her from that other world. It was as though she'd been born after that missing chapter. . . . The doctor was like a detective waiting in ambush for both of them at the end of a passageway, picking out the minute tracks with his magnifying glass. She walked alongside him in the covered tunnel of a corridor, her shoulder touching his white robe. A tall, mysterious, man. Her mother's eyes widened whenever he came into the room, and Naomi could detect an old yearning welling from deep inside her.

One afternoon, just after I'd taken off my white robe to go home, the duty nurse burst into my room all out of breath. "She's yanked out the infusion. Come quickly!"

We rushed to room nine. I stared at the empty bed and the mussed up sheets, horrified. The feeding tube was dangling in mid-air. A tendril off a tropical tree. A touch of wind that had made its way in through the open window was rocking it back and forth.

"Where is she?" I roared.

The nurse cringed. "I don't know."

"I gave express orders to watch over her. I said not to take your eyes off her for even a minute. These patients are very clever, and Paula is sneaky to boot. She was just waiting for the chance...."

"I don't know how it happened. I kept peeking in here every five minutes, and she was so peaceful today..."

"Put all the security guards on alert, and the entire staff too. We have to find her before she gets too far."

Instantly, the ward turned into a gushing beehive. The patter of footsteps down the corridor and a melange of voices shouting, "Mrs. Zimmermann! Mrs. Zimmermann! Where are you?"

I raced down the corridors like a little boy who'd lost a ball. In the bathroom, I found old Alfred, our oldest patient, by the sink, making faces in the mirror.

"Did you see her?" I shook him vigorously by the shoulder. Alfred looked me straight in the eye and his lips opened in a big smile as foxy as can be.

"Yes, yes, sure," his head became a relentless pendulum.

"Where?" I asked and it took my breath away.

"Right here," said old Alfred, stabbing at the mirror and leaving a fingerprint behind.

I pushed him away from me and his shoulder blades felt like stale cookies to my touch. Behind me I could hear his feeble cry, "Honest, doctor. I saw her there. She told me she was looking for something inside and that she'd be right out."

"Should I call the police?" one of the nurses tugged at my robe.

Friday night dissolved softly over the building. The white walls turned blue, then grey. I thought back over Friday nights in the country and it depressed me. Always the troublesome thought of a lonely Saturday, with nobody to share it with. On Friday nights I used to linger behind at the hospital. Only at the last minute, when there was no other choice, did I take off my robe, because Friday nights belonged to undefined longings, and to resentment over the fact that time was spilling out of its bottle, with no way of being pushed back in through the neck.

All those long years of vast insight wouldn't put the reins safely in my hands. I tugged at them, but they tugged back with a will of their own. The doctor turned into a dreamy butterfly catcher, only to discover that his net held nothing more than golden-orange spots.

Not right. Not true. I took off my white robe and dropped it to the floor, then rushed outside. Meanwhile, the deep blue had turned into a black salve spreading impassively over the walls and the trees.

"Paula!" I called out. "Don't run away from me!" My feet were deep in the thorny dark undergrowth and I noted how sorely neglected the garden was lately. I ran toward the white stain, like a ship washed up against an illusory lighthouse, and managed to adjust my sight enough to make out the silhouette of a human body. She was sitting on the ground, her legs crossed, her nightgown pulled over her knees.

"I've been waiting for you," she said in a clear voice.

"Come." I pulled her up gently. Her hand in mine was like a dry twig.

"Just a minute. Sit here," she commanded confidently.

I don't know why I gave in. I dropped down at her feet and crossed my legs the same way.

"You exert yourself too much. Rotting away like me. You've got to believe me. I know. Go cut away *your* infusion. Mine is easy to find. You gave me the shortcut. But you'll have to find your transparent tube yourself."

I didn't notice the search party coming in our direction. In fact they might have gone right past us if Paula Zimmermann hadn't cried out: "We're over here." And I didn't even feel ashamed when the hospital security guard and his assistant shone the straight rays of their flashlights right at us. When they picked her up to carry her back inside, I could hear her explaining amiably, "He's sick, you see."

Late at night, long after Naomi had gone to bed, there was a thumping at her door, working its way right into her dream. She shuffled out in her slippers, wrapping herself in her robe against the cold, and asked anxiously, "Who is it?"

"It's me, Doctor Adar."

He leaned on the door, out of breath. In a flash, she noticed one of the corners of his white robe peeping out from under his coat.

"Just look at you," she mumbled awkwardly.

"Could you turn a light on in here?"

She groped for the switch, and a sallow light spilled over them, outlining his haggard face. "Just a minute," she said, leading him in. "I'll go put the kettle on." She crossed the kitchen floor and opened one of the faucets. What did he want from her? She was ready. She'd waited so long and so patiently for the blow to strike and now that it had, there she was, clear-headed and filling the kettle. She wasn't even screaming. So totally composed. The end had been long in coming. It was the tragedy that her mother had been priming her for ever since childhood. The only thing left was to call Canada and make the arrangements. Her mind was a frenzied racetrack with the thoughts all buzzing around but she absentmindedly opened the other faucet too, and the hot water skimmed over her hands, till the ends of her sleeves were dripping wet.

Before going back into the room, she carefully buttoned up her robe, ran her hand through her hair to smooth it, and stole a look at herself in the window. Dr. Adar was sitting sprawled in an armchair. He hadn't even taken off his coat. Fingering the white cloth of his robe, he seemed to Naomi like a shy kid who'd mustered the courage to visit a house of ill repute.

Naomi came closer, her hands clasped together, like a student meeting the principal.

"When did it happen?" she asked.

"This evening," he answered weakly, still not lifting his head.

"Where is she now?"

"What do you mean? In her room. I found her outside. How did you find out already?"

"I was waiting for it to happen. She always warned us it would."

He put his hand to his head, rubbing it absent-mindedly.

"You don't understand, Naomi. She's all right. I put the infusion back in. She ripped it out."

Naomi slouched into the armchair beside him. Drops of borrowed time trickled out of the bottle. The Queen Bee had been given one more season to serve.

"She double-crossed me," Dr. Adar said bitterly. "She knew how important it was to me to keep her alive."

"Important for your sake or hers?" Naomi lashed out at him.

Dr. Adar hid his face in his hands and kept still. A heavy silence descended on the room. "I tried to take a look into that convoluted, frightening world of hers. She was so apathetic at first that I knew she didn't have it in her to rip it out. But you see, I did help her. I was the master who was exorcising those warped fragments in her soul. I gave her the courage to decide."

Dr. Adar rose from the chair and yelled, "Yes! Important for my sake too. You're like her. She understands. Do you know what she told me? 'Go cut away your infusion.' As though it were that simple."

Naomi didn't know how it happened. She took the doctor in her arms and for the first time in her life comforted a man. She was grateful that his face was buried in her shoulder, grateful that the only thing left was the stranger's head cupped in her hands like a fragile dish and the quivering collar of his coat.

And she thought about how the drone fled the hive for fear of being attacked by the workers. Sure his chest was broad and the tip of his stomach was a bit thicker, but his limbs were ill-suited for collecting nectar and he didn't even have a sting to protect him. He was the best man in the wedding entourage, trailing behind and begging, "Take me along with you."

I injected a muscle relaxant into the vein. It was a quick way of inducing sleep. That's what the books said. I watched the body sink dreamlessly under the white covers. It looked like a dried stem from last season's flowers. Shorn of its leaves, its buds and its flowers. The original stem, the one that broke ground years before in a land that never knew the taste of ashes. As a child I used to go picking wildflowers in the open fields of the countryside. Then I'd take them and press them in a big book. My mother still has it.

I placed the electrodes on the forehead, attached them firmly and pressed the switch. The entire body writhed under the sheet, as the electric current alternated between the negative and the positive poles. Whenever they can complete the circuit, they strive to do so. It's all the same to them if it means carving away a memory. It seemed as if the shadow of a shock ran through the lobe of my own brain too. I quivered. Naomi's hands clung to my head and I didn't recognize the feelings she was transmitting to me. I sank into a deep slumber in her chair, and when I woke I knew I'd had a dream, but I couldn't remember a thing. I lay there for a long time trying to direct the current backward, to recapture the warmth of that dream, but it was no use, and the bitter taste of something on the tip of my tongue lingered for the rest of the day. I didn't find Naomi in her bed but on the balcony, breathing in the crisp wintry air and slicing some cake for herself. I told her, "I fell asleep but I can't remember my dream." To which she replied, "Maybe it's better that way. That's the soul's way of protecting itself."

I appealed to Paula Zimmermann's sense of reason. I explained to her what an electric shock does. I was afraid she'd be frightened and put up a fight. Ever since that Friday night in the garden, she'd been very reticent, like a wounded water turtle who'd ventured onto land only to come across collectors of tortoise shells.

We put her under heavy guard, like some celebrity or someone whose testimony at a trial was expected to be decisive. From off to the side, I could see Naomi asking for permission to visit her, and the young nurse asking innocently, "So you'll watch over her now?"

I reassured myself. She couldn't feel anything now anyway. And I was doing what I was supposed to, in the proper sequence. I'd already written down "Treat with antidepressants" in her medical file. As for Naomi, I told her that the drugs increased neural conduction in the brain.

"Where do they conduct?" she retorted. "From nowhere to no-where?" The medical file was smothered in words. Slowly I shrank away, as I cast a human being into a familiar mold, and the pen trembled as it shaped the slanted letters. Didn't we have it backward? Just who was the patient and who was the doctor? Me who fancied myself a minor god, upholder of the family tradition, a doctor and a doctor's son? Now I saw the withered body, the nostrils sucking in the air and begging to stop. "Let's just wait and see," the nurse told me, but I refused to leave the room. That patient was mine. I almost said: that patient was me.

Who gave me the right to force her into prolonging her stay? Time on credit. Naomi, stoic as ever on the balcony. Not even the grey clouds above could dampen her mood. She'd hung my white robe up on the line, and it was swaying back and forth.

"How strange to see the robe without the doctor," she said. Maybe what she meant was the doctor without the robe.

"Where do you live?" she asked.

"Hasn't your mother told you?"

By the end of the day, I no longer gave any thought to the lack of insight the night before. My parents had thought the immigrants odd. They didn't understand their illnesses or the unspeakable pain they'd brought with them from Europe.

Naomi tiptoed into the room. "How did the treatment go?" she whispered.

"She's very quiet. Hasn't woken up yet."

"You said that when she does she might lose her memory."

"Don't you know she's been replacing some memories with others?"

Maybe she would replace the missing chapter with a happier one. As if she had spent those years between nineteen and twenty-four in some peaceful country, on the sun-streaked island of Martinique or the plains of Australia.

We both kept watch over her.

"There's nothing left of her," Naomi said sadly. I was overcome by pain. The flower in my little flower-bed had wilted, and I was powerless to help it. My father is dead. On the shelves back home, hundreds of his patients' files still lie waiting, and I didn't have the courage to throw them away.

I checked her forehead. Now that they'd cut off the currents, there was no sign except two tiny reddish blotches. When Naomi moved away for a minute to smooth the sheet, looking in the other direction, I patted Paula's forehead, as if to try and figure out the wondrous ways of react-ing the nerves of the brain have. But I didn't make it. Naomi caught me in the act and said in an expressionless voice, "You got there too late."

From the hospital, they headed straight home. Naomi was depressed and Gideon Adar could not find the courage to comfort her. "Her memory will come back," he said. "Amnesia is a common aftereffect."

"You break it all down into clinical terms," Naomi said bitterly. "You don't want to understand that she chose to forget. It's her way of getting back at you!"

Naomi had some cruel things to say, and it seemed to him as though she were testing him, though he had no idea what it meant.

It was early in the evening. Tel Aviv had opened its gates to one and all. He wanted to hide Naomi in the commotion, but she refused. When they entered her apartment she said, "You've forgotten to take off your robe again."

She's going to be irritable, he thought, and began taking it off, but she stopped him. "It's a very convenient mask," she said, taking the empty sleeve and pushing her face into it as if into a white tunnel. He was put off for a minute, but as soon as he felt her head rubbing against his arm he wrapped his other arm around it and tried to pull her toward him.

"I used to throw up when I was little. Everything I ate. Food was like stones, and every meal was torture. She used to scream and bang her fists on her head. Yigal would watch the performance and cry terribly." When Naomi was seven and Paula was beside herself, she took her to a well-known pediatrician in Tel Aviv. Naomi remembered the twilight and the trees rustling on the boulevard as though guarding a secret. Her mother cried. The doctor asked the child to leave the room, but she tried to eavesdrop through the closed door. She remembered when they finally let her back in. He took her face in his two warm hands and said, "You're a very nice little girl. If you're not hungry you don't have to eat. You'll learn to eat when you're ready." Deep inside, she was grateful to him all through the years. Her whole childhood was wrapped up in a drippy poached egg and a saucer of grated peeled tomatoes. That wasn't the end of it. The final seal was still engraved in her stomach. With the throbbing impact of life's ups and downs she could feel the inner tumult and would keep trying to get rid of it all, until not a trace remained. But to her last years Paula Zimmermann had been the priestess of the painstaking, ritualistic ceremony, which cannot tolerate even the slightest deviation, lest it all collapse.

Inside Gideon Adar's empty sleeve, Naomi stammered all this in her little girl's voice.

Her hands skittered over him, and she pulled off the other sleeve. Slowly, she opened the buttons, one by one, from the bottom up to his neck, then hung onto him as though to a big tree, its foliage all the way through to the top, as the tree itself remained taut.

"Now! It's the right time," Naomi whispered in his ear and pulled him onto the floor, right over the coat and the wrinkled robe. Frantically, he pulled off her clothing and her mouth hit his like a warm truncheon. He wanted to tell her something, but she put her finger over his mouth as her fluids rose toward him. The white body broke out of the dishevelled clothes, like the islands of Atlantis finally rising to the surface of the water. Every island of quivering skin yielded to his tongue as she uttered the soft sounds of sheer pleasure. The scholar turned savage as he ripped off her stockings, no longer able to bear the pain in his groin. Naomi swayed under him, as if struck by a frenzy. "Now, now," she moaned. His juices burst into her, surging again and again. A large stain spread over the wrinkled robe-bedding and the sharp odor of semen merged with the nectar of her innermost depths.

Early the next morning the telephone tore through their sleep. She listened without a word. Late last night, Paula Zimmermann had walked out of room number nine, climbed onto the roof of the hospital and thrown herself into the black abyss.

I closed the file. I thumbed through it and found some all-white pages, still blank. They had resigned themselves to being an empty chapter.

On the binding I read: 1784. A person might find chilling digits like those written on his forehead, or on his arm, or on his plot and tombstone. I wondered: was it just in order to tell people apart? You couldn't just engrave on the stone, "There's been a mishap here," after all.

Over those long months when she'd been close to me, perhaps more so than to anyone else, I'm afraid I committed the sin of trying to push my head in among the bars to discover, with scientific inquisitiveness, precisely where it had all gone wrong. I'd already asked myself whether Paula Zimmermann would not have stumbled anyhow, even without that missing link. Now she'd given us one more night to add to that obscure chapter.

I did not go into the cemetery. I waited by the low wall, telling myself that this was the great outdoors. I wondered whether they were burying her now on the other side, right next to where I was.

In the distance I could hear the sound of the spades smoothing the ground. Naomi was very quiet. Her brother had arrived on the night his mother threw herself over. Something had made him uneasy, and without informing anyone he got on a plane and came. It occurred to me that it was no mere coincidence that all these survivors had no more than two children. That's as many as they could emotionally handle. They couldn't chance having only one, in case anything happened to him, and two were as much as they had the strength for.

Even as I stood there behind the fence, I could hear her brother sobbing about how he'd arrived too late. Naomi had brought him over to meet me earlier, "This is Mother's doctor." Yigal looked at me, his face contorted with pain, and said, "Why didn't you watch her? Where were you?"

An uncontrollable warmth ran through me, and my flesh tingled with the taste of her searching kisses. My fingertips burned with her skin. As the mourners entered the gate, I wanted to tell the one on the stretcher, "Maybe you'll find some consolation in that."

I called my mother that morning. She was very old by then and was still living in the same house in the country, the one my father's family built at the end of the last century. She asked: "Is anything the matter, Gideon?" And I said, "No, everything's fine."

"When are you coming to see me?"

"Soon," I said. Then I stammered, ''I'll be bringing someone with me." I wanted to make my mother happy too that day, she was exasperated with me by then.

The mourners were leaving. I recognized the principal of the school where Naomi teaches, the neighbor who alerted me at the end of the summer, and other people who turned their eyes upward and whispered, "What a tragedy."

Naomi lagged behind. First she pushed a few bills into the hand of the cemetery attendant, then she turned to the faucet near the entrance and washed her hands. I saw how the water splashed frivolously into the puddle underneath. I could feel the muscles in my legs tense.

Slowly she walked out of the cemetery. Her hair was wrapped in a kerchief and her eyes were dry and ingenuous. The tear in her blouse, required by tradition, was just barely visible. Spotting me by the gate, she walked over and asked calmly, "Why don't we go home?"

Summer was over. Winter too. And another summer had begun. Gideon Adar was still taking on new patients. Madness did not disappear with Paula Zimmermann. "They complain about life and yearn for death," said Aretaeus of Cappadocia.

The bed in room nine had been taken over by a young man who thought of himself as a high-ranking officer in the army of Carthage. He had delusions of grandeur, of how he was going to accompany Hannibal on the march to to Rome. Within days of his being admitted, blankets and quilts began disappearing from the other rooms, until one of the nurses found him piling them high on his bed as if he were riding an elephant. Sometimes Gideon Adar would ask himself where the real world ended and who actually occupied the realms of madness. Finally he sighed. It's all just the whim of some invisible being, after all.

Naomi went back to school, back to filling up test tubes with phosphorescent dyes and explaining the basic elements of nature to her students. Once, an experiment went wrong, and a huge blast shook the classroom. The children were scared at first, then amused. And Naomi simply stared and stared at the black spot clinging to the ceiling.

One afternoon, Gideon Adar decided to surprise Naomi.

He took off his robe earlier than usual, left instructions for the duty nurse and walked out of the hospital. On the way, he bought a bouquet of wildflowers and put them down beside him on the seat of the car. As he drove, a bee was attracted to the flowers in the car. Gideon Adar did not dare to flick her away, and waited patiently for the bee to fly off on its own. As he entered the congested streets of the city, the worker bee disappeared without as much as a single buzz.

He climbed the steps very quietly, pulled the key out of his pocket and drove it into the lock. Naomi's probably asleep, he thought, or preparing tomorrow's lesson. He entered the hallway on tiptoe. He could picture himself scooping her up from behind, as the petals of her lips opened in joy or desire.

From the angle at which he now stood, he could see the kitchen clearly. The pantry door was open. Naomi was standing on a little stool, filling the shelves with stacks of cans. High as towers they rose to the roof of the cupboard. Tightly wedged among them were bags of various sizes and colors. Gideon Adar read the labels: sugar, flour, rice. There was a special place set aside for the loaves of bread, wrapped in nylon, snuggled up against one another, each loaf protecting the others.

Naomi did not skip a single one. One by one, she stroked them all, humming softly to herself. Then she climbed down off the chair, a loaf of unwrapped bread in her arm. She pressed it to her bosom, and still didn't notice him.

(1985)
—Translated by Miriam Schlesinger

Introduction to Yehudit Katzir's "Schlaffstunde"

With the word "Once," Yehudit Katzir's story "Schlaffstunde"—"Siesta Time"—opens, and, indeed, as it begins to unfold, "Schlaffstunde" has the air of a children's story, a fairy tale, or even of a distant dream. A reference to the "new Prime Minister Menahem Begin" places most of the events recounted in the story in 1977.[36] Yet time itself soon becomes slippery as the narrator silently evokes her memories of childhood summers with her cousin Uli as the two of them, along with others, attend their grandfather's funeral. In the world of "Once," the young Uli claimed there were barrels of sauerkraut hidden in the basement of a restaurant, barrels "that could last a long time in case of another Holocaust." The children's grandmother baked cakes that reminded her "of her home overseas," and always had a full supply of memorial (*yahrzeit*) candles "because there was always a *yahrzeit* for somebody in her family who had remained over there." When Uli swears the narrator to secrecy, the vow is taken "on the black grave of Hitler." Though born in Israel, in other words, these children are nonetheless Holocaust-haunted. Their own private hideaway becomes "espionage headquarters":

---

36. See page 152: " . . . we could hear Menahem Begin the new Prime Minister giving a speech about Auschwitz and Six Million, and then he announced he was willing to meet in Jerusalem with President Sadat. . . ." Begin became Prime Minister, and Anwar Sadat, President of Egypt, came to Jerusalem, in 1977.

124

Then we climbed to our espionage headquarters under the roof, which sometimes was Anne Frank's hiding place, where we'd huddle together trembling under the table and munch on potato peels and call each other Anne and Peter and hear the voices of German soldiers outside and drop onto the green velvet sofa which Grandmother brought with her when she came to Israel in the ship. . . .

For interwoven throughout the text of "Schlaffstunde" are suggestions of another work: Anne Frank's *Diary*.[37] Moments before she and Uli are about to make love for the first time, for example, the narrator describes herself as having

thought about Anne Frank and how the Germans caught her before she really had a chance to love her Peter, when she was exactly my age, and I said to myself, I will have a chance. . . .

Then heavy steps grated on the stairs and I whispered, The Germans, and I started trembling, and we held each other tight and clung to the wall, and the door opened. . . .

Though Israel in 1977 is of course not Amsterdam under the Nazis, the meaning of the trauma that awaits these children and its significance for their lives are deepened and intensified through the identification with Anne and Peter. In the end, the story becomes a kind of revisioning and reconceiving of Anne's *Diary* in the context of an Israeli childhood, the "Schlaffstunde" of the title assuming an evocative and unforgettable resonance.

"Schlaffstunde" appeared in Yehudit Katzir's first collection of short stories, *Closing the Sea*, published in Hebrew in 1990; it has been translated into Dutch, Italian, and English (by Barbara Harshav). Her novel, *Matisse Has the Sun in His Belly*, was published in 1995 (Hakibbutz Hameuchad). Born in Haifa in 1963, Katzir studied literature and cinema at Tel Aviv University, where she now teaches Creative Writing in addition to working as a reader for Hakibbutz Hameuchad Publishing Company.

---

37. In Amsterdam in July 1942, the Frank family went into hiding from the Nazis in a "secret annex" in Otto Frank's office building, along with the family of his business partner, Hermann van Pels. Peter van Pels was nearly sixteen, and many passages in Anne's diary describe her friendship with Peter and the awakening of her sexuality. (The Gestapo raided the annex on August 4, 1944; Anne died in Bergen-Belsen concentration camp in 1944–1945, and Peter van Pels died on May 5, 1945, just three days after the concentration camp Maunthausen in Austria was liberated.) See Anne Frank, *The Diary of a Young Girl: The Definitive Edition*, eds. Otto H. Frank and Mirjam Pressler. Trans. Susan Massotty (New York: Doubleday, 1991).

Schlaffstunde

Yehudit Katzir

Once, when summer vacation stretched over the whole summer and tasted of sand and smelled of grapes and a redhead sun into a gang of clouds and we galloped home through the ravine in a thunderstorm and the rain stabbed your tongue with mint and pine and the neighborhood dogs set up a racket, barking like uncles coughing at intermission in a winter concert, and suddenly spring attacked with cats shrieking and the lemon trees blossoming and again came a *khamsin* and the air stood still in the bus but we got up only for Mrs. Bella Blum from the Post Office, a dangerous-child-snatcher who comes to us in bed at night with the wild gray hair of a dangerous-child-snatcher and the narrow glasses on the tip of the sharp-as-red-pencil nose of a dangerous-child-snatcher and pokes dry-ice fingers into our faces, and only if we'd give her all the triangular stamps could we somehow be saved or if we prayed to God, who disguised himself as a clown in the Hungarian circus and rocked, balancing himself on the tightrope under the blue canvas of the tent, in high-heeled shoes and wide red-and-white checked pants and then disguised himself as an elephant, turned his wrinkled behind to us and went off to eat supper.

Once, when the world was golden through the sparkling Carrera vase in the living room on the credenza, which vanished perhaps with all

---

Schlaffstunde: Siesta Time.

the other furniture as soon as we left the room and we peeked through the keyhole to see if it was still there but maybe it saw us peeking and rushed back and a horrible gang of thieves was hiding out in the garage under the supermarket and only Emil and you could solve the mystery because obviously you were going to be an important detective they'd write books about and I'd be your assistant and we experimented with invisible ink made of onion skins and we heated the note in the candle so the writing would emerge and then we trained ourselves to swallow it so it wouldn't fall into enemy hands and we did other training exercises, in self-defense and in not-revealing secrets even if they torture you and tie you to a bed and put burning matches under your toenails, and we mixed up poison from dirt and leaves and crushed shells and we kept it in yogurt jars and we drew a skull and crossbones on them and hid them with all our other treasures.

When the summer vacation stretched over the whole summer and the world was all gold and everything was possible and everything was about to happen, and Uncle Alfred was still alive and came for afternoon tea and Grandfather and Grandmother went to rest between two and four and left us endless time, we snuck up the creaky wooden steps behind the house to our little room in the attic which was headquarters and we stood at the window where you could view the whole sea beyond the cemetery and you touched my face with your fingertips and said you loved me.

Now we're gathered here, like sad family members at a departure in an airport, around the departures-board at the entrance, where somebody's written in white chalk, two zero zero Aaron Green, funeral, and I look at the woman sitting on the stone bench next to you, a round straw hat shading her eyes and ripening her mouth to a grape and the sun polishes two knives of light along her tanned shins and then I go up to the two of you, take off my sunglasses and say quietly, Hello, and you stand up hastily, Meet each other, this is my wife. My cousin. I discern the sparkle of the ring and the white teeth among the shadows and touch her soft hand with long long fingers and say again, Hello. And the undertakers, busy at work like angels in their white shirtsleeves, bearded faces, sweaty, carrying on a stretcher the shrivelled body under the dark dusty cloth,[38] the head almost touching the fat black behind of the gravedigger, the legs dangling in front of the open fly of the second one, and a frosty

---

38. In Orthodox Jewish burial ritual in Israel, bodies are buried in a shroud rather than a casket.

wind blowing inside me, as then, and I seek the memory in your eyes
but you lower them to her, take hold of her arm and help her up and
my spy's eyes freeze on her rounded belly in the flowered dress and see
inside her all your children you buried behind the house, in the grove,
in the summer vacation between seventh and eighth grade, when on the
first morning, as every year, Grandfather came to pick me up from home
in his old black car, with Misha, the office chauffeur, who dressed himself
up in my honor in a white visor cap and a huge smile with a gold tooth.
Misha put my red suitcase in the trunk and opened the back door for me
with a bow and a wink and we went to pick you up from the railroad
station near the port. On the way, I stuck my head between him and
Grandfather and asked him to tell me again how he played for the king
of Yugoslavia and Misha sighed and said, that was a long time ago, but
I remember it as if it was yesterday. I was a child then, maybe nine,
maybe ten, and I played the trumpet better than anybody in the whole
school and one day they brought me a blue suit with gold buttons and
a tie and stockings up to my knees and a cap with a visor and said, Get
dressed, and they put me next to a flag and said, Play, and I played so
beautiful and strong and King Pavel came in and the flag rose to the top
of the pole and the trumpet for the king and he came to me and stroked
my head and asked, What's your name, and I told him, Misha, and
Mama was very stubborn, like Albert Einstein's mother, his father didn't
want him either, and then he was terrible in school and the teachers
called the father and the father said to him, Albert, you're seventeen
years old now, not a child, what will become of you, but when he was
twenty-six he met Lenin and Churchill and showed them the theory of
relativity and there were a lot of discussions and he became famous all
over the world, so when I hear about abortions I say, Who knows what
can come out of that child, why kill a human being. Misha sighed again
and lit a cigarette. In the distance you could already see the big clock
over the railroad station. At five to nine we arrived. Grandfather and I
went down to the platform and Misha waited in the car. Two porters in
gray caps leaned on their rusty carts, looked at one another from time
to time with half-closed eyes, and smoked stinky cigarettes from yellow
packs with a picture of black horses. I was so excited I had to pee and
I hopped around from one foot to the other. At nine o'clock on the dot
we heard a long happy whistle of the locomotive pulling five rumbling
cars. The porters woke up, stomped on their cigarettes with huge shoes
and started running back and forth along the platform shouting, Suit-
cases, suitcases. Terrified, I looked for your face among the hundreds of
faces, crushed and scared, against the glass of windows. Then the doors

opened with a hiss and you came down, the very first one, wearing the short jeans all the kids had and a green shirt with emblems on the pockets that only a few had and a checked detective hat they had brought you from England and no other kid had, and you stood there like that next to your father's black suitcase, and looked around with eyes scrunched up like two green slits under your dishevelled fair curls, and once again I felt the pain between my throat and my stomach that clutched my breath every time I saw you and even when I thought about you, and I shouted, Here Uli, Here Uli, and I ran to you, and then you saw me and smiled and we embraced, and Grandfather came too, and tapped you on the shoulder and said, How you've grown Saul, and he didn't take your suitcase because you were already thirteen and a half and stronger than he, and you put it in the trunk, next to my red one. And Misha took us to Grandfather's office on Herzl Street, whose walls were covered with big shiny pictures with lots of blue, pictures of beautiful places in Israel, the Kinneret and the Dead Sea and Rosh Ha-Nikra and Elat,[39] where there were rest homes, and the government paid him to send Holocaust survivors there, and I always imagined how they arrived there by train, wearing funny coats and hats with sad yellow faces underneath them like in the pictures they showed us in school on the day commemorating the Holocaust-and-Heroism, and they line up there in a long row with all their suitcases tied with rope, and everybody enters in a line and takes off his coat and hat and gets bright-colored clothes and an orange pointy cap, and they sit in chaise lounges in the sun and swim in the sea and eat a lot and convalesce and after a week grow fat and tanned and smiling like the people in the advertisements and then they're sent home because new survivors came on the train and are already waiting in line. Until once, on Saturday, we went with Grandfather and Grandmother and Misha to visit one of those rest homes, called Rosh Ha-Nikra Recreation Village, and there was no line of survivors at the entrance, and there was no way to know who was a Holocaust survivor and who was just a normal person because they all had fat, droopy pot-bellies and nobody looked especially sad, they were all swimming in the pool and gobbling sandwiches and guzzling juice and talking loud and playing bingo. So we made up a system to check who was a real survivor, but I didn't have the courage, I just watched from a distance as you passed among the chaise lounges on the lawn next to the pool and whispered

---

39. The Kinneret is the Sea of Galilee; Rosh Ha-Nikra is in northernmost Israel, near the Lebanese border, and Elat on the Gulf of Elat in the South.

into everybody's ear, Hitler, and I saw that most of the people didn't do anything, just opened their eyes wide in a strange kind of look, as if they were waking up from some dream and hadn't had time yet to remember where they were and they closed their eyes right away and went on sleeping and only one man, big and fat with a lot of black hair on his chest and on his back like a huge gorilla, got up and chased you all over the lawn huffing and puffing, his eyes red and huge, and finally he caught you and slapped you and shook your shoulders hard and barked, *Paskutstve holerye, paskutstve holerye,*[40] and you came back to me with red ears, and you didn't cry and you said it didn't really hurt, but from then on, every time they mentioned Hitler, in school or on television, I would think of the gorilla from the rest home instead of the real Hitler with the little mustache and dangling forelock.

In the afternoon we went down, as always on the first day of vacation, to eat in the Balfour Cellar, and the tall thin waiter, who looked like a professor, and Grandfather told us that many years ago he really had been a professor in Berlin, wearing glasses in a silver frame and a beard the same color and a black bowtie, gave a little bow because he knew us, and especially Grandfather, who was a regular customer, and pulled out the chairs for us to sit down, and quickly put menus in front of us and said, What will you have, Herr Green, even though Grandfather always ordered the same thing, roast with puree of potatoes and sauerkraut, and a bunch of purple grapes for dessert, and the regular customers around the tables knew us and smiled and waved at us with white napkins, and as I ate I watched the two plywood cooks hung on the wall in their high chef-hats and long aprons and black mustaches curving upward like two more smiles on their mouths, and they looked back at me leaning on half a wooden barrel sticking out of the wall and full, I was sure, of very very good sauerkraut. And once you told me that the restaurant had a secret cellar right underneath us and that was why it was called the Balfour Cellar, and in the cellar there were lots more barrels like those and all of them were full of sauerkraut that could last a long time in case of another Holocaust, and then the limping newspaper seller came in wearing a dirty gray undershirt soaked with sweat and yelled, Paper get your paper, until the whole restaurant was filled with his sour breath, and Grandfather beckoned to him and he came to our table and gave him the paper with a black hand, and Grandfather paid him twenty agorot even though right next door to the restaurant there was a clean kiosk that had

---

40. *Paskutstve holerye:* A Yiddish-Polish curse.

papers and soda and ice-cream-on-a-stick. Then we went back home on the steep road that went by the gold dome[41] and you could see the whole bay from there, and on the way we fooled around on the back seat and played pinch-me-punch-me and boxed and yelled and called each other names, and Grandfather suddenly turned around and said quietly and earnestly, Don't fight, children, human beings have to love and pity one another, for in the end we all die. And we didn't understand what he meant but we stopped, and Misha winked at us in the mirror, and told about Louis Armstrong, who was the greatest trumpet player and had the deepest lungs, and when Betty Grable who had the prettiest legs in Hollywood got cancer he came with his whole orchestra to play for her on the hospital lawn under her window. Then we got to the house, and Grandmother opened the door, her tight hairdo rolled in a braid around her scalp, and pecked each of us on the cheek and said, Now Schlaffstunde, which always sounded to me like the name of a cake like Schwartzwalder Kirschtorte or Sachertorte or Apfelstrudel, which she would bake because they reminded her of her home overseas, and the steamy fragrant café when outside it was cold and snowing, but Dr. Schmidt didn't allow her to eat them because she had high blood sugar which is very dangerous for the heart. So she only served it to us and Uncle Alfred and Grandfather, who always said politely, No thank you, and refused to taste a single bite even though he was very healthy. But sometimes, when he went to walk Uncle Alfred to the gate, Grandmother would cut herself a small slice and eat it with quick bites, bent over her plate, and Grandfather would come, stand in the door and observe her back with a tender look, and wait until she was finished, and only then would he come into the living room and sit down with the newspaper, pretending he hadn't seen. They went to their room, and we went out to the grove behind the house and stretched a strong rope between two pine trees and tried to balance on it like that clown we once saw when we were little and Grandfather took us to the Hungarian circus in Paris Square,[42] where there were purebred horses and panthers with yellow eyes and trained elephants and a beautiful acrobat with long blond hair and the face of an angel who danced on the tightrope with a golden parasol in her hand, and we decided we'd run away and join

---

41. The gold dome of the Bahai Temple on Mount Carmel, on which the city of Haifa is built.

42. *Paris Square:* In the lower city of Haifa, Israel's third largest city, sometimes called "the capital of the north."

that circus after we were trained, but now we only managed to creep along on the rope, and you explained to me that it's important to know in case you have to cross over water. Then we climbed up to our espionage headquarters under the roof, which sometimes was Anne Frank's hiding place, where we'd huddle together trembling under the table and munch on potato peels and call each other Anne and Peter and hear the voices of German soldiers outside and drop onto the green velvet sofa which Grandmother brought with her when she came to Israel in the ship, and when one of the two wooden headrests collapsed they bought a new sofa for the living room and brought this one here, because it's a shame to throw out a good piece of furniture, and suddenly you said in a pensive voice, Interesting what you feel after you die, and I said, After you die you don't feel anything, and we tried to close our eyes tight and block our ears and hold our breath to feel dead, but it didn't work because even with our eyes closed we could see colors and you said, Maybe by the time we get old they'll invent some medicine against death, and I said, Maybe you'll be a scientist and invent it yourself and you'll be famous like Albert Einstein. Then we played writing words with our finger on each other's back and whispering them. First we wrote the names of flowers, narcissus and anemone and cyclamen, and names of animals, panther and hippopotamus, and names of people we knew, but after a while you said that was boring, and it was hard to guess because of our shirts, so I took off my shirt and lay down on the sofa, my face in the smell of dust and perfume and cigarette smoke that lingered in the upholstery from days gone by, and I felt how your nice finger slowly wrote words we never dared to say, first a-s-s and then, t-i-t and finally w-h-o-r-e, and while I whispered the words in a soft voice between the cushions of the sofa I felt my face burning and my nipples which had just started to sprout hardening against the velvet.

In the afternoon Grandfather and Grandmother came out of the bedroom with pink cheeks, twenty years younger, and at five o'clock on the dot Uncle Alfred came and we never understood exactly how he was related to us, maybe he was one of Grandmother's distant cousins, and her mouth grew thin as a thread whenever his name was mentioned and Grandfather would roar with rage, Bastard, and we didn't know why they didn't like him, whether it was because he was poor or because he once tried to be an opera singer in Paris or some other reason we couldn't guess, and why they entertained him so nicely in spite of it, and Grandmother served him tea and cake, which he would drink and eat and smack his thick red lips and tell again, his eyes melting with regret, about how he was a student in the Paris Conservatoire and lived in a teeny-tiny attic without a shower and without a toilet in Place de la République, and ate half a baguette-with-butter a day, but at seven in the evening he would put on his only good suit and bowtie and sprinkle eau-de-cologne on his cheeks and go to the opera, where he would stand under a decorated lighted vault and steal the occasional notes that slipped out through the lattices and caressed the statues of the muses and cornices of the angels, and in the intermission he would mingle with the audience and go inside, because then they didn't check tickets, and find himself an empty seat in one of the balconies, and so with sobbing heart and damp as a clutched handkerchief he saw the last acts of the most famous operas in the world. And here he would usually stand up, sway like a jack-in-the-box, clasp the back of the armchair with his plump fingers, and burst into an aria from Rigoletto or La Traviata or the Marriage of Figaro, and his voice was frail and fragrant and sweet like the tea he had just drunk, and only at the end did it squeak and break like glass, and Grandmother's thin hands smacked one another in dry applause and Grandfather lowered his eyes to the squares of the carpet and muttered, Bravo, bravo, and we didn't know why Uncle Alfred was thrown out of the Conservatoire one day and didn't become a great singer in the Paris opera, and Grandmother wouldn't tell us, she only clenched her mouth even tighter, as if a huge frog would leap out if she opened it. And Uncle Alfred would sit down and sigh and wipe his reddish nose like a strawberry with a wrinkled handkerchief he pulled out of the left pocket of his jacket, and he would hold out his arms to invite us to ride on both sides of the chair, and hug our waists and tell about the cafés of Montparnasse and Montmartre, which was a meeting place for writers and artists and students, and from his mouth strange names flowed with a wonderful sound I'd never heard before anywhere, like Sartre and Simone de Beauvoir and Cocteau and Satie and Picasso, and then he'd caress your hair and say, You'll be an artist too someday, and stroke your back and say, Or a writer, and press his little white hand on your leg with the short jeans and say, Or a musician, and go on strumming with his fingers on your smooth bare thigh as if he were playing a piano, and he didn't say anything to me. He couldn't know that someday, on a steamy shuddering mid-summer afternoon, we'd be standing in the old cemetery at Carmel Beach, our shamed backs to his tombstone, on which were the words, in gold letters as he requested, of the Chinese poet from Mahler's *Lied von der Erde:*

When sorrow draws near,
The gardens of the soul lie wasted,
Joy and song wither and die,
Dark is life and so is death.
Now it is time, companions!
Drain your golden goblets to the dregs.[43]

Our backs to his tombstone and our faces to Grandfather wrapped in a
sheet, he hurrying to slip into an eternal Schlaffstunde next to Grand-
mother, who died in the winter many years before, but they didn't take
us to the funeral because they didn't want us to catch cold and miss
school, and our faces to the cantor whose closed eyes were turned to the
sky as he trilled his *El male rakhamim shokhen bamromin*,[44] and to your
father who had turned completely grey, muttering *Yitgadal v'yitkadash
sh'me raba*, and to my mother hiding her face in her hands, ripping her
shirt,[45] and to the old people responding Amen, their familiar faces
mocking me under their wrinkled masks, waving at me sometimes and
smiling around the tables in the Balfour Cellar which isn't there any-
more, and sometimes dozing off in the chaise lounges of the rest home
which was closed years ago, and here's Misha, who almost didn't get old
but without the visor hat and the smile with the gold tooth, and he's
wearing a black *kippa*[46] and noisily wiping his nose, and my gaze is drawn
to the shrivelled sharp face of a stooped little old woman which is stamped
on my memory as if it had accompanied me throughout my childhood,
though I can't remember where, and I turn to you and seek in your eyes
which don't look straight at me, in your worn-out face, in the white
threads in your hair, desire in me a sharp wild pain like the whistle of the
train now galloping along the shore on its way to the new station at Bat-

---

43. Mahler's *Lied Von de Erde:* The "Song of the Earth": a song cycle set to German
translations of Chinese poems. That Alfred should be performing Mahler seems utterly
appropriate; Mahler was a tormented outsider whose *lied* try to come to terms with the
reality of death.

44. *El male rakhamim shokhen bamromin . . . Yitgadal v'yitkadash sh'me raba:* "God full of
compassion . . . judge on high . . . Magnified and sanctified be God's great name. . . ." (the
mourner's prayer).

45. *Ripping her shirt:* A traditional symbol of mourning. See also Ruth Almog's "Invisible
Mending," in which the protagonist is tormented by her schoolmates for having had her
torn jumper repaired.

46. *Kippa:* A skullcap which he is wearing because of the religious service.

Galim, but only tatters of memories are pulled from me, connecting to one another with their tails like the colored handkerchiefs from the box of the magician in the Hungarian circus, and about a week after vacation started you didn't want to join the circus or practice balancing on the tightrope between the pines and you didn't want to play Anne Frank or Emil and the Detectives, you didn't want to play anything with me, you just sat under the big pine tree all day long and read little books with crinkled bindings and you looked worried and sad and full of secret thoughts under your checked cap. At first I tried not to disturb you even though I was insulted, but by the third day I had had enough. I waited until afternoon and when Grandfather and Grandmother went for their Schlaffstunde, I crept up behind you, grabbed the book named The Confession of the Commander's Lover with a picture on the cover of a soldier in a brown uniform with black boots up to his knees aiming a huge pistol at a blonde sprawling in the snow between his legs and wearing only panties and a bra. I hid the book, and said I wouldn't give it back until you told me what was going on. You looked at me strangely through your long light lashes and said, Swear on the black grave of Hitler that you won't tell anyone in the world ever. I swear, I whispered solemnly, and to myself I imagined a deep black hole where the big hairy Hitler of the rest home was standing. Then you told me that recently, ever since you started reading those books, it swelled up in your pants and became so hard you had to rub it with your hand until a kind of white liquid sprayed out of it and that was the most wonderful feeling you ever had in your life like the explosion of a shooting star, but afterward you were worried because in school they explained to you that women get pregnant from it, and when you wash your hands it goes into the pipes of the sewer along with the water and flows into the sea and a lot of women swim in the sea and it could get into them under their bathing suits, and not all of it would go into the sink either because among millions of little seeds some twenty or thirty were bound to be left on your hand, and sometimes you had to go on the bus afterward or to basketball or scouts, and it could get on the money you paid the driver, and from the driver's hands to the tickets he gives the girls and women of all ages, and then they go back home and to the bathroom and tear toilet paper and wipe themselves and it gets inside them and they don't even know, and now thousands of women are walking around the streets with babies from you in their swollen bellies, and not only here in Israel, because the sperm can be washed away in the water and even go as far as Europe. An ashamed spark of pride glimmered in your eyes for a moment and died out. I sat silently awhile and thought,

chewing on dry pine needles. That was a really serious problem. Mean-
time you were tossing pine cones, trying to hit the tree trunk opposite,
thunk, thunk, thunk. Suddenly I had an idea. I stood up and ran to the
kitchen, opened the drawer next to the sink which had all kinds of things
you need in a house, matches and Band-Aids and rubber bands, and took
out a few plastic sandwich bags Grandmother used to pack food for the
road when we went on a visit Saturday to one of the rest homes, and I
ran back and gave it to you and said, Here, do it in this and bury it in
the ground. From that day on, the worry and the pride disappeared from
your face and we were friends again and played all the old games and
only sometimes did you suddenly stop and give me long pensive looks,
and at night I'd creep into the kitchen and count the bags to know how
many were missing, and I'd go out barefoot to the fragrant dark grove
with gloomy treetops and the sound of rustling and chirping and howl-
ing and mysterious hissing, and I'd find the places where dry pine needles
were piled up and the earth was loose, and I'd dig with feverish curious
hands and panic and bring up the plastic bags from their graves and look
at the wonderful liquid in the moonlight for a long time. One day you
add the crinkled little books to our treasure and I said, I don't need this
garbage anymore, I can invent better stories myself, and I said, You'll
surely be a writer someday, and I remembered that Uncle Alfred had said
it before I did. So we tore the pages out of the books and sat down to
cut out the words, especially the coarsest ones, and pasted them into
scary anonymous threatening letters to the gang of criminals under the
supermarket and to Mrs. Bella Blum of the Post Office, and we gorged
ourselves on the chocolate we had stolen earlier from Grandmother's
kitchen, where she kept it for baking her cakes, and it tasted a little like
almond paste, and suddenly you touched my face with your fingertips,
as if to wipe off a chocolate mustache, and you went behind me and
wrote slowly on my back, word after word, I-love-you, and hugged me
tight. You lay on the sofa, and I lay down on top of you, my face in the
soft shadow between your shoulder and your neck, a smell of paste and
starch from your green shirt, and your damp fingers stroked the back of
my neck for a long time, trembled, hovered over my hair. Stuck together
without moving, almost without breathing, only our hearts galloping like
horses in a mad race, and I slowly stroked your face, as if I were sculpting
it anew, your fair curls and your smooth brow and your eyelids and
underneath them is a whole world and your little nose that a finger could
slide down like a ski to your lips, where a hot draft breathes on my
frozen finger, and you pull up my shirt, your cool hand on my back
down and up, then up and down to that nice place where if we were cats

our tails would grow out of, and I put my mouth on your mouth, taste the stolen chocolate, our tongues meet, circle, and push each other like two panicky wrestlers, and I tug the shirt up off your smooth chest and my shirt up off my breasts, to press my nipples hard from the cold against the warm soft skin of your panting belly, and I feel a sweetness between my legs as if honey had spilled and a little of it drops on my panties, and that makes me open them and move back and forth on your thigh, and you hug tight and suck my lips like lemon drops and you put my hand on the hard bulge in your shorts and your face becomes serious and fragile so in it I can see what no one before me has ever seen, and I breathe fast-fast like a little animal without memories, my melted belly stuck to yours the sweetness in my panties more and more until it hurts until I can't and suddenly those spasms inside me the first time so strong and sharp and long and then shorter and faster like flutterings but I don't shout so they won't wake up and I want it never to end but finally it does end and I fall on you breathless as if I had run the sixty-yard-dash, and I see that you too are half fainted, struggling to swallow air, your face burning, and I get off you and lie beside you and discover a big spot on your pants and, excited, I inhale the sharp smell rising from the two of us, a smell not like any other.

Then you looked at me with flashing green eyes and you smiled and kissed me on my cheek, and you wildly pushed aside the hair stuck to your brow and sat up and took off your shirt in one movement and said, Take off yours too, And I took off mine, and you laid your head on my stomach, and we rested like that awhile, my hand stirring your damp hair, and fingers of sun pierced the chinks in the shutter and spread golden fans on the walls. Then I stroked your back and said your skin was soft as velvet, and you said mine was soft as water, and you kissed my stomach and drew strange forms on it with your lips, and you said, When you lie on your back your breasts are as flat as mine, and you licked my nipples, and your tongue was a little rough like a cat's, and you licked and licked until they got hard as cherry pits, and again I felt sweet and smooth between my legs and wanted it to go on as before, but Grandmother's voice rose from downstairs, sharp and probing, like the periscope of a submarine, Children, where are you, five o'clock tea and cake. We put on our shirts fast and came down and you went to change your pants, while I looked in the gilded mirror in the vestibule. My eyes sparkled like cups of sky, and the whole world, the furniture in the living room and Grandfather and Grandmother and Uncle Albert looked far away and unreal but sharp and clear, as on a stage.

That night I couldn't sleep because I missed you too much, you were sleeping quietly in the room at the end of the hall and maybe your body was dreaming of me. I wanted so much to come to you in the dark and hug you and hear you breathing, but Grandmother was always strict about you sleeping in your father's old room and me in my mother's room, next to their room, so I controlled myself and thought about tomorrow, about the ceremony we planned down to the smallest detail after dinner, when Uncle Alfred had gone and Grandfather and Grandmother sat down in the living room to watch the Friday night news on television, and we whispered back and forth in the kitchen, and we could hear Menachem Begin the new Prime Minister giving a speech about Auschwitz and Six Million, and then he announced he was willing to meet in Jerusalem with President Sadat, and Grandfather said, At last that idiot came out with something good, and Grandmother called us, You should see this, important news, but we knew that tomorrow's ceremony was much more important, and especially what would come afterward, and there was no way I could stop the film that kept repeating over and over on the dark screen, the film we starred in. And suddenly, from their room, I heard Grandmother scream in a whisper, Aaron, Aaron, and Grandfather woke up and said gently, yes, Minna, and Grandmother said she couldn't fall asleep, and she told him quietly, but I could hear every word, that in the morning, as she was walking around in the supermarket with the cart to buy food for the Sabbath, she suddenly felt that her mother was standing next to her, in a black fur coat, the one she wore years ago when they said good-bye at the railroad station, and her face was as pale and tired as it was then, and she told her something, but Grandmother didn't pay attention because she said to herself, It's summer now, why is Mother wearing a fur coat, and before she could understand, her mother wasn't there anymore. I've been calm ever since, Grandmother went on in a harsh whisper, I'm sure it's something very bad. From her face I know something awful is going to happen. Grandfather didn't say anything, he just sang her something very quiet, a tune of yearning without words, and repeated it over and over until it filled me completely, until I fell asleep.

The next day was the Sabbath. Grandfather and Grandmother woke us early to go with them to visit the rest home in Tiberias,[47] and were surprised when we muttered from under the covers that we were tired and wanted to stay home, but they gave in. I remembered what I had heard at night from their room, and I thought to myself, How can ghosts wander around in our supermarket, and why didn't Grandfather

---

47. Tiberias is on the Kinneret (the sea of Galilee) and is known as a resort area.

comfort her and tell her it was all her imagination and nothing bad would happen, and suddenly I thought, Maybe that whole conversation didn't happen and I only dreamed it, and I decided not to tell anybody, not even you. Grandmother made hard-boiled egg sandwiches for our lunch, and prepared food to take on the road, and my heart began to pound when I heard the drawer next to the sink open and Grandmother whisper to herself, Funny, I remember there was a whole package here. Finally she wrapped it in waxpaper because Misha was already honking for them outside, and pecked each of us on the cheek and said, We'll be back by seven-thirty tonight, behave yourselves, and they left. As soon as the hum of the motor disappeared around the corner, we leaped out of bed and met in the hall, and we started to do everything exactly according to the plan we concocted last night down to the last detail. First each of us took a long and thorough bath, shampooing our hair and cleaning our ears. Then we wrapped ourselves in our sheets, which we tied at the shoulder like Greek togas, and I put on perfume from all the bottles I found on Grandmother's dressing table, and I smeared my lips and cheeks with a lot of red, and my eyes with blue. Then we cut off the tops of the pink flowers Grandmother had bought for the Sabbath, in the golden vase on the credenza, and we plaited two wreaths for our heads. Then we went into the kitchen but didn't eat breakfast because we couldn't swallow a thing, but from Grandmother's hiding-place for candles, next to the hiding-place for chocolate, we stole six *yahrzeit* candles,[48] she always kept it full of them because there was always a *yahrzeit* for somebody in her family who had remained over there, and from the sewing box covered with flowered cloth we took a pair of scissors, and from Grandfather's linen drawer we took a white handkerchief, and from the pantry a glass of wine, and from the library a small Bible your father got as a Bar Mitzvah present from his school, and barefoot we went up to our room in the attic with all those things. Then we closed the shutter on the day and on the cemetery and we made it absolutely dark, and we lit the *yahrzeit* candles and put them about the room, which was filled with the shadows of scary demons dancing on the ceiling and the walls, and we left one candle on the table, and we put the Bible next to it, and you asked, Are you ready, and I whispered, Yes, and my heart was pounding, and we stood facing each other, and we put one hand on the Bible and we raised the other with thumb and pinkie together as in the scouts' oath, and I looked straight into your eyes

---

48. *Yahrzeit candles:* Memorial candles; a "Yahrzeit" is an anniversary of a death ... "who had remained over there," i.e., who had been killed in the Holocaust.

where the flames of the candles were burning and repeated after you
slowly, solemnly;

> I swear by God and by the black grave of Hitler,
> I swear by God and by the black grave of Hitler,
> I will never marry another woman,
> I will never marry another man,
> And I will love only you forever,
> And I will love only you forever.

Then we hugged each other and almost couldn't breathe because we
knew that that oath was strong as death[49] and to make it even stron-
ger we cut the words out of the Bible and pasted them on a sheet of
paper in the light of the candle. The two Gods we found right away
in the creation, and woman in the story of Adam and Eve, and grave
in the part about the Cave of Machpelah.[50] Then we found man and
swear and I and of and you and another and love and the and black
and will and never. The rest of the words, Hitler and marry and
forever, we couldn't find so we pasted them together from separate
letters. When it was all ready, you wrapped the glass in the handker-
chief, put it on the floor and stamped on it hard with your bare foot.
The glass broke and a big spot of blood spread over the cloth. You
dipped your finger in it and signed your name under the oath. Now
you, you said. I took a deep breath, picked up a piece of glass, and
scratched my big toe hard, from the bottom, so nobody would see
the cut, squeezed a drop of blood onto my finger and signed a shaky
signature next to your name. Then we wrote the date, the regular
date and the Hebrew date, and the exact address, Presidents' Boule-
vard, Mount Carmel, Haifa, Israel, Middle East, Continent of Asia,
Earth, Solar System, Galaxy, Cosmos. Now we'll tear the oath in two
and each of us will keep the half with the other's signature, I said
what we had planned to do, and you were silent for a moment and
suddenly you said, No, let's wrap it up and bury it under the big pine
tree, someplace where we can always find it. I thought to myself that

49. *Oath was strong as death:* Compare the Song of Songs: "Love is as strong as death, and
jealousy cruel as the grave" (8:6).

50. *Cave of Machpelah:* Which the patriarch Abraham purchased as a burial place for his
wife Sara, in Hebron, and where all the Biblical patriarchs and matriarchs, other than
Rachel, were eventually buried. See Gen. 22.

we were forbidden to change the plan, but I didn't say anything. We folded the paper in the aluminum foil of yesterday's chocolate and put it in an empty matchbox, which we wrapped with more paper and in a plastic bag you had left over from the ones you stole from the drawer, and we went downstairs. We dug a deep pit with our hands next to the trunk and hid our package, more important to us than anything in the world, but when we covered it with earth and stamped it down with our feet and piled pine needles on it, I became very sad all of a sudden, and I didn't know why.

When we got back to the room, the *yahrzeit* candles were still burning and the demons kept jumping wildly on the walls. I knew what was about to happen but I wasn't scared. I thought about Anne Frank and how the Germans caught her before she really had a chance to love her Peter, when she was exactly my age, and I said to myself, I will have a chance. We took off the wreaths and the Greek togas and we spread one sheet on the sofa underneath us, and we lay down, and covered ourselves with the other one, and I caressed your whole body which was warm and breathing fast, and I walked my tongue among hills of light and soft shadows and paths of soap and sweat under the sheet, and suddenly you were over me on all fours and looking at me with sparkling yellow eyes and a savage smile, and I wanted that to happen, and I whispered, Come, and you asked, Does it hurt, and I said, No, and I could hear your heart drumming on my breasts rhythmically I-love-you-I-love-you, and I was filled with tremendous pride.

Then heavy steps grated on the stairs and I whispered, The Germans, and I started trembling, and we held each other tight and clung to the wall, and the door opened, and in the opening in a halo of light stood Uncle Alfred. They apparently forgot to tell him they were going away and that he shouldn't come today for tea. He looked at our sweaty bodies and the handkerchief spotted with blood and the pink flowers scattered over the floor and the *yahrzeit* candles, and he rubbed his strawberry nose in embarrassment, and his eyes were fixed on some point on your stomach, maybe your belly button, as he stammered, What's this children, it's forbidden at your age, you shouldn't, if Grandmother finds out. We covered ourselves with the sheet and looked at him cautiously and silently like cats. He lowered his eyes to the shiny tips of his shoes and went on, Of course I'll have to tell her, who would have thought, children, cousins, and God Forbid there'll be a baby with six fingers on each hand, or two heads, or a little tail like a pig, this is very dangerous, who would have thought. And he wagged his head from the right shoe-tip to the left shoe-tip, as if he were setting up a shiny-shoe contest.

Then he looked at you again, and said with no stammering now that he was willing not to tell anybody on condition that you agreed to meet him here, tomorrow afternoon, so he could talk to you and explain what a serious thing it was we had done. Why only him, I burst out to defend you, and Uncle Alfred said he regarded you as responsible and that with your sense and talent he hadn't expected anything like this from you. I agree, you said quietly, and he left. As soon as the door closed behind him we jumped off the couch, stood at the window again, with one hand on the Bible and the other in the air, with thumb and pinkie together, and I repeated after you the oath we composed on the spot:

> And even if we have a baby
> With six fingers on each hand
> Or two heads
> Or a little tail like a pig
> We will love it as if it was a completely normal baby
> With no tail at all.

Then we dressed and cleaned up everything fast before Grandfather and Grandmother got back home. Except the dark red spot, blossoming on the green velvet, that we left as a souvenir. Before I fell asleep, I could hear Grandmother whispering into the golden vase on the sideboard, Funny, I remember buying flowers for the Sabbath, and Grandfather comforting her gently, Well, my memory's not what it used to be either, how could I forget to tell Alfred not to come today for tea.

In the middle of the night I felt horribly nauseous, ran to the bathroom and stuck my finger down my throat and suddenly I felt I was throwing up sand, enormous amounts of wet sand, it filled my mouth and gritted between my teeth, and I spat and threw up, threw up and spat, and then something else was vomited up from me with the sand, and I looked into the toilet. A tiny black dog floating stiffly on his side, his legs spread out, his gums exposed in a creepy smile, watching me with a gaping dead eye. In horror I slammed down the lid. Outside it was beginning to turn light.

I wandered around among the trees with my hands in my pockets, kicking pine cones. You'd been up there for more than half an hour, closed in the room. What did he have to tell you that took so much time. I couldn't control myself anymore. I went up very quietly, opened the door a little, and peered in. The two of you were sitting on the sofa. With big opera gestures Uncle Alfred was explaining something to you that I couldn't hear and from time to time he put his cotton hand on your leg. Then he wrapped his arm around your shoulders and put his face which was always flushed, almost purple, close to your face which was ashen. Suddenly he looked up and saw me. A shadow passed over his eyes. I fled downstairs. I lay under the big pine tree, right over the oath we buried yesterday, and I looked at the green sparkling needles that stabbed the clouds which today were in the shape of a huge white hand. I waited. Time passed, more time, a lot of time passed, and you didn't come down. I remembered the dream I had last night, and I shivered with cold. At last the door opened and Uncle Alfred came out breathing deeply as he went steadily down the steps. He buttoned his jacket and rang the front door bell. Grandmother opened the door, said, Hello Alfred, and he went into the house. Then you came running out, you lay down beside me, hid your head against my belly, and muffled your howls of anguish. Your whole body shook. I held you. What happened, what did he tell you, I whispered. We have to kill him, you cried. Your hot tears were absorbed by my shirt. I had never seen you cry like that. But what happened, what did he do, I asked again. We have to kill him we have to kill him, you wailed, your feet kicking the ground. But what did he do, hit you, tell me what he did, I pleaded. You lifted your burning wet face where the tears and the snot were running but you didn't care, and you said quietly, Today I'm going to kill him. I looked into your red eyes, with two black pits in them, and I knew that today Uncle Alfred would die.

Within minutes we had a fatal solution of poison made of shells ground up with two ants, a mashed piece of pine cone, and yellow dog-doo. We mixed it all up with pine tar so the ingredients would stick together. My job was to ask Grandmother if I could make the tea today, and to pour the poison into Uncle Alfred's cup. I chose the big black cup for him so I wouldn't confuse it with another and also because I thought the poison would work better in a black cup. I added five spoons of sugar and stirred it well, trying to hear what they were saying in the living room to make sure he wasn't telling on us in spite of everything. They were talking very quietly and only separate words reached me, Dr. Schmidt, chest X-ray, diagnosis, and Dr. Schmidt again. They were talking about diseases. I calmed down. On the tea cart I also put the special two-layer Schwartzwaldertorte that Grandmother baked and I didn't understand what it was in honor of, maybe it was his birthday today. As soon as I entered with the tray, they shut up. Uncle Alfred said, Thank you, and a sad smile clouded his face. You came in too, your eyes dry now, and we huddled together in the chair, waiting with awful tension to see him drink and die on the spot. First he greedily polished

off three pieces of cake. Then he sipped noisily, smacked his lips, faced
us, and declared, Now I will sing you the first Lied from Mahler's Lied
von der Erde. He cleared his throat twice, clasped his hands on his
stomach, and started singing in German which we couldn't understand.
His voice burst out of his chest as a solemn trumpet blast, rose to a great
height both gold and trembling like a tightrope walker, and suddenly it
fell and plunged into a dark abyss, where it struggled with fate, pleaded,
prayed, shouted like a hollow echo, whimpered, abased itself, the
face that of a drowning man, tears flowed from his eyes and from
Grandmother's eyes too, she understood the words, and even Grandfa-
ther blew his nose a few times, and we looked at each other and knew
the poison we mixed was also a magic potion, and we held our breath
to see him sink into the carpet in the middle of the song, but Uncle
Alfred finished it with a long endless shout and his arms waved to the
sides and hit the credenza, and the gold vase teetered a moment in
surprise and then slid off and smashed on the floor into sparkling slivers.
Uncle Alfred sat down, panting heavily, and whispered, Sorry, and Grand-
mother said, It's nothing, and she came and kissed him on the cheek and
Grandfather didn't look at the squares of the carpet and didn't murmur,
Bravo, but shook his hand and looked into his eyes and said, Wonderful,
wonderful, and Uncle Alfred took another sip of the poisoned tea, and
stood up to go, and said to us, Good-bye, and caressed you with his
gaze, but we didn't answer, we only looked at him with hatred, and they
accompanied him to the door, and wished him good luck, and Grand-
father patted him on the shoulder and said, Be strong, Alfred, and Uncle
Alfred said hesitantly, Yes, and the door closed behind him and Grand-
father and Grandmother looked at each other a moment, and Grand-
mother nodded her head and brought a broom and dustpan and swept
up the slivers.

   At night I woke up to the sound of coughing and an awful screech-
ing laughter and I heard Grandmother telling Grandfather in the kitchen,
Now I know what she said, now I know what she wanted to tell me then.
And the awful laugh was heard again, as if it weren't Grandmother
laughing but some demon inside her. I got up to peer from behind the
door, and I saw her sitting at the table, her long hair disheveled and in
her nightgown and her mouth stained with cherry juice and chocolate,
a knife clutched in her fist over the ruins of Alfred's two-layer cake, and
Grandfather in pajamas grabbing her wrist and pleading, Enough, enough
now, you've already eaten too much, and Grandmother struggled to free
her hand and the screeching voice of the demon burst out of her, Just
one more little piece, just one more little piece, and Grandfather held her

and cried, Don't leave me alone, Minna, please don't leave me alone, I can't make it alone. I ran away from there to your room. Your breathing was heavy, uneven. I got in under your blanket and hugged you and put my head next to yours. The pillow was soaked.

The next day we went with Misha and Grandfather and Grandmother who sat in front, her braid now pinned together, and Misha left them off at Rambam Hospital and took us to the beach at Bat-Galim, and we took off our clothes and had our bathing suits on underneath, and Misha looked like a lifeguard with his visor cap and broad chest, all he needed was a whistle. He sat down in a chaise lounge at the edge of the water, and you ran into the sea with a spray splashing colorfully and you plunged into the waves, and I ran in behind you and also plunged because I wanted to feel what you were feeling, and my eyes burned and I swallowed salt water, and when I came back to the shore, you were already standing there and shaking your curls, and we sat down on the sand next to Misha, leaning against his sturdy legs, and we watched the sea and were silent because none of us had anything to say. Then I asked Misha to tell us again how he played for the king of Yugoslavia because I knew how much he liked to tell it, and I thought maybe that would save the situation. He was silent a moment, and suddenly he said quietly, It wasn't I who played for the king, it was another boy, he was also called Misha, and he played better than I did, so they chose him to wear the uniform with gold buttons, and the trumpet sparkled in the sun, and the flag went up to the top of the flagpole, it was so beautiful I'll never forget it, and King Pavel came and patted his head and his mother cried so they had to hold her up, and I stood there in the line with all the children and I cried too. He wiped his nose, and then he went on, as if to himself, But that Misha isn't here anymore, Hitler took him, all of them, all of them, my parents too, my brothers and sisters, I'm the only one alive, the sixth child, the one they didn't want, because Papa and Mama got married very young, they were cousins, but the family decided to marry them off at thirteen, that's how it was done in those days, and every year they had a baby, every year a baby, until Papa said, enough. But then they went for a vacation in Austria and when they came back Mama was pregnant again. Misha fell silent and lit a cigarette, and then he said out of the blue, Your grandfather is a fine man, there aren't many people like him. We quietly watched a young man who finally managed to walk on his hands and a man who threw a stick in the water and his big dog charged in barking and swam and brought the stick out in his mouth and the man patted his head. I took an ice-cream stick and drew a house and a tree and the sun on the wet sand, and the waves came and erased my picture. And the sea slowly turned yellow and we got chilly so we dressed and went to get Grandfather and Grandmother, who were waiting for us at the entrance to the hospital with gray faces and looking suddenly very old.

A few days later Grandmother told us that Uncle Alfred had died in the hospital. She wiped her tears and said, He had a disease in his lungs and the operation didn't succeed. But we knew the real reason, and we didn't dare look at each other as we walked with Grandmother, who was weeping for Alfred and for herself and with Grandfather, who was weeping for Grandmother, and with our parents and the other three people we didn't know, behind the undertakers busy like angels in the white shirtsleeves and sweaty faces, carrying the shrivelled body on a stretcher under a dark grave-cloth, the head almost touching the fat black behind of the first gravedigger, the legs dangling in front of the open fly of the second one, and I thought, It could be anyone under the cloth, maybe it's not him, but when we got to the open grave the cantor said his name and a desperate crying burst out of me because I knew you couldn't move time backward. And you stood silently on the other side of the black grave, and I knew Uncle Alfred would always be between us, and after the funeral your father would take you home, long before the end of summer vacation because Grandmother already didn't feel well, and in a few months, in the winter, she would die too, and Grandfather would close the office on Herzl Street and move to an old people's home, and he would go on talking to her all those years as if she were still beside him, and we would never again be together in our little room under the roof, and only sometimes, before sleep came, you would crouch over me on all fours and look at me with yellow pupils and I would whisper to you, Come, and I would feel your heart drumming on my breasts, until the last flutter. I wipe my tears and go with all the old people to put a little stone on the grave, and now everyone is turning to go, but I stay another moment at Uncle Alfred's yellowed marble, I know you're standing here next to me. Up close you can see that I too have lines at the corner of my mouth and many gray hairs, and the two of us read by heart the lines from the first *Lied* of *Das Lied von der Erde,* whose words we didn't understand then, and I put a little stone under the words and you put a little stone and then you put your hand on my shoulder and say, Let's go. My mother and your father are walking in front of us, whispering about the city's plan to destroy the old house and dig up the grove to build an expensive apartment building on the site, and I see the ground, which can't still be holding all we buried there, it will split open and the high-rise will crack and collapse. Misha comes behind us and sighs and says, If you could only go backward in life, even one minute, and I know exactly what minute he wants to go back to. And at the gate stands the stooped over old woman whose shrivelled face is so familiar, and she grabs my sleeve with a trembling hand and screeches, Maybe you don't remember me but I remember your grandfather very well, he was a regular customer of mine, in the old Post Office. You're Mrs. Bella Blum of the Post Office, I whisper and my heart turns pale, and for a split-second I see eyeglasses on the end of the sharp nose, gray hair, icy fingers reaching out for the necks of children and triangular stamps, and I remember the anonymous threatening letters, and I glance over at you, but you're looking at your shoes covered with dust and you say, I have to go, we have a meeting at the factory, and once again I touch her soft hand under the purplish straw hat. Suddenly a strong wind comes from the sea and snatches the hat off her head and rolls it down the path, and she runs after it among the tombstones in her fluttering flowery dress, with her rounded belly, with the strips of her chestnut hair, flinging out her full arms to catch it, but the hat mocks her, it flies into the sky like a purple butterfly, and just as it's about to light on the sharp top of the cypress, it changes its mind, flips over twice and lands on the tombstone of Abba Khushi the famous mayor of Haifa, and you and Misha and all the other men volunteer to get it for her and you jump around among the graves, but the hat is already far away from there, crushed and ashamed between Hanoch ben Moshe Gavrieli born in the city of Lodz and Zilla Frumkin model wife and mother, who lie crowded next to each other, and all of you are flushed and sweating, but the hat pulls away again with a splendid somersault and soars, and you chase it, look up and wave your hands, like survivors on a desert island to an airplane, then the hat loses its balance and spins around itself like a dancer with a jumble of purple ribbons and lands with a bang outside the gate and lies on its side and laughs with its round mouth, and she runs to it, heavy and gasping and bends over and picks it up and waves it high in the air and brimming with joy she turns to you with sparkling eyes, I got it, I got it.

(1990)
—Translated by Barbara Harshav

Introduction to Shulamith Hareven's "Two Hours on the Road"

Shulamith Hareven's "Two Hours on the Road," from her collection *Loneliness,* conjures up an Israeli landscape that perfectly fits the kind of difficult and tortuous emotional transitioning Ada, the story's main character, is faced with having to undergo. On the highway to Jerusalem, Ada drives past the low hills and fields of Latrun junction but is suddenly paralyzed by fear, unable to go further, to make the winding, demanding, ascent into the steep Judean mountains to get home. For when she does arrive home she will have to confront the changed circumstances of her own life.

Juxtaposing "Two Hours on the Road" with Nurit Zarchi's "Madame Bovary in Neve Tsedek" suggests just how profoundly both Israel and the sense of possibilities for women's lives have changed over the generations. In "Madame Bovary in Neve Tsedek," set in the pre-State days, the writer's husband went abroad to "collect money from diaspora Jews for the Building of the Land." A few decades later, Ada's husband is making the same trip, this time to encourage *aliyah,* immigration: "There goes Shmaryahu again to bring the Jews of the world to Israel, and here comes Shmaryahu again, still without the Jews of the world. Maybe next time." The husband in Zarchi's story drowns; in Hareven's, Ada, "perfectly calmly, says to Shmaryahu, who is preparing for another trip abroad, that she would rather he did not return from there to their apartment." Living in a little house on the sands of Tel Aviv, Zarchi's character imprisoned herself in her bed. By the end of "Two Hours on

148

the Road," it is clear that middle-aged Ada is ready to face that difficult uphill drive to Jerusalem and the emotional complexities of the new stage of her life. One is also tempted to suggest that Ada is a great deal more equipped to do so than is her husband, for the story also suggests that an emotional vacuity is the driving force of public men committed to an illusory Zionist cause.

The first woman to be elected to the Academy of Hebrew Language (in 1979), Shulamith Hareven is one of Israel's most prominent, prolific, and multi-faceted writers—a commentator for Israel's leading newspaper, *Ha'aretz*, and the author of sixteen books, translated into fifteen languages. In "The Limits of My Language are the Limits of My World," Hareven has written brilliantly and eloquently about the structure, characteristics, inherent values, richness and uniqueness of the Hebrew language, its concision and "urge for laconism." In "On Being a Levantine," she argues with elegance and passion for the vital importance of Middle Eastern peace for the future of Israeli literature:

> I am a Levantine because I'm language-struck, and the rocky, sensuous, luminous languages of the Levant took root in me far more naturally than the languages of the West, which sometimes sound too soft for my ears. I am a Levantine because I write Levantine books. Because when I go to Egypt, I suddenly understand a great number of scriptural and linguistic concepts that were closed to me before, and this is happiness. Peace with our neighbors is the lifeblood of language-struck types like me, because we wish to return the language to its Semitic roots—in other words, rescue it from extinction.[51]

Politically engaged ever since she served as a combat medic in the 1947–48 siege of Jerusalem, when she was seventeen, she served in the Israel Defence Forces as an officer, worked with Jewish refugees from Arab countries in the transit camps in the 1950s, and was a war correspondent during the War of Attrition and the Yom Kippur War of 1973. As a longtime active member of Peace Now, she reported on conditions within Arab refugee camps during the uprising known as the *Intifada*.

---

51. "The Limits of My Language Are the Limits of My World," and "On Being a Levantine," in *The Vocabulary of Peace: Life, Culture, and Politics in the Middle East* (San Francisco: Mercury House, 1995), pp. 26–49, 81–87.

But, says Hareven, "I draw a very distinct line between my public activities and my literary work. I view my writing as 'craft' in the medieval sense of the word. Participation in the press enables me to influence the contemporary scene in Israel, while keeping my literary work strictly separate." Among her most recent works are haunting, spare, and lyrical reconstructions of the life of the ancient Hebrew tribes in *Thirst: The Desert Trilogy* (San Francisco: Mercury House, 1996), gracefully translated by Hillel Halkin.

Hareven lectures frequently at the Israeli Academic Center in Cairo, and has been a Writer in Residence at Hebrew University, Oxford, Ohio State, and Cambridge. She was elected one of "One Hundred Women Who Make the World Move" by the Parisian *L'Express* in August 1995. She has been married to Alouph Hareven since 1954 and has two children and five grandchildren. She lives in Jerusalem.

Two Hours on the Road

Shulamith Hareven

Past Latrun,[52] between the low hills and the mountains, Ada, without warning, finds herself driving into fear.

Ada slows down. Her foot feels heavy on the gas pedal. She can't drive anymore. Together with her, we feel how stuffy the car is, how the world is boxing her in. Ada quickly turns the handle to lower the window, then raises it again. Ada is very frightened. The cars speeding toward her seem about to veer out of their lane, ballooning in size as they threaten to collide with her.

The car behind her honks a sharp warning and passes her a little too quickly. Ada brakes and pulls off onto the shoulder. She is covered with sweat. The hitchhiking soldier in the passenger seat looks at her in surprise.

"What's the matter?"

Ada shakes her head vaguely to say: nothing.

"Something wrong with the car?" Impatiently. He's in a hurry.

"The car is fine."

The soldier mumbles something that sounds like a curse and quickly bails out to look for another ride, slamming the door behind him. He is sweaty and hatless. The shirt of his fatigues hanging out of his pants does not conceal his paunch. He has no time. Already he is standing on

---

52. *Latrun*: Opened after the Six Day War of 1967, the road to Jerusalem from Tel Aviv and the coastal plain passes the Latrun junction, site of Emmau (Luke 24: 3–31) and the Monastery of the Trappist Fathers, before curving and climbing into the mountains.

the side of the road with his hand out. Now he is squeezing into the cabin of a pickup truck that has screeched to a stop, beside two other men. We will get along without him.

The sweat trickles into Ada's eyes and streams from the back of her ears down her collar in a steady flow. Ada feels very bad. Her fear translates into bodily signs. The tips of her fingers and toes are very cold. Ada is pale. She cannot start the car, cannot drive another inch. All of the traffic seems aimed at her. Don't start the car, Ada, we tell her. Rest. Wait. The traffic is heavy now, and if you're unsure, it's best to take no chances. Ada unfastens her seat belt and sits there, exhausted.

It is six-thirty in the evening and the highway is full of cars.

Now a word about the drivers. They turn to look as they pass, making querying hand movements. Most of them do not stop. Each car that passes rocks Ada's car, with Ada inside, like a little tornado or earthquake. Ada does not want them to stop. It's all right, she signals with her hand, keep going. The cars speed by, going much too fast, *ffasst, ffasst, ffast-ffast, ffasst.*

It is six-thirty and many drivers are returning home. The cars keep racing by ffasst-ffast, nonstop. The sun is setting quickly. To the rear, the fruit trees of the monastery at Latrun[53] are golden in the light, row after row of neatly planted trees, each a curly bronze whorl. A low fence runs on into the distance along the right-hand side of the road, like a very clear sentence, in the last light.

Ada reaches into the back seat for her pocketbook and places it on her knees. One after another, a handkerchief, a tissue, and a little bottle of cologne pass through her hands. Also in the back is a thick folder of scientific publications. Ada does not know when she will be able to edit them. She daubs cologne on her forehead, but the usual refreshing feeling is missing. Ada steps shakily onto the shoulder and walks back along the fence side of the car, which she leans on for support. She opens the trunk and pulls out a jerrycan, intending to splash some water on her face and hands. In the end, however, she pours the entire contents of the can on her head and all over herself, as if taking a lukewarm shower. At first she does this without meaning to; then, with a growing sense of relief. Rivulets of water run down her hair, coiling it into ringlets, and onto the shoulders of her dress.

---

53. Christian legend holds that this was the site of the house of the thief crucified with Jesus; hence in the Middle Ages it was called *Domus Boni Latronis* ("House of the good thief"), corrupted into "Latrun." It is now the site of a Trappist monastery.

Ada feels better. She replaces the jerrycan, slams the trunk shut, walks back to the front of the car, and leans against the right side of the hood, her white dress dripping water. She still cannot drive. A puddle collects on the pavement around her feet, all reddish gold in the sunset, like an odd celebration, a celebration of the end. Ada stands there: propping herself up, exhausted, golden. The sun has become less definite and her panic is not so acute. We can worry less about her. It is the end of sunset in the Latrun valley, in a soft and rather aloof landscape that does not detain the traveller. A white car stands parked on the right side of the road—between the car and the fence a middle-aged woman dripping water, the shoulders of her dress turning gray and clinging damply to her body. She is resting. We are waiting.

Ido sits by the driver of the very dusty Jeep, which stops near the Latrun junction. The driver is shod in sandals consisting of soles and a single strap and is dirty with engine oil. The driver and Ido are silent, two people who have spent so much time together that they have said all there is to say and are now simply fellow travellers. Ido's sandals are caked with dust. One of the straps is hanging by a thread, about to tear. Ido is returning from guiding a desert Jeep tour in Sinai. His face is unshaven. By his side are an almost empty knapsack and a rifle.

Ido is named after Ada, because Ido's mother is Ada's best friend. Ido's mother is a woman of many committees and commissions who changes hairdos every week. Ido's mother is the only person with whom Ada can really laugh out loud, the way you can laugh with someone who has known you since childhood. Ada and Ido's mother do not need many words when they talk. And that is all we will say about Ido's mother, because she is not on the road with us and does not belong to our story.

What does belong to our story is the fact that when Ido was a baby, Ada, in the days before she was married herself, was often his baby sitter. She held him in her arms and taught him such first words as *light*, *hot*, and *water*. Ido, an alert and quiet infant, looked now at the ceiling from which hung the bulb that Ada's finger switched on and off; now at the steam from the kettle; now at his own chubby brown hand that Ada held beneath the faucet; and now, concentratedly, at her mouth trying to follow her lips which said: "water." Ada liked teaching babies their first words, and Ido has liked Ada ever since, because she had known just how to be with him, whatever age he is. When Ido, thin and excited, celebrated his bar mitzvah, Ada did not dream of kissing him, but Ido stood on tiptoe and planted a kiss on her cheek before fleeing from his amazed family. Then he grew up and went into the army. Although now that he is discharged he no longer lives with his parents, he and Ada always enjoy their rare meetings. Ada is not sentimental and feels no need to play a tribal mother. The hopelessly disarming encumbrance of childhood has long ceased to come between them and they can talk. Ido likes Ada, more than he likes her husband, Shmaryahu, who always has a driven look. Shmaryahu's blue eyes seem frozen to him, focused on some other world. Ido and Ada's daughters were never friendly.

Is Shmaryahu with us on the road too?

Perhaps.

Ido gets out of the Jeep, slings his knapsack and rifle over his shoulder, and raises his hand idly: good-bye. The driver of the Jeep swings around at the intersection to head back toward the southwest. He takes out a pair of sunglasses and puts them on. Ido, on the other hand, who is now walking eastward, takes off his dust goggles. We are delighted that he is walking eastward.

Ido crosses the intersection and keeps walking straight ahead in the direction of the mountains. His pace is neither quick nor slow, and he enjoys stretching his legs after several days of driving. The after-sunset light illuminates him from behind in dull bronze tones. The light falling on the roadside is no longer strong; a first pallor rises from the fields. Ido halts to look for something in his knapsack. He is thin and not especially tall and is wearing a polo shirt that is too small for him and stained with diesel oil in the midriff from an emergency repair in the desert. His shorts are ragged and very short. Ido is a little hungry, but not terribly. He finds a slightly discolored apple at the bottom of his knapsack and takes a bite of it. Actually, he has plenty of time. After the torrid heat of Sinai, the air is pleasant. Ido walks slowly along the roadside by the low ongoing fence. Ido likes to feel his body, the muscles of his legs.

Ada is still leaning against her car. The drivers slow down and ask her if she needs help, and she continues to wave them on gaily. Ada decides that if she still can't drive by nightfall, she'll hitch a ride to Jerusalem. Meanwhile, she'll wait to see what happens. She isn't in a hurry. There's nothing wrong with standing by the roadside. Actually, she feels all right except for having to drive. The cars speed by, *ffassst-ffasst, fffast.*

Ido, who has spied the parked car from afar, decides to walk to it. It stands to reason, he thinks, that if its driver has a problem, he may be able to fix it and catch an easy ride to Jerusalem. He tosses the rest of his apple into the oleander bushes by the roadside and continues walking eastward. The passing cars fan him with warm air.

Ido suddenly realizes that the car is Ada's and covers the remaining distances quickly. He puts an arm around her. Ido chatters gaily as a sparrow. He and Ada stand together on the side of the road; Ido talks and Ada simply smiles. A big red automobile whizzes by and screeches to a stop on the shoulder ahead of them. In it is a couple Ada knows.

They turn to look back, swivelling their heads as far as they can, and smiling broadly, ludicrously, as a communication of vigorous friendship. The man gestures with his hands. The woman rolls down her window and sticks out a disembodied head. She has on too much lipstick.

The disembodied head calls out: "Ada! Need any help?"

"No, no," answers Ada, anxious to be rid of them. She already has Ido, smile and all.

"We've got a performance in Jerusalem," shouts the woman's head apologetically, and the red automobile sets out again. We'll get along without it. Ada and Ido smile at each other.

Ido says, "So what happened, Ada?"

"I don't know what happened. I just can't drive."

"Are you sick?"

"I don't think so. The road just frightened me all of a sudden, so I stopped."

"Want me to drive?"

"I'd appreciate it."

Ido does not hurry. Every movement is deliberate. He circles the car to its other side, moving easily, and opens the door. Ido puts his rifle in the backseat, on top of Ada's folder of manuscripts, lays his knapsack next to it, sits down behind the wheel, and stretches his legs. He leans forward to open Ada's door and says: "I've been driving nothing but Jeeps for a week. What a treat your car is."

Ada sits down beside him and shudders slightly. The sun already has set, and the drop in light and temperature makes her shiver. She feels sad that the light has gone; she thinks of darkness as one of those bad times that only being old enough can get you through, with a measure of resignation. Ido has not started the car yet. He asks if she is cold. Ada is not certain. Ido asks why all that water. She tells him about the jerrycan. Ido takes off his shirt with its streak of diesel oil and begins wiping her slowly, thoroughly: first her head, then her face, then her arms, then—still unhesitatingly, though perhaps a bit too forcefully—her back and chest. Ada breathes slowly, quietly, relaxing under his hands. Ido tosses the wet shirt into the back seat. The once neatly empty seat now looks a mess with the folder, the grimy knapsack, the rifle, the discarded shirt. But Ido sits erect, a compactly built young man. His skin is tanned and dry. His vertebrae stick out like a long, stiff string of beads.

"I thought I'd dry out more quickly in this heat," says Ada with her eyes closed.

"It's because of your long hair. My mother would never go pouring jerrycans of water on herself. Her hairdo has to last all week. Have you seen the Eiffel Tower she has now?—no, not a tower, it's like a beehive. More power to her. But you don't need a hairdo. You have hair."

Ido says "hair" as though saluting. Ada smiles. Her eyes are closed.

"Look, something must have happened."

"Something did. Shmaryahu and I separated three days ago," says Ada with her eyes closed. "And you," she adds, "are the first person to hear about it."

Ido whistles lightly and looks at her.

"Is it final?"

"Yes."

Ido asks Ada if she feels good about it. Ada says that it was she who wanted it.

Ido asks, "How many years has it been? Twenty-two?"

"Twenty-three."

"Does my mother know?"

"Not yet. I told you, right now you're only one." Ido feels suddenly awkward. It's all a little too much for him, too much for his years. He says, "Well, talking won't get us to Jerusalem."

Ido puts the key in the ignition, turns it, and starts the car, which takes to the road, gliding forward gaily in the long line of traffic. It seems content to be its old self again. Ada looks straight ahead through half-shut lids. The air is growing gray. All colors are fading, even those of the cars on the road. We are aware of shapes now, rather than colors, moving shapes, blurry at the edges, in a lightless halo of haze like thin dust in the air, as though a curtain were covering and blotting out the earth. The fields darken quickly.

A recent flashback: three days before all this, Ada, perfectly calmly, says to Shmaryahu, who is preparing for another trip abroad, that she would rather he did not return from there to their apartment. We are sorry to hear this, but Ada is neither sorry nor surprised. She expected it. For several years now she has noticed when setting the table, she forgets Shmaryahu's knife and fork, or sometimes his glass. That she goes to sleep and gets up in the morning looking straight ahead, as if there were no one else in the bed with her. That she immediately heads for another room to get dressed, and so does he. That their nightly battles over the blanket have been settled long ago by separate blankets. That Shmaryahu's frequent trips, his returns, the turn of his key in the door, his heavy tread with two suitcases and an overcoat over his arm—all have ceased to sound any depths and have become a mere nuisance. There goes Shmaryahu again to bring the Jews of the world to Israel, and here comes Shmaryahu again, still without the Jews of the world. Maybe next time. Ada can no longer bear the awfulness of hope. When she tells him she would rather he didn't come back, there is no violence in what she says, but the contrary: now life will be easier. Shmaryahu does not argue. I'll phone you from New York, he says, from the hotel. We'll talk it over. He takes his two suitcases and leaves, only his jaw a little slacker than usual, as if he were chewing on something.

Ada and Shmaryahu have no children left at home. Their older daughter is married, and their younger daughter is studying in Beersheba. We are concerned about them. You will have to tell them, Ada, we say: How will you do it? How will they take the news? So far, Ada has no answers. Meanwhile, she has not told anyone. Shmaryahu has not called from New York either. Perhaps he is calling now and the phone is ringing and ringing in their empty apartment. Let it ring. Now she has told Ido, who is driving her car and feeling both awkward and glad. He never much cared for Shmaryahu. He never shared his parents' sentimental opinion of the man. Ido drives, his eyes on the road, very much in charge. He is thinking that all these years it was he, not his parents, who had it right: Ada was never happy with her eminence of a husband. So who saw it all along, eh?

Ido would gladly get Shmaryahu off the road and out of this part of the story.

It's Ada and Ido, unmistakably in one car. Ido says, "We'll get there before night."

And yet he switches on the headlights. In the hazy twilight, between day and night, the cars are phantasmagorical. Ido is in need of a clearer definition of light.

Ido is an excellent driver who misses nothing. The lanes of cars surge on like a herd of heavy gray horses; now the left lane moves ahead, now the right. Now the traffic bunches up even more: something is holding it up, perhaps a tractor or a stuck car. Ada cannot bear the tension of the cars coming toward her in their passing lane, *ffasst*, as jauntily as if they owned the world; every car-shape seems about to crash into her, more out of thoughtlessness than spite. She does not know how Ido can drive without thinking of such things. Once more the traffic breaks free and flows faster. The orchards are hard to make out in the no-light.

The massed mountains are in front of them now. Look, over there on the left are the lights of the gas station at Sha'ar Ha'gai where the climb begins. And over there on the right, in the dusk beneath the ruined Turkish khan, is the old beauhinia tree, heavy with hanging pods. Ido steers the car into the steep ravine through which the highway to Jerusalem runs, stretching in his seat; he can already smell the scents of the city, of wind, mountain, and many pine trees, of air that you can drink in large gulps. The change is total: coming from the desert, he is keenly aware of the difference. Hills rise on either side of them; the one on the left is closer to the road, the one on the right, farther off. Along its flank runs the road from Beth-Shemesh, which feeds into the highway and joins it.

The highway heads into the night. The air is truer now. Soon the shapes of the cars will be swallowed up and converted to many quickly moving lights in the deep earnestness couched between the mountains. Up above stand in a row the lights of a village, like fishing boats that have set sail on an ocean of darkness. Soon the cars will thin out; each car rampaging up or down the ravine will be noisy and violent, the sound reverberating into the distance while the ravine waits to calm down again. Night will close over the road, a high, stern night whose moon has set long ago. Pine trees will turn black and rustle slowly, part of the nocturnal essence. Only in the first light of dawn will they reappear by a road swabbed bright with phantom water, as fresh as on Creation's first day, with bicycles and partridges. The pines will yawn and awake to their own green. And then with much noise, will come the slow trucks shifting gears. And again, the racing cars.

Keeping his eyes on the road, Ido asks Ada what it's like to be separated for three whole days.

Ada says she doesn't know. Ido cannot quite believe that. But we can. Ada tells Ido's unbelieving shoulder that she really has no idea. Ido does not understand how you can have no idea about something so important. Ada says that she wishes she felt something, anything, sorrow or anger or relief, but that she doesn't feel a thing. Except for this sudden fear of the road. She is sure to get over it in a day or two. It will pass. It has to.

"What have you done these past three days?"

"Nothing special. Read manuscripts, made notes. This morning I returned a batch to the publisher in Tel Aviv and took a new batch. I shopped for groceries. I spoke on the telephone. What does anyone do?"

Ido says with a smile that he's happy to see that Ada is wearing her white dress with the gold belt. He remembers her wearing it to his bar mitzvah. Ada can't believe he remembers.

"And how I do!" says Ido, embarrassed to glance at her. In fact, he tells her, that whole year, and all the years before and after his bar mitzvah, he was crazy about her. And scared to death that his mother would find out. Or that Ada would. He says this without daring to look at her. His imagination is already at work while he expertly pilots the wet-haired woman in distress sitting next to him with her eyes shut. Ido tries keeping his mind on the road. That's where it belongs.

Ada is happy. She moves a little nearer to him. When she opens her still half-shut eyes, she sees the thin brown body very close to her, sun-bronzed legs almost black, calm hands resting on the steering wheel. Be careful, Ada, be careful. But she hasn't another field of vision at the moment. Ada wants Ido now, hard; perhaps she has wanted from him the moment he appeared twenty kilometers ago. Ido casts a quick glance at her. Cunningly he reaches out as though to check if her car door is locked. But Ada's body is there to meet him. It's not your imagination, Ido.

"Why don't you rest that wet head of yours on me, you'll feel better. And if you stick your hand in my knapsack, there's one more apple there."

Ada pulls from the knapsack a pair of torn underpants, a dry soap container, a map fitted to a plastic folder, a crushed matchbox, and a bruised apple. She carelessly wipes the apple on her white dress, and Ido is pleased with her. Ada and Ido take turns taking bites from the apple. Her hair dampens his neck and shoulder and excites him a bit, making him bite his bottom lip. Their bodies were never strangers to each other. As a child he clung to her no end. And yet. The hunger is now very clear.

Ido suddenly realizes that all this will vanish into thin air once they reach Jerusalem and decides to plunge ahead.

"Listen. I'm going to pull over soon and we'll walk to the top of that hill."

"Here?" wonders Ada. It has never occurred to her before to stop her car on the highway to Jerusalem in order to go mountain climbing.

"Not right here, a little farther on. There's a real nice saddle up above us." Ido is afraid that Ada will say no, but Ada does not say anything.

Ido, responsibly, says gruffly:

"Just don't fall in love with me, because I have a girlfriend. You've met her. Her name's Ilana."

What an idiotic thing that was to say, Ido. Ada stiffens for a moment, then reflects that actually it makes things easier: all at once everything is less important, because Ido is less important too. Fine, so there's Ilana. So what. She remembers Ilana from one of those Saturday coffee klatches at Ido's parents' house: a boyish haircut, an Arab dress from the souk,[54] and an unpleasant voice.

---

54. *Souk:* The open-air Arab market.

Ido pulls off the road and cuts the engine. They stop. Seat belts. Windows. Doors. Air.

The car stands parked on the shoulder once more. It hasn't gone very far and here it is again.

The evening air is warm and dark, suffused with the smell of gasoline. Once more the vehicles speed by, *ffasst, ffasst, ffasst-ffast, fffasst,* rocking the car with each gust. Ido remembers to take the triangular reflector and stand it behind the parked car, so that for a moment it seems to Ada that they've just stopped for some repair. Ada regards the reflector as though it were a tombstone for something not yet identified. Reality seems to have broken up into little particles that she can't fit together again. The cars flash by with people hurrying home to their dinners and well-lit rooms. On her right, close enough to reach out and touch it, is a rocky trail. From a car you can't reach out and touch anything. Ada has her doubts about the mountain. But it's only Ido, after all.

"Up we go," says Ido, urging her on like a tour guide.

Ada climbs slowly up the mountain, which exudes the hot day's smells of pine trees and thyme and gasoline fumes and much dust. Even the insects on the pine roots are caked with dust. Ido takes big strides from rock to rock, as sure-footed as on a city sidewalk, skipping quickly and erectly with his rifle over his shoulder. Ada has to grab at something now and then to keep from slipping. She is embarrassed to be out of breath and to have to keep stopping to get her wind. It is not really a hard climb.

"Come on," Ido encourages her with a smile. "Come on, Ada, we're almost there." Here, on the mountain, he has no peer. A king.

Ada is afraid with a whole confused ocean of fears. Midway in life, as at its outset, you do not trust your body not to fail or disappoint you. Ada is glad that it is getting dark quickly. Ido seems to know the place well (Ilana?): a very bent pine tree spreads its low branches above a rockface flat as a table, a warm rock covered with pine dust and pine needles. The front of the rock drops off sharply, and Ada warns herself not to slip, because you can tumble from here all the way back down to the road.

Ada and Ido on a rockface, beneath a spreading pine tree, on top of a not very high hill. The abandoned car is almost exactly beneath them, its triangular reflector shining behind it, every detail of it familiar: the upholstery, the dashboard, the broken ashtray that hasn't been fixed for years. Everything in the car is familiar. The noise of the big highway echoes louder up here, deafeningly. But it's only Ido, after all.

"It's kind of funny to be carrying something like that around since your bar mitzvah," says Ada, as though looking for an opening.

"Better late than never."

That too, of course, is not the right phrase; but Ido's face close to hers is flaming now, his dark eyes are very earnest, and words in themselves have no value. Ada is thrilled by his new face. She could have lived her whole life and never seen it. We say: of all Ido's faces, Ada, this is the one you will remember. Ido puts down his rifle within reach and turns to her. But this is so sudden, Ada thinks. Ada drops to her knees and he quickly kneels down by her side. The rock feels warm beneath her back. High up above his shoulder the sky looks unkempt: the terrible, ravaging sorrow of a night in the mountains, as though all of life existed only on a very thin, narrow strip, a flimsy bridge that alone was habitable; take a single wrong or careless step and you were banished to dead dirt where no man lived. Down below, the cars speed on and on, bringing their passengers home, a long, narrow swath with nothing beyond it. Ido's face, a long, sharp jawline in need of a shave, the tense look of a man in danger. There is a possible wound in this, Ada thinks. And an innocence.

Something in her gives now, bursts hotly, like pity. She hugs him hard; and indeed, all that is left for her to do is to step into that great sea she knows so well and let herself be taken by a wave and yet another until she picks out the biggest wave of all and rides it, breaking, back to shore; but the big wave eludes her this time, as if some dreadful, all-levelling sorrow has reduced all things; and she becomes Ido's silent witness, with no regrets.

Ido checks and rechecks his rifle, which has pine dust in its barrel, blowing in it over and over. Ada gathers her almost dry hair and shakes dust and pine needles from her dress.

"I was too excited," he says apologetically.

"So was I, Ido." Ada's voice is very low. She is still full of an endless tenderness that fills her completely. So much Ido. And that new face.

Ido does not know what to say. He touches her forehead, her mouth, bashfully. Suddenly he jumps to his feet.

"Damn, I see some police down there by the car. I better get down and calm them before those mothers break into it and you've got a problem."

Now Ada too sees the fierce blinking blue light down below on the roadside, as if sniffing her car. We say: they won't break in so quickly, Ido, but we know that you want to get away from her. That it's all so terribly sad.

"Go on down. I'll follow you."

Ido plunges quickly downhill in leaps and bounds, as if nothing can knock him off his stride. There is a note of finality in his descent. I've lost him, thinks Ada. From now on there will always be a great self-consciousness between us, as between people who have gone too far. When I'm invited to his wedding with that Ilana of his, or with some other Ilana, there will be a problem. I've lost Ido, Ada thinks. Tomorrow I'll visit his parents, and when I take off my sunglasses, he'll count my wrinkles with open curiosity. And the day after that, with a triumphant show of sorrow, he'll take note of my first gray hairs.

Ada, in her fears, does not understand Ido, who has just persuaded two policemen in a slightly hoarse voice that everything is all right. Writing off their suspicions, they return to their vehicle and drive off with a slam of its doors. Quickly it merges with a long line of traffic that slows down for it, the fierce light winking on its roof, tinting the mountainside with a moving blue stain. Ido is now a dark shape against the car, waiting for her to come down. He is rather mortified. He thinks he has lost Ada forever, because he had his chance and disappointed like a baby. Ido is angry with himself; he stands there, full of dark fury. The sandal that was about to tear has torn. Ido removes it and goes on standing with one shoe on and one shoe off. He braces his bare foot against the side of the car, which is still giving off heat. Bad. Ido waits, angry with himself.

The breeze arrives at last. At first they hear it dragging at the dry thistles with a sharp rustle, then whipping the pine boughs, which take a long, a very deep breath. Ada stretches herself: she can feel the strength run back into her wide-awake body, every bone of which feels aired by the wind. Ada looks down and knows that never again will she see the road from this angle; from now on she will drive without stopping, without looking up from the thin life-strip of the ravine. She will keep to the straight and narrow. Ada lightly touches a pine tree, almost in farewell. But now she can drive, and that is what she decides to do. She needs only to get to the bottom, not quickly like Ido, not by leaps and bounds, but to get there. And to tell him to sit next to her while she starts the car and drives the last few kilometers to the city that broods quietly over its mountains, one more car to have arrived among the houses and the flowerbeds and the traffic lights. And to open her seat belt, and let Ido off by his house, and say the inevitably awkward good-bye, because the two of them, really, what an idea. And then home to a house that Shmaryahu would never come back to, to be by herself, and begin at last, three days late, the job of tallying and mourning.

(1985)
—*Translated by Hillel Halkin*

Introduction to Mira Magen's
"Gerbera Daisies at Half-Price"

The conflict enacted in "Gerbera Daisies at Half-Price" dramatizes one that is pervasive in contemporary Israel: the split between traditionally religious and secular ways of life. With the same sensitive attention to detail that characterizes all of Magen's stories, "Gerbera Daisies at Half-Price" portrays a modern young secular anthropologist leaving her husband and seeking to become a *khozeret b'teshuva,* a "returner to repentance," a practicing Orthodox Jew. She and her child move into a religious neighborhood, a kind of foreign territory whose customs, values, noises, fragrances, are vividly evoked in the story.

But the pivotal issue for the narrator becomes not one of the possibility of authentic religious faith, but rather one of how to live with one's own eroticism. In her view, the apparently casual, café society of the secular world gave only the appearance of sensuality. " . . . we used to walk around practically naked," she says, "wearing shorts and thin shirts that reached only about an inch above our navels and were cut down to the middle of our backs," but the nakedness was an illusion: "the truth is," she goes on, "we were always covering up, concealing, trying to be what was expedient, not what we really were." Instead of the physical nakedness revealing the self, it masked it: "we were always posturing." In contrast, in the religious neighborhood where men and women are, in the words of the collection's title, "well-buttoned up":

Babies wriggle their way around underfoot from apartment to apartment, babies wriggle around in wombs, and breasts are always full . . . Here, though everyone is wrapped up in layers of fabric, life is really naked, always touching their flesh, filled with the smell of sperm and blood and milk, and they don't use creams and bleaches to battle their flesh, they live within its circles, they give birth, nurse . . .

Can she really become part of that world, however? The Hebrew word *teshuva* means not only "repentance," or "return"; it also means "answer." In Israel, when those who have "made teshuva" leave the religious world to return to that of the secular, they are described as *khozrai b'sheh'ai'la*—those who have "returned to the question." That phrase seems a profoundly apt one to describe the narrator's state of mind at the end of "Gerbera Daisies at Half-Price," an ending that suggests more questions than answers.

Gerbera Daisies at Half-Price

Mira Magen

What a jerk you are, you said as I buckled the big suitcase and fumbled with the zipper of the black bag we once bought in London. You couldn't understand how someone might suddenly choose to narrow their horizons. Even though we already talked it over, you thought that the chances I would actually dare to get up and leave one day were even smaller than the chances of rain in August.

Seven months have passed since then, but I remember quite well the silence between us after that "what a jerk you are." You stood at the door and didn't even offer to give me a hand when the zipper of the black bag insisted on getting stuck halfway, and I didn't see any point in explaining to you yet again that I was sick of the infinite horizons of our life, of all the scurrying around in that vast emptiness we call freedom, in telling you for the umpteenth time that I was leaving for a life hemmed in by a fence whose wires you can touch, a place where everyone knows where they must stop, where they can get hurt if they don't, and not everything is exposed to the wind.

I left five pairs of jeans in the closet, taking with me only my skirts and Ori, the only child born to us in the dozen years of our marriage. You didn't protest. What did you have to offer him? You knew very well that raising a six-year-old boy doesn't begin and end with a goodnight kiss. Ori didn't ask a lot of questions, as if this were the way of the world that mothers leave and children go with them. He packed his cars and boxes of Lego, without an iota of curiosity. He didn't ask why we were going or what about Daddy or even where we were headed. He was glued to the TV up to the last minute, participating in the fates of the Walt Disney cartoon characters on the screen, as if real life was there.

We didn't dramatize our parting. I gave you my hand at the door. You pressed it impassively, a lawyer pressing a client's hand, said good luck, and followed us downstairs carrying the suitcase. Ori sat down in the back seat of the taxi and checked out the steering wheel and the dashboard, not even spreading the fingers of the hand he waved at you. When I looked out the back window, you were still standing there, hands thrust into the pockets of your jeans, the wind plastering your black shirt to your ribs, and when I looked back a second time you were no longer there, as if Ori and I were leaving for a two-day trip, the indifferent farewell of people practiced in respecting each other's sudden whims.

It's the anthropology of the thing that attracts you, you said. After you get to know them and write an article or two, you'll get sick and tired of it.

You were wrong. I'm not here because of my degree or my interest in anthropology. Seven months have already passed and I haven't written a word.

Haya Horovitz's and Leah Grossman's doors are open. Life flows from both sides of the staircase, intermingling. Babies wriggle their way around underfoot from apartment to apartment, babies wriggle around in wombs, and breasts are always full. Everyone here is involved in the pot of cauliflower cooking on the stove, in the right amount of paprika to be added, in the price of skim milk, and in the period that's already six days late.

These are not my strong points. My cooking is mediocre, I have no remarkable cauliflower and broccoli recipes, and my period is very regular. In any case, I haven't been with a man for seven months.

That's what'll break you, you told me, you're no nun and you won't be able to do without it. But until that first Saturday visit of yours, you were wrong. Seven months since July. My wardrobe consists only of skirts and more skirts—straight lines, wide hems, each with matching kerchief. Now my face looks like what it really is, older, nothing conceals the crow's feet from my eyes to my temples. The top layers of my jars of face cream have become brittle, so rarely do I break through them to spread the cream.

It's January 8th today and very cold. Winter doesn't seem to be even half over yet. I arrived here in the middle of July, but it's as if someone had stretched out that whole summer and moved it backward. Yes, those Friday afternoons of May and June have become so distant. Friday afternoons, always in the same coffee house with the same people, Ori dashing among tables with their dogs and their children, we in our protective sunglasses, exhaling straight streams of smoke, the sun shining on our mugs, our naked arms, exposed necks. Talking about art, comparing genres and structures, analyzing the authenticity of the hero of the latest book to reach the shelves, never oblivious, even for a moment, of the position of our legs, the immobility of our elbow and hand cradling the chin, our outstretched legs encased in frayed jeans—paying homage to anything that smacked of youth. We get up to go only after the waitress begins piling chairs on one another, and then only on the way to the car do our face muscles relax from the strain, the rearview mirror of the Fiat reflecting the slackness of our fatigue. We're short-tempered with Ori. Who has patience then for his banging his toy car on the nickel plating of the back seat?

But that woman, her thighs chafing as she crossed the pedestrian mall from east to west, had walked by when the afternoon was still at its peak and coffee levels had not yet dropped past the midpoint of our mugs. She was carrying full plastic bags in both hands. Gerbera daisies sold for half price on Friday afternoon were peeking out from one of them, the edges of their leaves already beginning to wither. She marched straight ahead, wearing a checked blouse and a faded flowered skirt, the cheap fabric obeying the commands of her heavy body, rolling, widening, stretching. She had on clumpy flat shoes like the ones girl soldiers wore, her swollen veiny legs encased in thick stockings, and she was hurrying along to get to the number twenty-four bus three hours before the lighting of the Sabbath candles. Look, I said to you then. You looked at her and asked, what's to see, and turned back to the table. I didn't have the guts to get up and follow her but that's what I wanted to do, to understand what impelled her forward with all those bags, ignoring the goings-on in the street, free of the need to make an impression.

From the window I can see the yard that extends from the outer wall of the kitchen and the sign forbidding cars to enter on Saturday.[55] The children outside are playing hide-and-seek. Ori stands next to them watching, wearing an embroidered Armenian cap I bought him in the Old City.[56] Persuading him to cover his head was difficult. He asked why and to tell the truth, I didn't have a satisfactory answer. Eliezer, the

---

55. In many religious neighborhoods, automobile traffic is prohibited on the Jewish Sabbath.

56. *Old City of Jerusalem*. Ori is asked to cover his head in accordance with religious practice.

Grossman boy, tries to lure him into the game but Ori, like the son of new immigrants, stands off to the side learning their language. The younger Grossman is wide-shouldered like his father; one day he'll have the same sturdy legs and thick neck. But he inherited his mother's blue eyes. His gaze is open and clear, not like his father Yehiel's whose eyes were usually cast down at the ground. Once, perhaps two days after I came to live here, Yehiel Grossman opened the door of the building on his way out as I was coming in. The sudden light dimmed his vision, and the surprise caused our gazes to meet. His eyes were two dark green circles, which he quickly averted from me to the iron grating at the entrance used for scraping mud from shoes. He backed up against the wall, allowing me to pass through the entire width of the doorway. Although it isn't dark yet, the street lamps in the yard have been lit and Eliezer Grossman leaps high into the air trying to reach the metal plates that enclose them.

Do you remember that light bulb you changed in the bathroom? A month or so before I left the house, you replaced the burned-out ceiling bulb with a hundred-watt bulb that lit up the bathroom with the cruel, white glare of a spotlight. I stood there in that light, a woman of forty-one plus, the mirror reflecting me precisely, treating me with brutal honesty. Standing that way in the bathroom, having just discovered a new line in my forehead and bags under my eyes, I heard Ori's baby sitter arrive, a budding young beauty of sixteen. I realized then that what was degenerating in my body was just beginning to blossom in hers and the order of things infuriated me. There I was, fingers full of moisturizing cream to rub in around my eyes, and in the living room, there was a baby sitter with dark curls fanning out over her shoulders, and it suddenly became obvious that all the concoctions in the world were useless, that this battle can end only in my defeat. It seemed so absurd to try to deflect my body from its natural course, to force it to be moist, to produce youthful follicles from its pores, and there, under that hundred-watt spotlight, it occurred to me again that real life was wherever the woman with the gerbera daisies was going. I wiped the expensive cream from my fingers with a tissue and turned off the light.

Ori is standing in the bushes pulling apart the stem of a rose. The white petals float onto his shoes. He raises the plucked stem to the last light of day, examining the naked stamens. Picking flowers on the Sabbath is forbidden, but he doesn't really have a handle on all the rules yet. The embroidered circles on his Armenian cap glitter in the light of the street lamps. He still hasn't made any friends here but he doesn't have any enemies either. From time to time Eliezer Grossman comes to visit him, mostly for a taste of the foreign. He spills all of Ori's cards onto the floor, marvelling at the whales and dinosaurs, and then looks around, puzzled by the fact that there's only Ori and me, that each room has only one bed, and the bathroom is never occupied.

You chose to come to us on a Saturday, of all days. You parked the Fiat two blocks away from here but I heard the jingling of your keys from the curb. I didn't open the windows after you left. The smell of you lingered in the small living room, for hours, your aftershave, the cigarettes you carried in your pocket, the leather jacket you didn't take off, your jeans. You returned to the Fiat an hour before the Havdalah blessing[57] and I stood in the living room breathing in the lingering smell of you.

You sat on the sofa. The hallway outside was permeated with the strong smell of cholent left simmering on hot plates all Sabbath long, and herring being served for the day's third meal. The odors seeped into the apartment through the space between the door and the floor.

How can you stand it? you asked, looking as if the thick air was suffocating you. I said that here the available light and air were distributed among so many people that it really was very close. I wanted to tell you that it was occasionally hard for me too to endure the smell, and I had almost vomited during my first few days here, but that asymmetrical line appeared on your forehead, the one so familiar to me, the one with more than a hint of scorn, and I launched into a fervent speech instead.

Look, I said, barely restraining myself from touching your arm, we used to walk around practically naked, wearing shorts and thin shirts that reached only about an inch above our navels and were cut down to the middle of our backs, but the truth is that we were always covering up, concealing, trying to be what was expedient, not what we really were. We talked about freedom but walked around imprisoned in our posturing. Here, though everyone is wrapped up in layers of fabric, life is really naked, always touching their flesh, filled with the smell of sperm and blood and milk, and they don't use creams and bleaches to battle their flesh, they live within its cycles, they give birth, nurse, count the days of their *niddah*. . . .[58] I stopped to catch my breath and did not continue.

---

57. *Havdalah:* The ritual marking the end of the Sabbath and the beginning of the secular week. The ritual includes blessings, a braided candle, fragrant spices, and wine. The song Yehiel Grossman sings below is one of the concluding melodies of the ritual.

58. *Niddah:* The days of menstruation, and directly afterward, during which women are forbidden by traditional Jewish Law to engage in intercourse or have physical contact with their husband.

You picked up two Lego blocks from the floor and clicked them together. The line in your forehead lengthened, joined by a thin wrinkle that formed on the right side of your mouth. You didn't say a word as you separated and re-joined the blocks five or six times until you grew tired of it. If it hadn't been for those lines on your face, I would have told you about Leah Grossman who comes here often to teach me how to pray. She sits in the kitchen with me, her wide behind draped over the sides of the stool, encircling it like the tire of a semitrailer, her big breasts usually crushed against her thighs as she bends to tend to the babies that have straggled in after her. Her stockings, not completely opaque, are lined with the prints of greasy little fingers that grasp at them from the floor. And it always seems to me that her side of kitchen is brighter. Maybe because of the light shining from her eyes.

They live above us. Her endless steps, heavy and muffled, joined in the evening by those of her husband Yehiel, are absorbed by our ceiling, like the echo of thunder from a distant storm. His wide shoulders fill the staircase, but since that time we bumped into each other in the doorway, I always wait to go out until he has finished coming up or going down.

Saturday afternoon, two hours before twilight, I could already hear the keys to the Fiat jingling from the sidewalk and the sound of your white Reeboks on the ground, the faint squishing of rubber against asphalt. I opened the door, you put the keys in your pocket, and we didn't shake hands. Ori, in his white Sabbath shirt and Armenian cap, got up from the caravan of toy cars he was steering into the kitchen and went to you.

Hi son, you said, hugging him tightly, and then you looked around, saying, you're more serious about this than I thought. You looked at the candlesticks encrusted with wax drippings, at the white tablecloth, and finally at my kerchief and my unmade-up face.

Even though it wasn't cold, you didn't take off your jacket. Most of the time you kept your hands in your pockets, and sat with your legs crossed in those jeans I loved, the blue-black pair that fit snugly over your hip bones and stretch tightly over your firm thighs. At one point, you took out a cigarette, remembered,[59] and put it back in your pocket. Although most of our comments to Ori were meant to fill gaps in our conversation, you were in no hurry to leave. I sliced the store-bought English cake for us, and you dunked yours into your coffee and waited

59. Smoking is forbidden on the Sabbath.

for it to stop dripping, looking at me as if we had never met before. I tried to assume the serenity of Leah Grossman. I didn't move my hands which had dropped onto the arms of the chair, and I didn't hide my fingernails, cut down to the skin. I didn't straighten up or raise my head to smooth out the wrinkles on my neck, but I must admit to myself that it was not because I was tranquil. I've invested a great deal of energy in subduing those old habits.

We did not discuss the future. You asked only once, so, reached any conclusions yet? Then I asked about friends I hadn't seen for seven months and you became more relaxed as the gap widened between us and the people we talked about.

But my real meeting with you occurred after you left. I didn't open the windows, the smell of you lingered in the living room for hours, and the indentation in the sofa made by your firm ass, and those jeans . . . I have nothing made of denim. My fingers hungered for the feel of that rough fabric and the warm skin under it.

You drank two cups of coffee, ate a slice and a half of the English cake, and left before it was dark. Ori went downstairs and walked to the curb with you, then stayed in the yard, his white shirt glowing amidst the darkening bushes. All the men were in the synagogue and in these final languorous moments of the day, the women in their festive head coverings leaned against their doorways in the forced idleness of the Sabbath. These leisurely moments were woven into those that had come before and those which would follow. Tomorrow the leftover squash would be fried, the cholent would be thinned into soup and the "clean" days between menstruations would continue to be counted. You didn't ask if there was a man in my life and I didn't ask what about you. How strange that we, who had been so obsessed about sexual desire, worshipping it, believing it to be the driving force of all things, could sit there facing each other, man and wife who had shared the same bed for years, without even our little fingers touching.

That's what'll finally break you, you're no nun and you won't be able to do without it.

I was sure that you were wrong, but after you left, I listened for the first time in months to the men's voices filling the staircase as they returned from synagogue. Ori came up with them, carrying a sprig of rosemary he had picked in the yard for the Havdalah blessing of the spices. He became immersed in picking at the braided candle, shaking the wicks so that the flame set bright spots dancing on his smooth cheeks until it was doused with wine. The strong voice of Yehiel Grossman filtered through the ceiling, *Al tireh avday Yaacov* ["fear not, My servant

Jacob"], he sang, the combined noise of all the children unable to drown out the words.

Ori asked if you would ever come to live with us, saying that here all the fathers live with the children and the mothers. He spoke nonchalantly, as if this were a fact he had suddenly noticed rather than something he wished for.

Daddy is not religious and it would be very difficult for him to live here, I said, and he asked what does religious mean.

Religious means believing in God and carrying out all of His mitzvoth. What about you?

I said yes, I was religious, but the truth of the matter is that I had no answer. God was still nothing more than a concept that my neighbors were so graciously trying to instill in me. Haika Horovitz said that it would eventually come to me and Leah Grossman said that faith is like love, it comes from here, pointing at her left breast, under which her generous heart was buried.

Darach cochav m'Yaacov ["A star will emerge from Jacob"], Yehiel Grossman sang and, feeling suddenly weak in the knees, I went into the bathroom to see in the mirror what you had seen on my face. Using some cream with the consistency of hardened butter, I tried to smooth away the crow's feet. *Tsaveh yeshuot Yaacov, al tireh avday Yaacov, al tireh* ["Command salvation for Jacob, fear not my servant Jacob"], his voice filtered through the bars of the high window of the bathroom and I was suddenly struck by the realization that you couldn't have gone seven months without sleeping with a woman. This sudden flash of recognition almost toppled me onto the sink, and touching the cold porcelain, I had a vision of a woman's smooth shoulder peeking out from under the big patchwork quilt we bought at a crafts bazaar and your fingers drawing circles on the unfamiliar shoulder, embracing it. Despite the cold, I was sweating, unaware of the water the soft soles of my slippers were absorbing. Only when my feet were completely soaked, did I notice the water dripping from the toilet pipe, overflowing into the corridor that led to the bathroom.

Despite all the rags I spread on the floor and then wrang out into the bathtub, I couldn't keep up with the speed of the leak. Ori tried to contain the water with a squeegee, but the drops rapidly joined together into a thin line, carrying with them scraps of rust from the burst pipe and painting the floor orange.

Go up to the Grossmans, I told him, maybe they can stop this flow until I can get a plumber.

Ori was excited by the unexpected opportunity to visit the Grossmans. I heard him leap up the stairs and knock gently on their door. They didn't hear him, and only when he dared to knock with his whole fist did the door open, the clamor of children and the clatter of dishes being washed bursting from the apartment into the hallway.

Wearing his black Sabbath trousers and a white shirt, Yehiel Grossman squeezed between the sink and the toilet and ran a thick finger over the crack. The large knots of his *tzitzit*[60] were prominent against the shirt stretched tightly across his back. After examining the length of the pipe, he got up, looked down at the floor, and said, it has to be replaced. He suggested that in the meanwhile, we paste something on it temporarily. Not even once did he raise his eyes from the orange stream absorbed by the rags I had spread on the floor.

Ori followed him upstairs again, but did not come back with Grossman when he returned with a tube of glue, a thick brush, and a rubber bowl. The door to the apartment was left open and the cold wind that blew in made the lampshade in the living room dance. I did not close the door because of the *yechud*—the fact that we were alone together—and I put one of Ori's aluminum cars between the door and the jamb so that it would not close by itself.

From the narrow bathroom corridor, I saw him squeeze a rubbery snake of glue into the bowl and bend down to the burst pipe. I sneezed twice, from the dizzying fumes of the glue or from the cold wind, and took off my wet slippers. My bare feet in their transparent stockings left circles on the cold floor.

Yehiel Grossman leaned against the sink, looked at the floor, and said the pipe had to be replaced as soon as possible. I asked if he knew a good plumber, embarrassed by my naked feet. He smoothed his unkempt beard with a wet hand, gripped it, smoothed it again, and looked at me, saying, they all rob you blind. The green of his eyes was as strong and hard as nettles.

The smell of the glue blended with the strong odor of his body and the lingering smell of you. I held my dripping slippers, thinking of the delicate instep you were stroking now and your hand moving up along her calf. Yehiel Grossman's eyes were fixed on the damp spot on the floor

---

60. *Tzitzit:* Fringes, worn by some religiously observant men in accordance with the commandment to Moses, "Speak to the children of Israel and tell them to make for themselves fringes on the corners of their garments throughout the generations . . . you shall have it as a fringe, so that when you look upon it you will remember to do all the commands of the Lord . . . you will not follow the desires of your heart and your eyes which lead you astray" (Numbers 15: 37–40).

one tile away from my feet. I'll think of something, he said gathering his bowl and brush. With a quarter-turn of his shoulder at the door, he said, have a good week. He immediately averted his face and was swallowed up by the darkness of the hallway. The door inched its way back toward the jamb and banged against Ori's small car, staying open a crack.

Ori was brimming with excitement when he returned. Do you know how many beds they have? Maybe nine, would you believe it? He held up nine fingers of hands that were miniature versions of yours, the same flat, elongated structure with slender fingers and long rectangular nails. Two of the nine beds pitched and tossed at night, groaning and squeaking, becoming still only very late. Leah Grossman came in from outside two or three hours after the Sabbath had ended, filling the staircase with the smell of soap mixed with that of the liquid used to clean off unscrubbed porcelain and cleanse women of their contamination.

That night, I dreamt that Yehiel Grossman was wearing your blue-black jeans, inflated and enlarged to his size and the hand I placed on the coarse fabric stuck onto it. The jeans were smeared with the same kind of yellow glue he had used to seal the hole in the pipe, and I couldn't remove my hand. When I woke up, my right hand was numb and heavy, pins and needles running along the length of my arm. I clenched and unclenched my fingers until the pins and needles were gone but I didn't manage to shake off the dream. I suspected that perhaps I was coming too close to the fence that marked off the boundaries of life here. I had to stop in time.

The line of light was like a conductor's baton being waved over the building, life bursting forth from it all at once. The water flushed from the toilets flowed through the pipes from floor to floor, the babies shrieked, the men buttoned their jackets on the way downstairs to the synagogue, and the children went up and down, bringing fresh bread and milk. Doors opened and closed and the sour smell of sheets filtered into the hallway. I opened the window to the cold wind, a faint scent of perfume rising from the sprig of rosemary lying on the table, and the quite obvious fact that there was a woman sleeping beside you now was suddenly bearable. I drank some hot milk with honey, Ori squeezed two packs of cards and a sandwich made with Sabbath challah into his schoolbag and he went to wait for the minibus that takes the boys to school.

The building quieted down like a sandstorm subsiding. The bathroom floor was dry and the yellow glob of glue rested on the pipe like a giant wasp. I took some anthropology articles from my suitcase and browsed through one on Eskimo birth and death rituals. A morning in mid-January, known here as the Hebrew month Tevet, a name I had not yet gotten used to. The western window was dark with clouds, the eastern one still filled with sunlight that turned the upholstery of the sofa to gold. I still did not have the slightest idea of the essence of God but on that particular day more than on many other days, I felt that it was no longer so far off. The sun from the eastern winter flickered on the photograph of the sturdy Eskimo, illuminating flat expanses of ice. I was thinking that in the afternoon I would tell Ori about those people who live on infinite fields of snow, lying with him on the carpet the way you used to, so we could build a large igloo from white Lego blocks, when there was a knock on the door.

A wide, white plastic pipe was pressed under Yehiel Grossman's arm. His other hand held a blue tool box.

I asked if a plumber was on the way.

No, it's a pity to waste the money, I'll fix it, he said, staring at the pipe as if examining it for the first time.

I didn't mean to impose upon you, I said, I'll pay you for the pipe and call a plumber.

They all rob you blind, he said again, his eyes wandering restlessly from the pipe to me and back to the pipe.

The bathroom was too narrow for his large body. He removed his jacket and draped it over the shower curtain rod. Under the jacket, he was wearing a white shirt that perhaps had once been his Sabbath shirt but had been demoted when the sweat began to fray the collar, wearing away a line across its width. I couldn't offer to help him, nor could I return to reading about the Eskimos while he was stretched out there on the floor working, so I went into the kitchen and, peeling potatoes, I heard the old pipe squeaking as it turned in its grooves.

It was cold. The apartment door was open, swinging back against the jamb, the wind occasionally widening the crack, then blowing the door back against the jamb once again. From the corridor I asked if he needed anything, and I saw his wide back and thick neck wedged into the space between the sink and the toilet.

Nothing, he grunted into his beard. The carelessly rolled-up sleeves of his white shirt fluttered around his elbows like two white doves.

Here's some tea, I said, noticing how his jacket absorbed the steam rising from the glass I placed on the hamper. Some cookies too, I said.

Yehiel Grossman did not respond. He struck the pipe with his wrench to shatter the old glue that had hardened on the plastic, pieces of the hard white crust dropping onto the floor. Then he rose, wiped his hands with toilet paper, drank the tea, and listened to his wife Leah's long strides moving across the ceiling. It's about ten o'clock, maybe ten-fifteen. Life here is already at its peak and you are just getting up, I thought, stretching your body and reaching out your naked arm to the woman beside you. Even at the height of the winter you sleep only in your underpants, training your body to remain healthy, thin and flexible, strengthening it against the cold. Then push-ups, the exercise bicycle, and a cold shower. Your youth is perpetual, even though with the passing years you invest more in preserving it.

Although Yehiel Grossman did not leave a drop of tea, the cookies remained untouched. I was still suspect in all things related to *kashruth*,[61] so I smoothed out the cellophane wrapping to show him the kosher stamp printed on it in white vowelled letters saying, strictly kosher.

He smiled for the first time, his cheeks widening, pulling his lips up with them to reveal a mouth of crowded teeth. It began to rain outside, small splatters painting circles on the small, dust-covered bathroom window. He took a cookie and said the blessing *Borei minei mezonot*.[62] He didn't shake off the crumbs that dropped onto his beard as he chewed. Leaning against the hamper, he ate the cookie, looked at the window and listened to the rain.

Another glass of tea? I asked.

A strip of gray sky moved through the space between the open window and the wall. You can watch and smell the rain for hours. You always say that it's the sky making love to the earth. Once, as we were watching the rain together, you said there's something so sensual about wet earth, and you closed me in your embrace and drew me to the bed. Yehiel Grossman gazed with near astonishment at the small square of rain. In the morning he had prayed *Mashiv ha'ruach v'morid ha'geshem*, saying, *Natati metar artzechem b'eito*,[63] and now, like a child, he was amazed that his prayer for rain had been answered.

Okay, another glass of tea, he said, eyes on the window.

All of his large beard was reflected in the mirror over the sink when I returned to the corridor with the tea. My face joined his in the mirror

---

61. *Kashruth:* Jewish dietary laws.

62. *Borei minei mezonot:* The blessing recited before eating cakes and pastry.

63. *Mashiv ha'ruach v'morid ha'geshem:* "Thou causest the wind to blow and the rain to fall," a phrase added to the liturgy between the autumn holiday of Sukkoth and the spring festival of Pesach (Passover)—in the hope of rain for the winter.

as if we were in a framed family photo. I don't know if he was staring blankly, musing about the rain, or whether his stare was deliberate, but the strong green eyes were on my white face, and on the strands of my fair hair not concealed by my kerchief, and on my throat, already revealing wrinkles not covered by my collar.

Tea, I said, waiting for him to move from the opening so I could put the glass on the hamper for him. He stood solidly in the doorway, his back to me, his eyes fixed on the mirror, and did not move. As I tried to steady the glass on the small tray, his shoulders moved suddenly in a complete circle and he turned to me, his barrel chest almost overturning the tea.

Are you a married woman?

Not even the span of a hand separated the buttons of his shirt from the tea I was holding.

No, I said, the tea spilling from the rim of the glass onto the tray. Yehiel Grossman shifted from the wall to the pipes, knelt down on the dusty floor in his black pants, and struck the pipe, the wrench breaking off flat pieces of glue, scattering them around the bathroom. I went to the kitchen to turn the cutlets frying in the pan and did not return to tell him that I had been confused, that we were not divorced, and that I have not stopped being your wife even if we haven't been together for seven months.

It rained harder. Hands hurried to gather the laundry from the lines and to close windows. That "married woman" was like an annoying sting which continued to irritate me despite my efforts to ignore it. The cutlets were overdone, their edges charred and blackened, the air dense with the smell of burnt oil. I opened the window and a big gust of wet wind burst into the room, mixing some of the odors, and carrying off others. The wind cooled my forehead and penetrated my back, but did nothing at all to ease the sting.

The window screen was covered with rain, transparent strands of water trailing down its length and gathering on the sill. This morning could have been perfect, I thought. Only an hour ago all had seemed right and proper to me. In spite of everything, I seemed to be absorbing the gentle stream of life that flowed toward me here, already feeling a sense of tranquillity. And suddenly a jagged rock had been thrust into the stream, disrupting the flow.

Why didn't you wait with the other woman? You could have held off till I reached some kind of decision. I understand that passion must have its release, but why bring her home and bed her down in the indentations made in the mattress by my body? The cold wind did not even touch the fire burning my face. I opened all the windows so wide that they banged against the wall, the noise blending with the blows of the wrench. What did he mean by "married woman?" Yes! I am a married woman and my husband is now gazing at the rain, saying to the woman next to him, "Watch the earth being screwed."

Why did you ask what you asked? I surprised him at the bathroom door. He was rubbing his hands together, peeling strings of glue from his skin. He did not move from his bear's crouch, did not turn his heard toward me. What difference does it make to you whether I'm married or not? I persisted.

All at once, he withdrew his glue-smeared hands, and leaning on his large knees, turned his head to me, all the skin visible through and above his tangled beard flushing. Forget it, he said and returned to the pipe.

I don't understand, I said, entering the bathroom filled with his heavy breathing. The wind struck the windows, driving the rain up against them, and slammed the apartment door.

He rose, took his black jacket from the shower curtain rod, and said, I put contact glue on it, you have to wait twenty minutes for it to dry and then connect the pipe. I was standing between him and the bathroom door, blocking his way. I still haven't gotten an answer, I said, pressing up against the bathtub to let him pass, but he was in no hurry to leave. He groped at the pack of cigarettes sticking out of his jacket pocket and said, in the world you come from, flesh is master. Here, the soul conquers the body, but we too are only flesh and blood . . . we sometimes suddenly weaken.

He became silent and crushed the pack of cigarettes through the rough material of his coat, fingered the matches in his pants pocket, and then said, don't touch the glue until I come back, and left. He didn't go up to Leah and his babies and he didn't put on his jacket. From the window, I saw him cut across the width of the yard, the wind hurling large drops at him from the trees, widening the wet spots on his shirt. He inhaled deeply on his cigarette, his head bent to the ground, his shoes squashing wet beds of black foliage, his jacket gathered under his arm like a bedraggled black cat.

Do you remember that woman with the gerbera daisies at half price, the fat one with the varicose veins who marched straight ahead? I was suddenly reminded of her as I watched this man smoke his second cigarette, the soles of his shoes filling with mud. How naive the assumption is that theirs is a world of still waters where people flow smoothly through life the way blood flows through the arteries of a baby.

He returned in exactly twenty minutes, bringing with him a wet, black branch which he thrust between the door and the jamb. Smelling of rain and cigarettes, he crossed the hallway and again hung his jacket on the curtain rod.

You have the chance to put things right now, I said to myself, tell him that you're a married woman and make it easier on him and yourself. I stood at the bathroom door thinking that, now that his face was turned to the pipes, this was the right moment to tell him and get it over with. I removed a wet leaf from the jacket hanging on the curtain rod and asked if the glue was dry enough. He threaded one pipe into another and said, the glue is okay.

I looked at his large behind and thought about your hard, narrow hips. I didn't understand how I could even have dreamt of him wearing your jeans. When he undresses, there's a deep red line at his waist from the pressure of his belt, while your ribs can be counted even through your shirt. How red and deep is the line cut into his flesh by his belt. Beads of sweat glistened on his neck in the space between his large skull-cap and his collar. I couldn't control the sudden pity I felt for this big man kneeling on all fours linking pipe to pipe, the toilet on his right, the sink on his left, and the large circle of his rear end between them.

Who knows at what dizzying speed his blood courses through his body, churning, overflowing, with no outlet? Standing over him, my hand absorbed the heat of his scalp and sank into the thick, cropped hair. The skull-cap rolled onto his shoulder and landed on the dusty floor. Yehiel Grossman froze like a turtle in its shell, didn't stir from his crouch. Only his shirt stretched over his ribs, barely containing the flesh that was expanding from breath to breath.

Relax, Yehiel, I said, massaging his heavy, damp neck with my cold hands. Suddenly, he shifted his knees from the floor, straightened up, lifted his skull-cap, squeezed out of the space between the toilet and the sink, bent over the tub, and, turning on the cold water, placed his feverish head under the flow. He didn't touch the clean towel I had put on the rack for him. Dripping all over, he wiped himself with the gray satin lining of his jacket, uttering not a word as he hurriedly gathered his wrench and glue and put them into the blue tool box. He went abruptly to the apartment door, pulled out the black branch that had been thrust there, and, shoving it up against the jamb, locked the door from the inside and came toward me from the bathroom corridor. You know, there is a kind of blind moment when a person is only a body, the way a cat is unimpeded by ideas or values in that split second before pouncing on the bird that has shaken a branch. That's how he was as he came toward me from the corridor. And, from the moment he pulled the piece of wood from the door, I became like the Havdalah candle dipped in wine,[64] everything suddenly fizzling out inside me. His arms embraced me like a heavy winter coat. He drew me to him and I passed a cold hand across his sweaty forehead and said No, Yehiel, removing his hard hands from my shoulders, saying it doesn't matter, Yehiel. Three or four times I told him it doesn't matter. Pale as the porcelain of the sink, he held my hand between both of his, rubbing it between them and when he finally unclasped them, my hand dropped, red and hot.

Yehiel Grossman washed his face under the bathtub faucet, the water pouring over his wild beard. He washed and washed, neck bent, the cold water flowing over his head onto his back and chest. Then he lifted his skull-cap and rubbed it on his pants. He turned, shoved his wet shirt into his pants and buckled his belt over it.

I should have given you the name of a plumber right away, he said, his eyes looking as if they wanted to drill a hole for themselves in the floor under the flat pieces of glue. I looked at him and knew how much, from now until his dying day, he would try to please God, but no matter what he did or how great his efforts, he would always feel guilty. I've already told you that in this place, the boundaries are marked, the horizon is finite. The woman with the gerbera daisies can hurry along quickly and far, but ultimately she'll have to step on the brakes. She'll be in for it if she doesn't, and there are usually warning signs.

He put his jacket on over his wet shirt, buttoned it, and began scraping pieces of glue off his pants, his thick fingers trembling as he separated the glue from the fabric. I wet the towel, saying let me do it. I rubbed the black gabardine and he, with all of his bulk, stood beside me like a lost child and let me clean his pants for him.

Don't torture yourself, Yehiel, I said to him, the impulse comes from your God. He created us with it.

Why *my* God? What about you?

I'm still void of God. I made so much room for him inside me, I removed everything, and He has not entered, I said, gathering my hair and tying my kerchief around it.

And God will not enter, he said, God is within. He removed his skull-cap and again rubbed it on his pants, examining it in the light to see that it was clean.

---

64. Part of the Havdalah ritual.

Then maybe I'm sterile, I said, looking at the dense, dark sky that filled the window.

Yehiel Grossman put the old pipe under his arm, took his blue tool box, turned the key in the door, and listened to the sounds in the hallway. Don't flush the toilet for three hours, you have to let the glue set, he said and left, closing the door after him. Exhausted, I sat down on the cold bathroom floor. My legs trembled incessantly, even when I pressed them hard against the wall.

Ori came home at noon, his cap wet with rain, its embroidered circles darker. He scraped off the charred edges of the cutlets with his fingers and told me something about school. The rain trailed transparent threads along the window screen, the sprig of rosemary shook as if it were cold, and I didn't hear a word he was saying and I couldn't eat a thing.

When you finish, I'll tell you about the Eskimos and we'll build an igloo with your Lego, I said to him. What's an igloo, he asked, chewing his cutlet quickly, and later we built a luxurious igloo from the white tiles. You should have seen how skillfully he connected the pieces. We got stuck only when we reached the arched ceiling, and what finally emerged was a flat-topped igloo, and Ori said, only Daddy knows how to make a real arch.

It drizzled the whole afternoon, the sound of it silenced by the life that flowed from the doorways into the hall. Only in the late evening, when the building had once again quieted down, could the gentle murmuring of water gliding down the window be heard. How fortunate for the earth and the rain that they can do it endlessly, I thought, picking up the telephone to ask you, so, how's the rain?

Not what it used to be, you said, rain should be watched by two.

Then you were silent and it rained harder, large drops splattering on the window pane, rolling down its length. Since you were silent, I said that sometimes it was hard for us without you, and since you continued to be silent, I said that without you all the igloo ceilings we built were flat, apparently because only you know how to make a real arch. I don't know if what I heard then was you laughing or the rain creeping across the kitchen screen or both.

(1994)
—*Translated by Sondra Silverston*

Introduction to Yehudit Hendel's "Apples in Honey"

"A Stone of Wrongs was in Jerusalem; whosoever has suffered a loss should turn to it," says the Talmud in *Baba Metsia*. The lines serve as the epigraph for Yehudit Hendel's powerful 1991 novel whose name, *Mountain of Losses*, can also be understood literally as "Mountain of Wrongs." For the "mountain" is the site of a military ceremony where the young casualties of Israel's many wars lie buried. And where the price of those many wars is most keenly felt.

Mountain of Losses pivots around one father's visit to the grave of his son, killed sixteen years ago, when he was nineteen:

> "He'll always be 19," Maeera said, but Shmulik Ron didn't hear her, because that's what he said to me later, standing near his plot. He'll stay 19, always 19, he said.
> "Mine is 21," said the man at the nearby plot.
> "Yes, everyone here will stay young," said Shmulik Ron.
> "Of course, they'll have eternal youth," said the man in the next plot.[65]

If the *Shoah* haunts the work of many of Israel's writers today, so does the anguish of war. In the decade of the nineties, that has meant

---

65. *Har Ha'to'im [Mountain of Losses]* (Tel Aviv: HaKibbutz Hameuchad/Simon Kriya, 1991), p. 31 (my translation).

the emotionally paralyzing Gulf War, the ravages of the *Intifada*, the seemingly endless, and some argue, purposeless, bloodshed in southern Lebanon. The wars penetrate the Arabic poetry of Israeli Arab Nidaa Khoury, the Hebrew poetry of Dahlia Ravikovich and Maya Bejerano, the English-language poetry of Karen Alkalay-Gut, Rachel Tzvia Back, and Shirley Kaufman, as well as the Hebrew prose of Ronit Matalon and Yehudit Hendel.

First published at the conclusion of *Mountain of Losses*, "Apples in Honey," one of the most moving of Israel's war narratives, was also included in Yehudit Hendel's 1996 collection, *An Innocent Breakfast*. Like many of the stories in *An Innocent Breakfast*, "Apples in Honey" explores the collision between the present and the past, the painful issues of memory and of loss. At the heart of the story is a vivid paradox: just as the young men who are buried in the military ceremony retain an "eternal youth" as those who mourn them age, so the more deaths there have been, the more lush with growth the rectangular-shaped cemetery plots, each like a small garden, become. That lushness helps to explain the obsession in Hendel's novel with planting and with flowers.

Throughout her long career as a writer, Hendel has focused not on the triumphant reborn nation, but rather on its most vulnerable people. Her earliest collection of stories, *They are Different* (1951), takes place against the background of the 1948 War of Independence. But unlike the work of her male contemporaries such as Aharon Megged, Hanoch Bartov, and Moshe Shamir, Hendel's perspective is that of the "other," the new, insecure immigrant, meeting the native Israelis. The protagonists of other of her early stories are victims of the Holocaust and men wounded by the War of Independence. *The Yard of Momo the Great* (1969), reissued in a newly edited version as *The Last Hamsin* (1994), paints a portrait of a multiethnic subculture in a courtyard in Haifa's lower city; the courtyard is peopled by characters broken by their personal losses and by history, isolated in their individual dreams. The novel's main character, Saul, is a young man who comes to Israel from Poland after the Holocaust; working in Haifa port, he moves from room to room in the courtyard, no more able to find a "home" than to understand the traumas of his own war-torn childhood. For Saul, as for most of the novel's characters, whether they are Holocaust survivors or Jews from Eastern countries, Israel is less a true home than a kind of limbo— what commentators have described as a "place to exist, between the sea and the funeral parlors."

Born in Warsaw, Yehudit Hendel came to Israel in 1938. Her first novel, *The Street of Steps*, was performed as a play at Habima National

Theatre in Tel Aviv; *The Yard of Momo the Great* was televised. She was awarded the Agnon Prize and the Israel Prize for her contribution to Israeli literature. Works in translation include *The Street of Steps* (New York: Herzl Press, 1963); "Zili and My Friend Shaul," in *The New Israeli Writers: Short Stories of the First Generation* (New York: Sabra Books), pp. 61–76; "A Story with No Address," in *Translation: The Journal of Literary Translation* (Spring 1993), pp. 113–120; "Low, Close to the Floor," in *A Married Woman and Other Short Stories from Israel* (New Delhi: Star, 1995), pp. 49–52; "The Letter That Came in Time," in *Stories from Women Writers of Israel* (New Delhi: Star, 1995), pp. 103–132, and "My Friend B's Feast," in *New Women's Writing from Israel* (Portland: Vallentine Mitchell, 1996), pp. 66–89.

In the version of "Apples in Honey" included in *Mountain of Losses*, the author's experience is directly connected to that of the mourners. "When I was working on *Mountain of Losses*," the story begins, "I used to go there sometimes, and this week I went again." In the more recent version, the opening phrase is changed to "That summer . . . ". But the sense of intimate and profound connectedness with the young widow of the narrative remains. " . . . there's never anybody here on this day, I'm always here alone," she tells the visitor.

Perhaps, a younger version of the narrator, she still is.

Apples in Honey

Yehudit Hendel

That summer, I'd go there sometimes, and this week I went again. It was a hot day at the end of summer. A hot wind blew from time to time, stopped suddenly and returned suddenly, full of dust, and when I entered, the place was empty. Not a living soul. I thought of wandering around a bit and then, on the other side behind the shed, I saw the gardener standing and talking with a young woman who sat bent over the stone, moving her head as she spoke, a head wreathed in balls of red curls, glowing like balls of fire in the *khamsin* light.

As I said, the place was empty. The paths had just been swept, sharpening the clean, orderly lines of perspective, and in the heavy, *khamsin* light it looked more colorful and shining than ever, wrapped in a thin pink coat from the fresh watering and new blooming, almost a shining sheath of shining lacquer. And it was very quiet. Not even a sprinkler moved. But as I went along the path everything seemed full of rustling and talking and raspy sounds, rising from both sides of the path from the colored patches of the dense vegetation, as if someone there were grinding glass under the earth.

That was in the most beautiful section, the newly flourishing section from the Lebanon War which was laden with a rich growth of living flowers and silk flowers and velvet flowers and flowers of thin copper plates and flowers of burlap and flowers of gauze and rustcolored bandages and long serrated cacti with fleshy shoots like explosive caps and tops shaped like an axe.

The woman lifted her face to me.

Do you have somebody here? she asked.

She clasped her knees to her body, didn't take her eyes off me.

I've got somebody here too, she said.

Her knees were really up to her body, but she didn't take her eyes off me.

My husband, she said.

I understand.

Yes, my husband.

I understand.

She turned half her body to me.

My husband, she repeated a third time.

It was quiet. Her eyes were fixed on me, pale, very bright, wide open in dark brown lashes that had nothing to do with the balls of fire, and I don't know, maybe because of the quiet, I said I came here sometimes, hadn't seen her.

Yes, I come once a year, she said. Her voice was low-pitched, almost masculine, almost basso, and she spoke like someone continuing a conversation that had been broken off.

And it usually falls on a hot day like this, a *khamsin*. Always on a hot day like this, a *khamsin*. She banged her knees together, clutched her leather bag to them. And I sit alone. Sometimes with the gardener.

I said I had met him here, the gardener.

She fixed me again with bright, wide-open eyes, raked her hand in the air with a quick movement.

I'm talking to you like I know you, she said.

Maybe we did know each other once.

She laughed, repeated the nervous gesture in the air.

Yes, could be.

Maybe, I said.

She laughed again, covering her knees with both hands. Then she shifted her eyes from her knees and moved closer to me on stone frame surrounding the small, beautiful garden. She smiled.

He's a good man, the gardener.

The sun apparently blinded her, since she was facing the wrong way, and she closed one eye, and now she looked at me with one eye round as an animal's eye.

I said: Yes, a good man, the gardener.

She changed eyes, blinking, bent farther over the stone, and opened a cactus coiled up near the stone pillow. Apparently she saw me looking at the date on the pillow. No, no, I come on our anniversary, that's the day I come here, once a year.

Now, too, she spoke slowly, emphasizing every word.

I don't come any other day. Why should I come any other day?

It was quiet, and even quieter between one word and the next.

And I said, it always falls on a hot day like this, a *khamsin*. In fact, it was a hot day like this then too, a *khamsin*. She banged her knees together hard, pressed the palms of her hands on them, and said it was impossible to talk about it. I said she didn't have to. She said: I can't talk about it.

You don't have to.

Yes, but when you think.

Better not to think.

That's it, better not to think. That doesn't always work. You understand.

Yes, I understand.

It was quiet. She bent over a bit, leaning forward, unzipped her purse, pulled out a pair of big, gray glasses, and put them on.

Believe me, you learn it, and aside from that, time—

I couldn't think of anything else to say.

It was quiet. She zipped up her purse and put it back on the stone.

Yes, time. You think time can . . . ?

I could see her dark lashes drop and open all at once through the big glasses. She took them off a moment and straightened up again looking around leaning her head back, the way you look out a train window. In the meantime, everything, almost alive, years, almost alive, she said, turning around to me, and the word *almost*, echoed in the empty garden, hit the air like a pneumatic hammer, and I felt something heavy in my ears and some desire to cover my ears. It seemed that was what she did too, but the wind waved her hair, exposing her ears and they suddenly looked small, almost like a little girl's ears. Her eyes moved slowly, wandering over the garden, as if the garden were fleeing behind her, and I thought I should say something but I didn't know what. The light became even lower. The sky a bottomless dome. The blooming roses and chrysanthemums in the beautiful garden burned like scarecrows, and I wanted to tell her that there are ways to be, and something about the length of the day and the length of the night, and the simple truth of death and loneliness when that truth comes from the earth and enters your feet and climbs on you through the soles of your feet. Suddenly I remembered the old custom of women to measure their lovers' graves with strings, and then they folded the strings, doubled them, and made wicks for wax candles in honor of their lovers from the wrapped doubled string, and at night, in little cans, they lit the wax candles and all night the long wicks burned in the cans and the wind was forbidden to put out the fire in the cans, and I wanted to tell her something about the cans. But she sat quietly, gathering up her hair that was waving from side to side on her neck, moving her fingers slowly through her hair as if the strength had gone out of her hands.

That's it, she said. Her hair was now gathered on the back of her neck and she put her hands back on her knees. In the light you didn't see her eyes, only the lenses of the glasses. She smiled weakly and took off the glasses, closing one eye again as if it were more and more blinded. It really was very hot. The air grew heavy, taking on an ashen color, stilling the movement of a hot dry wind that suddenly approached from some unknown gate, covering that clean, well-swept expanse with a cloud of dust. You smelled a thin odor of smoke and resin. Stone tablets looked taut enough to burst. The fresh paths were filled with arteries of lead and the broken sound of broken flutes approached as if it were going into a cave. The woman facing me pressed her hands to her knees as if she wanted to say, quiet, quiet, but the sound of broken flutes just grew louder, the leaves over the garden plots folded into burned strips of paper, scattering torn petals all around like grains of oats, and I saw the slight trembling of her hands on her knees. Once again she seemed to want to say something, but I didn't hear what, only how she closed both hands on her knees. The sound of broken flutes grew even louder, the light became really low, almost touching, and in the low light the stones suddenly seemed to be moving, waving like curtains, changing that strange architecture of cut off limbs and turning into a thick dough over the colorful fermentation coming from cracks in the earth, contorting the precision of the well-chiselled tablets, and the paths, the markers, the signs at the corners of the paths, the cracks of radiance and the broken screens, and you couldn't identify any stone now. The roses seemed to be plastic, and the grass full of heat worms, and when the wind passed as it had come, the black inscriptions on the stones still ran around in the air a moment and after a moment only the young woman was seen sitting alone, quiet, in the weary garden. Now too her hands were folded on her knees and she sat in silence.

She opened her eyes, looking at me with a special intimacy.

I'm lucky, there's never anybody here on this day, I'm always here alone.

That really is nice, I said.

Yes, it's nice. And I'm always scared they'll come all of a sudden. But you see, God watches over me, until today that hasn't happened, every year I'm here alone, sitting like this, alone.

Her eyes were fixed on me all the time, with that special intimacy that exists only between strangers.

It doesn't bother you that we're talking, she said.

No, of course not, it's nice, I said.

She said, Sometimes, you know—
Yes, of course, I know.
It's that, when you sit there, looking—
Of course, I understand.

She quickly rearranged her clasped hands, and asked if I had to go and I said, No, I've got time. She said: I'm glad. Then she said: Sometimes, you know, you want to talk. The light fell on her face, where two thin serpents of sweat ran down, and she wiped them off with the palm of her hand. Nothing special, just, to talk; she smiled in pain—You know, and I said certainly, I know. She smiled again in pain—you always think everything happens to other people. Even when it happens to you, it's like it happened to other people. Her face now rested between the palms of her hands and she lifted it a little, turning aside. There was some noise and stones rolling around as in an execution by stoning, and she straightened up, looked, and took off her glasses a moment, putting them back on immediately, shifting them as if she couldn't put them on right. She had long, beautiful, mocha-colored hands, and I looked at her hands which were encircled with wide copper bracelets and rings, a ring on every finger, sometimes two, and when she lifted her arms, the bracelets dropped toward her elbow, linked together making a plate of thin copper. She smiled, bringing the bracelets close to her wrists while looking at me through the sparkling lenses. Then she bent over and took out a blue Hebron glass pitcher, put it next to the stone pillow, and said something about the glass and asked if it was beautiful, and I said to her it was very beautiful. Then she said she wanted to bring velvet flowers because she very much liked making velvet flowers, especially since fresh flowers would fade tomorrow and she only came once a year, and I said yes, that's how it is. She said: Yes, that's how it is, and stopped a moment, once again moving the glasses that gleamed like two tin tablets. What can you do, that's how it is, she repeated. Her eyes lit up with a strange passion and she shook her head, passed her hand over her throat, and once again I looked at her hands and at the bracelets, and every movement changed their position, making a dull noise of copper striking. They were very beautiful bracelets, and I noticed that every bracelet was set with different stones, and there was a bracelet with yellow amber and a bracelet with red amber and a bracelet with turquoise and a bracelet with small blue lapis and a bracelet with pink coral stones, as if she had a collection of bracelets on her arms. She said: Yesterday, I almost made baked apples, every year I want to do that and I don't, bake apples. She laughed a little—That's what we used to do every year on this day, bake apples. Her voice was parched a moment, and I said that was really good, baked apples. She said: With raisins and nuts, you know that, and I said it was really good with raisins and nuts. She said:

And cinnamon, of course cinnamon, and you burn the sugar a little, it's very good when you burn the sugar. She moved away a bit on the stone. We didn't put in honey, but he called it apples in honey, she said. She spoke very quietly now, the shaded dark lashes grew wet from one word to the next, and I said I also make that sometimes, especially at the end of summer. She asked why at the end of summer. Her face grew tense, firm, and I didn't know why I had said that or why at the end of summer, and I felt I had to say something and I didn't know what, and I said it was best to make it with Grand Alexanders, and that I always looked for Grand Alexanders. She listened quietly, and I said it was good to peel a thin strip around the apple so it wouldn't burst when it was baking. Now too, she listened quietly. Once again her hair was undone and waved from side to side, and she pressed it, clasping it to her scalp, then she stuck her hand in her hair and wound the ends around her finger.

It's really hot, she said.

Her face was wet and she wiped it with the palm of her hand, moving her hand from her forehead to her throat a few times, then she put her hands down on the surface of the little garden and wiped them with leaves. Her head swayed a bit and for a moment she seemed to be dozing, and I thought about the plants that hoard water in their stems, producing giant thorns for defense. Suddenly I remembered a friend of mine who wanted to be buried under his table in his cafe, and they told him: It must be somewhere else. And he said: how can I be somewhere else? Under my table, he said, under the table, and even broken up it's all right even taken apart it's all right even with one leg it's all right, and I looked at that strange cemetery, at the stone pillows and the beautiful gardens. Within the emptiness the black letters and the white spaces ran around, moving within air pockets, and that's how she sat too. Her hair still moved from side to side and she pressed it to the back of her neck, then she leaned over, hastily opened her bag and hastily closed it again right away, and seemed to take some hairpins out of it, because she started sticking pins in her hair. It took her time to do it because the curls kept opening up again and fell on her throat and maybe the pins weren't strong enough to hold the burden of her hair, and she plucked off a branch, smelled it, and then stuck it in her hair, then plucked another one and held it close. It had the sweet, rotten smell of soft wood and she stroked her face lightly with it, and I said she had beautiful hair and beautiful hands. She laughed a little: The bracelets, you mean the bracelets, and I said the bracelets really were very beautiful. She moved away a bit on the stone—Yes, every year, he would bring me a bracelet that was his anniversary present. Her bass voice suddenly broke like a watch that falls to the ground, and she straightened up and stretched her back—But I don't wear them, only when I come here. She stopped, rotated her wrist He loved it when I had bracelets on my hands, so when I come here—her eyes became big, yellow, an owl's eyes, unmoving, and I saw her taking out the bracelets at night and putting them on the table and arranging them in order, and in the morning putting them on in order, and looking at her arms and some bracelets are missing on her arms, and she moves them and counts the missing bracelets.

Her throat was taut and she sat, looking straight ahead.

This is from the first year she said, pointing to the bracelet near her wrist, the one with the big, yellow amber stone which her hand stroked a few times, and I understood that they were put on in the sequence of the years, and the second year he bought her the red amber, and then the turquoise, and then the lapis, and then the coral, and I tried to guess what he would have bought her the year after. Her face was still impassive and you saw only the eyes, and it occurred to me that that was what she was thinking now too and that was certainly what she did this morning and how she went to the mirror, standing, looking, and the amber and the turquoise stones, the blue lapis beads and the pink coral return in the mirror, and she doesn't get the dates right, or the years, and she counts the years, and suddenly I didn't see her but only the bracelets shrivelling, narrow, thin, closing on her like handcuffs.

She turned around to me now, making a noise that sounded like laughter, but wasn't.

Usually my arms are empty, I told you, all year long I walk around with empty arms, she said. She laughed briefly again, and I said she really had beautiful arms and they were beautiful even without the bracelets, and I tried to imagine how they looked without the bracelets but I simply couldn't. The copper stabbed my eyes like needles and I felt a slight pain in my eyes, and I didn't even see her arms but only how the bracelets wrapped one of them, then the other, and her shoulders, her stomach, her chest, and she was sitting all wrapped as in a giant rack. No, no, I said to myself, it's the quiet, it's very quiet, it's the strong light, it's the strong light, how they sparkle, the bracelets, in the strong light, and how she's dressed up for him, living or dead, she dressed up for him, what a beautiful dress she put on for him, maybe she even washed her hair for him, its shine is so fresh, and how it waves burning on her head, making a living crown on her head. She said: I don't wear the rings either, not the rings either, and I tried to imagine her fingers without the rings. She had mother-of-pearl colored polish on her fingernails and I saw how delicate her fingernails looked. Suddenly I remembered the story of the apples in honey and the small annual celebration. She said: For our tenth anniversary he said he would bring me one with garnets, and I tried to guess when the tenth anniversary should have been, and what he would have bought on the ninth, the eighth, the seventh, but the needles stabbed my eyes, the amber got mixed up with the turquoise, the lapis with the coral, and I said to myself: No no, so much light, you can't sit in such light, I said to myself, that was what she was doing now too, the tenth, the ninth, the eighth, and like me she was counting backward and the count was short, and she was saying it will get longer, every year this will get longer, the bracelets will get short and the counting will get longer, and then the arms will get shorter too. But she sat quietly, playing with the bracelets that made the banging sound of copper and a dull ding dong ding dong and I thought I might have met her once in the street at the corner and hadn't recognized her, she had empty arms and I hadn't recognized her and I said to myself: No no, not that, it's not her, it's the light, impossible in such a light, and it's a mistake, it's all a mistake, but the bracelets were already running around in the garden mixing with the fresh beautiful blossoming, with the black letters and the white spaces and the rings too, and suddenly I remembered empty of all body and his house empty and empty his soul and his prayer returning empty, I remembered don't leave me empty-handed, oh don't leave me empty don't come empty, and I said no no, the air shrivels and we walk empty, why did I remember that? Where did I hear that? Many years had gone by since I heard that, we stand poor and empty, I heard that, I was a little girl when I heard that, it was always in summer, when my mother would murmur that, and our little wooden house was across from the Muslim cemetery and the windows were open and I was afraid of the cemetery, and I said let's close the windows, but she said, it's not the open windows, it's the bell, it's empty, it rings empty.

Something wrong? said the woman. She was playing again with the branch in her hand, and I said I was tired and it was late and I had to go. She smiled. Of course, of course, and if you come next year you'll find me here. She sounded very quiet, almost calm, and I said I would remember the date and come, certainly, I would come. Since she didn't answer, I said it really was a very hot day and that wind . . . and I wanted to come in the evening but I was afraid it was closed in the evening.

She went on playing with the branch in her hand, passing it over her face, They don't close a cemetery, she said.

When I left, I saw the gardener arranging his tools in the shed, lining up the hoes and the spades, the spare faucets, and a heap of new seedlings. He smiled when I asked about her. Come next year he said, she'll be here. He locked his shed. She always comes at this time, every year.

(1991, 1996)
—*Translated by Barbara Harshav*

Introduction to Ronit Matalon's "Photograph"

As Ronit Matalon's short story "Photograph" opens, a woman—presumably Israeli—is sneaking illegally into the Gaza Strip while the *Intifada* rages. But more than the law is broken in this story: the social pressure that keeps Palestinians and Israelis bitterly divided is undermined as well. For it is a Palestinian friend who helps her sneak in, and it is the disappearance of other Palestinian friends that she is determined to learn about. In this sense, as well as in its laconic and unsentimental style, Matalon's is a highly unusual short story whose stimulus was her own experience covering the Gaza and West Bank from 1985 to 1990 for the weekly supplement of Israel's prestigious newspaper, *Ha'aretz*.

Ronit Matalon's background is Mediterranean and Levantine: her parents were from Egypt, and her grandparents from Italy, Lebanon, and Egypt; she speaks Hebrew, English, French, and Arabic. Born in 1959 in Ganei Tikva, a new immigrants' town near Tel Aviv, she studied literature and philosophy at Tel Aviv University. On the faculty of the Camera Obscura School of the Arts in Tel Aviv since 1993, she also continues to write for *Ha'aretz* and serves on the Council for Culture and Art of the Ministry of Education, and on the Forum on Mediterranean Culture for the Van Leer Institute in Jerusalem.

She began publishing her short stories in the 1980s, mostly in the literary journal *Siman Kri'yah* but her much awaited and heralded first collection of stories, *Strangers in the House*, did not appear until 1992, and her novel *The One Facing Us* appeared in 1995. She received the Prime Minister's Award for Literature in 1994. *The One Facing Us*, which continues her fascinating exploration of the connections between narrative, autobiography, and photography, was published in English by Metropolitan Books (Henry Holt), translated by Marsha Weinstein, in 1998.

Photograph

Ronit Matalon

First they put the black cowl on my head, just a cowl, a kind of veil, slightly pushing on my back with a long sharpened pole toward the gap in the huddle of bushes.

Ahalan, ya Nurit, *ya* Ronit, *ya* Madame, said Khaled, a young companion. His eyes were white. His clothes were different.

The photograph as a reflection of the times interests me, I said, as we pulled out our papers, mine yellow, his rose, mine red, his blue, mine white, his white, everything matching. Khaled was pleased: an unusual fit, I could've searched for hours, he said gently. Is anyone with you?

I spread my fingers open and he silently counted. One by one, like the cars of a mountain train, the children came crawling through the gap in the bushes, getting their clothes nicely dusty and presenting their fingernails to Khaled to inspect. *Habibi*, Khaled exclaimed in surprise, red gummy bears!

Khaled, I said.

Yes?

I have a personal request.

It's okay, everything is personal, said Khaled.

No, seriously, I said, seriously. A friend of mine and his wife have disappeared. I telephone and people tell me strange things. Every time I come close, it's as if little animals nibble at my toes. You think it'll be okay for you to . . .

195

Don't insult me with questions like that, he said, I have demons of my own.

So we drove the blue Mercedes to my dead friend's family home and we easily managed to locate the place. The light was dim, deflected, and the begonia plants were burning in the windows, not many of them . . . just a few. Khaled explained: In this gloomy desert, I suddenly come across a specific photograph . . . and it blows the winds, the spirits, of life into me. And I blow the winds of life into it too. It's not as if the photograph is alive—I don't believe in photographs that "live"—but it has that something I need to arouse life in me, wake up the spirit of adventure.

I believe it, I said, I really do. Meanwhile the children had fallen asleep and we were glad that they were spared the most difficult part— though not out loud, Khaled admitted it also. He too trembled for a moment as he registered the words "The most difficult part." We went on like that. What does all this have to do with me, I asked. I keep seeing a house that's all inside, nothing external, a climbing vine, pomegranate, flattened iron gate.

This is the house, he said. I looked at it to erase any remaining doubts. It was in one piece, its face sealed like a blank slate. I left everything behind me and came into the house, all alone, repelled, but with a sense of obligation. Khaled entered later on, after he peed. He bowed toward two black female ravens, the sisters of my dead friend. I kissed the palms of their hands, hating the ground they walked on: I love Gaza more than a second skin, this expiation for the ass of the world. I know my friend, and perhaps even his wife, were murdered last night, I said. One of them clutched a long candlestick that lit up the coarse brown wall. Not enough, she decided. I tried again: I need photographs of him, even something like an ID photo, so I won't have an image of his severed head with me for the rest of my life. It's that simple.

They didn't approve or disapprove. They turned the back of their neck to me, that bare section underneath the hairline.

I was lucky I had my excellent position, lucky that I could hide from the suffering behind my own importance, lucky for the sudden transparency of Khaled as a good-for-nothing middleman, lucky I tilted my head slightly when they laid his death on me, lucky that we searched the nooks and crannies of the dark room after the photographs were taken, lucky, lucky, lucky.

We didn't find a thing. Our minds drifted more and more toward the unnatural darkness. We answered the dead's sister's questions after

all, claimed the darkness was unnatural, the wall silent, the stone scream-
ing, the dead living through his death and dying through his life: stuff,
stuff, and nevertheless, when a man is at stake and not some object,
there's a completely different fate contained in the powerful evidence of
a photograph. When you look at the photograph of a bottle, the stem
of an iris, a chicken, a palace—only the concrete reality is involved. But
a body, a face—and even more so, often the body and face of a beloved
soul?

We were close to giving up, feeling heavy, sitting on stools and
waiting only because it was the polite thing to do. We suddenly spotted
something on the rough walls of the cavernous room: a flickering on the
walls, brown, white, that seemed like giant close-ups of his face, inter-
mittently appearing and disappearing, when we concentrated. Did they
all see what I saw? Could I have caught something triggered in the
memory of someone else?

One of the sisters, the bony one, pulled on my coat. Look, she said.
She was holding up a pair of man's pants. They were stiff, as if someone
was actually wearing them; rigid from mud and coagulated blood.

They're his, she said. No one knew what he thought when he was
alone. Everyone mistook him. You, too. They knew nothing. They all
thought he was one thing and he was something else entirely. Then that
moron went and married that American girl who used to go around
kissing the wounds of the poor. So what. She's dead, too.

I fell to her feet. Have pity on me, I said, don't kick me when I'm
down.

Khaled turned aside. With his finger, he drew a path leading to
the house of the parents of the young wife, the stranger. They got
married five months ago in a friend's home, a doctor. Her fine hair
grew yellow in the summer, one arm crushed an orange flower on her
skirt, the other hand covered her ear to hear better. My friend stands
on her right, his face radiant. His mouth is agape, his eyes con-
tracted—apparently from a sense of danger—but the expression on his
face defies analysis.

We stood there, Khaled and I, in the entrance of the home of the
young wife's parents, next to a strange winter garden, too strange—just
like in dreams I hate, said Khaled. This time our paths were separate: the
blackberry bushes over there, the tall white flowers, the muslin curtains,
all instructed us not to interfere with the intimacy of this experience.
Khaled promised to handle the situation, even though, he said after a
moment's silence, even though he doesn't have much trust in young

photographers who run all over the world determined to capture current events, unaware that they really serve as agents of death.

My intention was different, I said.

Khaled wrapped the metal lock chain around the gate. He was kind to me for the first time. The intention is always different, always different, he said. But death has to find some place in society—if it's not to be in religion anymore (or there at least to a lesser degree), it has to be somewhere else. Maybe the same image that tries to protect life really creates death.

I climbed high up on the metal gate so I could watch his image walking away. Goodbye, dark companion, ally of the moment, thanks to your openness we could see everyday life in a place already beyond simple sorrow. Goodbye, attentive ears that occasionally, selectively, would sharpen. Goodbye, half-torn Reebok shoes. When the news will cover the great and the obscure, your memory will stand as an emblem of human-ness.

All this time, the dead wife's parents were watching us through the living room window, standing side by side, look-alikes. A lock of hair from the mother's bun dangled loosely on her nose. She was playing with something in her hands. A handkerchief? A scarf? The edge of a curtain?

The father's head was leaning on the window ledge, his fingers supporting his forehead and holding a cigarette. He's not from around here. He's from Cleveland.

You could come in or not, it's all the same. The vase of Hebron glass will forever be secure in its place in the middle of the table on the handmade oval tablecloth. The straight-back chairs will always face one another, red, said the mother.

I felt profoundly sad. I knew the young wife well and only fear stopped me now from asking about the circumstances of her death. The mother stood in front of me, her arms supporting the rolls of her stomach, her head bent toward her chest, particularly her chin. She was whispering in a colorless monotone, and I bent down to hear what she had to say. After my daughter made this hole her home, this depressing town, we had to believe so we came, brought what was ours, we adjusted ourselves, we made everything fit in. Those pictures you see? She's in all of them.

Where? I asked.

To see a photograph well, you have to look beyond it or close your eyes. The photograph must be still. It's not a question of balancing considerations—but of music. We get to complete subjectivity only in the state of trying for silence. Don't say a word, close your eyes, let every detail emerge by itself and take its own form, said the mother.

Now I saw: how many dozens of photographs there were stuck one on top of the other. They were everywhere—on the wallpaper, on little labels on all their possessions, framed on the heavy sideboard. I took off my shoes, sweating and shaking from fear: in all of them I saw a Madonna and Child, Madonna and Child, Madonna and Child. That's her, the mother's voice spoke from behind me. She's in both of them.

Forgive me, cried the father, forgive me, is this a photograph or drawing? He tilted my elbow, wiping his face with his tattered hat.

Shh . . . I said to him . . . Shhh. I had to understand, the intensity of the knowledge tore me apart. I knew that whether I laid my eyes on the Madonna or the Child didn't matter. The young wife would come to life again through the power of my look alone, whole, undamaged. She gathered up the hem of her dress with her fingers, drew a lock of hair behind her ear, and stepped out of the photograph toward us, into the strange big room. I could see her, with that same pale bird-like figure and secretive smile. She emerged from the Madonna or from the Child. I recognized her well, but I had to stay silent about what I saw. I had nothing but the look.

Gaza, 1990.

(1992)
—Translated by Gal Keidar with Miriyam Glazer

Introduction to Selected Short Stories by Orly Castel-Bloom

Reviews of the short stories and novels of Orly Castel-Bloom have included such words and phrases as "audacious," "charmingly whimsical," "innovative," "hilariously parodic," as well as "iconoclastic," "violent," "apocalyptic," "razor-sharp," and "quintessentially Tel Aviv" in style: "laconic, mocking, and self-derogatory." She has been viewed as "simply zany, a clever punster," as well as a "postmodernist oracle consciously reaching beyond moral or ideological points of view." While her very short short stories have been compared to cartoons, some readers were overwhelmed by the violent fantasies of her novel *Dolly City* (1992), in which a doctor-mother is so obsessively worried about the possible dangers that might beset her baby that she compulsively subjects him to medications, operations, chemotherapy until indeed she does wreak havoc on his body. For critic Ariana Melamed, however, *Dolly City* reveals "a persistent and determined" effort "to expose the terrifying epic of motherhood to its core, with no compromises, restraint or cliches." Castel-Bloom's third novel, *The Mina Lisa* (1995), is a brilliantly complex and imaginative play of illusion and reality that examines both the paradoxes, compromises, pains, and solaces of a contemporary woman while also examining what it means to be a contemporary writer as well.

The stories here are like glances at everyday Israeli life reflected in the distortions of a fun-house mirror, particularly if one has a strange idea of "fun." The tensions of life at war. The tensions of a writer's

200

life. The tensions indeed of Israeli life as a whole. Born in Tel Aviv in 1960, Orly Castel-Bloom studied film at Tel Aviv University. Her publications include the short story collections *Not Far from the Center of Town* (1987); *Hostile Surroundings* (1988); and *Unbidden Stories* (1993); and the novels *Where Am I* (1990), which won the Prime Minister's Prize for Literature, as well as *Dolly City* (1992), and *The Mina Lisa* (1995). She lives in Tel Aviv.

Her fiction has been translated into German, Dutch, French, and Italian. For reviews of her fiction, cited above and published in English, see Rochelle Furstenberg, "A Postmodernist Oracle," *Modern Hebrew Literature* 16 (Spring/Summer, 1996), pp. 40–41; Dan Miron, "A Handbook to a New Prose Language," *Modern Hebrew Literature* 13 (Fall/Winter, 1994), pp. 32–34, and Anat Feinberg, "What an Intoxicating Madness!" *Modern Hebrew Literature* 8/9 (Spring/Fall, 1992), pp. 13–15.

A Thousand Shekels a Story

Orly Castel-Bloom

We weren't actually at starvation's door, although even that depends on
how you look at it—the house was in ruins, windows missing, the living-
room armchair shot to pieces, a crack in the wall, the kitchen a shambles,
cupboards falling apart, furniture which had given up the ghost a long
time ago—but I could smell it coming.

Apart from which my husband told me, "You're a wreck." This
being the case, first thing in the morning I phoned and asked to speak
to the editor-in-chief in charge of all the editors and chiefs and men-
tioned my full name—which is so long that it's ridiculous. I told him
about myself and said that I had an unprecedented offer for which I
wanted a four-figure sum, monthly.

I made an appointment with him in an air-conditioned café and
pushed my way through crowds of people I didn't know and who for
some reason embarrassed me greatly. When the coffee arrived I explained
my proposal to him.

"Listen to me," I said to him, "and then say whatever you've got to
say, I'm listening anyway. I'll just take in your tone, my feelers will grope
for the gist of your reply—yes or no, and afterwards, sir, we'll say good-
bye, either forever or not."

"I'm all ears," he said.

"Let me have a car, let me have money, neither a little nor a lot—
budget me—let me travel round and about the country. Yes, we'll begin
with round and about the country. Let me see what's going on. Believe

me, I haven't left the house in years, I'm in urgent need of contact with the outside world. And I'll pay it back, the outside world, by describing it with amazing accuracy, with flashes of brilliance. Let me travel, let me wander, and I'll bring you a story a week, a thousand shekels a story."

"Yes?" his eyebrows rose like two hills.

"Could you concentrate, please?"

"That's my side of the bargain, and what do I get in return?"

"A story a week, weren't you listening to me?"

"Certainly I was listening, that's why I'm asking you what you're giving me in return."

"I don't understand you."

"That story's for you—release, therapy, autotherapy, what do you want of me?"

"What kind of talk is that?"

"Sorry," he said. "We don't need a weekly story. Every day there are hundreds of stories and parts of stories in the newspapers. I've got reporters poking into the pockets of every Minister in the government, I don't need a literary angle on plain reality."

I called another newspaper and repeated my offer over the phone. I expanded it. After all, it wasn't asking much and the rejection stung me. I said: "Let me travel round the world, with my daughter and my husband. I'm Orly, I'm a wreck. But I've got eyes, sir. A thousand shekels a story. And not a penny less. That's my last word."

He said, "Let's see an example. Go to the refineries on your own account and bring me an example. Or not. Go wherever you like. Go to the Jordan Valley, to Masada, to Arad, to the Dead Sea. Wherever you like."

"Tell me, what is this? I'm not prepared for you to give me tests. Either you take me now as I am, or I'll go to Avigdor from the rival paper, or somewhere else. Either sign me up on a blank contract with no strings attached or else," and I took out a hammer and a rolling pin and banged on the table.

"Okay, okay," he sighed, "let's meet."

We arranged to meet at a café on the promenade, next to the sea. I repeated my offer and the waiter came and removed the melon rinds and the remains of the salad.

The man sitting opposite me lit a cigarette and thought. In the meantime a few thoughts crossed my mind which I thought were quite off the mark, but today I know they did me no good.

"Listen," I said, "all I want is a page in your newspaper and a thousand shekels a story. Come on, give."

He went on looking at the sea in silence. My wrinkles deepened. Five o'clock in the afternoon, the sun was directly opposite my face. I dried my sweat with a paper napkin.

"Well," I said.

He shrugged his shoulders.

"What do I know."

My worst fears were realized. I had made the man miserable. I had depressed him. The whole idea from beginning to end suddenly seemed futile to me. I asked him to forget the conversation had ever taken place. But he said that actually he liked my offer, and we should talk about it again in a couple of days time.

I walked up the steps to Hayarkon Street, and began going down all the streets perpendicular to the sea in the direction of Ibn Gvirol, the desolate street where the bus s.t.o.p. is situated. I stood at the bus stop and waited for a bus. When I got home I saw my husband watching a five by five video movie.

"Where is our daughter?" I asked.

"Sleeping," he replied, and demanded a full account of the conversation.

I falsified everything on purpose, because I'd already forgotten what had happened, and immersed myself in the television set. My husband filled me in with regard to the plot and I asked questions and he answered them.

A few days passed and the man didn't call. I personally wasn't waiting for a call, but the economic situation was.

The bank clerk came for coffee at six o'clock on Wednesday evening and asked when we intended covering the overdraft.

"Never," said my husband and stroked his cheek.

"Why don't you shave?" she asked.

"I don't like it."

"You know," she said to him, "you make awfully good coffee."

He looked at me, because actually it was me who had the made the coffee.

"She made it," he said.

"So what?" she said.

"What?" I said.

"If there's anything you want here," said my husband with a smile, "take it—don't be shy."

"Really?" said the bank clerk.

"Take whatever you want."

"Have you got a few crates?" she asked.

"Maybe the neighbors have," I said.

"Why don't you put your salary in the bank every month like everybody else?" she asked.

"I'll tell you," my husband began telling her, and hinted to me that I should make myself scarce. I took my daughter and went down to the woods. From there I went on with her to a café, and from there to the pub. The drink warmed my heart and I stopped wishing I was dead. My distress faded, I calmed down and hugged and kissed her and explained a few things to her from an objective point of view. She looked at me and I kept saying to myself that there was no other way, what other way could there be? My heart was like the skin of a camel, flat as a rug.

When we went home I saw the bank clerk's '86 Fiat Uno driving off in the direction of the main road.

"*Salamaat*," I said to her.

"*Salaamtek*," I said to her again.

"*Tislam*, peace be with you, lady."

I went inside, and I saw my husband standing there with his three brothers, all playing snooker.

"I got an extension of eight years," said my husband. "In the meantime the interest will rocket, but who cares. In eight years time we'll leave the country."

His brothers looked daggers at me. They accused me of hypocrisy, of self righteousness, of bad literature, of perversity.

I told them I agreed with every word they said, and I made tehina with lots of parsley. They all ate well, they finished the lot, they polished their plates clean, I didn't even have to wash the dishes, I put them straight into the cupboard, and to hell with them.

It was a long night. I looked at the stars scattered over the sky like salt on my wounds. I prayed for redemption, for the Messiah to come. What's going on here—I wondered. I'm not a woman, my husband's not a man. Soon I'll die, I'll turn into a picture. Everyone will forget me and I'll forget them.

I'll go away, I'll disappear, I'll vamoose, I'll evaporate. I'll die. That's it. Au Revoir and good-bye. No more. When. Finito la comedia. Twenty years from now, I'll die. I won't exist. I love moments of fellowship between people, they move me to tears. But open moments, like my sitting here on the balcony, send me way out. I love these open moments. When the dome of heaven really functions like a dome, it's terrific.

(1993)

—*Translated by Dalya Bilu*

The Woman Who Went Looking for a Walkie-Talkie

Orly Castel-Bloom

There was a war on, and everyone wanted to feel part of it. Lots of people bought walkie-talkies, and some of them even started driving around in military-colored Jeeps. The roads grew dangerous, only people who put up flags were allowed to drive in the left lane and on the open highway, the others kept their mouths shut and travelled by bus with tickets at a fifty percent discount.

Even when the war was over people went on buying walkie-talkies. They had bulimia, they couldn't control themselves.

There was a woman—neither tall nor fat—who was dying to have a walkie-talkie in the house. She knew that it wasn't enough to buy one walkie-talkie, you had to have at least two in order to transmit. The woman didn't care, she only wanted one instrument, but nobody wanted to sell her one, they said that walkie-talkies were like socks, shoes, or gloves, they came in pairs, and she had better find herself a partner.

Nobody wanted to be her partner, because they had other things to do. For example, to restore the market to the prewar norm. The woman didn't know what to do. What do you think she should have done? When you have to buy something with a partner, it's a problem. You can't always find someone with whom to split a loaf of bread in the grocery store, so why should you find one for a walkie-talkie? But there

206

was a war on, and in wartime people come close to each other, some of them even bend over, and others lift their skirts.

The woman wanted one walkie-talkie, and there was nothing she could do about it.

One day she happened to be on Basel Street in Tel Aviv, and an inscrutable Chinese man was standing there peddling solar heaters at a considerable reduction, and single walkie-talkies for fifty shekels; twenty-five new shekels and twenty-five obsolete old shekels. The woman jumped at the chance, and began hunting through the Chinese man's boxes for a walkie-talkie as good as new.

She had forty new shekels. The peddler agreed to meet her halfway and come down to thirty—so they struck a deal.

The woman switched on the walkie-talkie and began to talk. She opened her mouth and never closed it again. She walked along the coast, from Tel Aviv to Haifa, sometimes on the beach and sometimes in the water, and she talked and talked, and the people whose frequencies she got onto didn't know what to do, they couldn't get any work done. In Netanya she stopped for coffee, on that square of cafés next to the park that goes down to the sea, where they sell pizza for twenty shekels, and she ordered espresso au lait—even though there's no such thing except in Herzliah Pituach. The manager of the café didn't know what to do with this crazy woman taking up a table and asking for espresso au lait; there's a limit to the nonsense a person can put up with from his fellow man, and people who've got problems should get themselves seen by professionals.

The woman had nothing left to say. She murmured her life history into the instrument twenty-five times, her origins, her wishes, she recited passages from books she knew by heart, and then, when all else failed, she began singing songs whose refrain and first verse she knew. She went through all the festivals, she sang songs from long ago, and she gave the people whose frequencies she got onto such a headache that they were forced to transmit on other, impossible channels.

The woman went on babbling—it was incredible, the woman must have swallowed a radio—and her walkie-talkie began shooting off sparks it was so overloaded, but nothing had any effect on her amazing confessional capacity.

A little after Zichron Ya'akov the walkie-talkie itself asked her—in words, in fluent Hebrew—to stop, because it was on the verge of a nervous breakdown, it couldn't stand it, why didn't she get off its back, for pity's sake! She wasn't the only one, it had other customers too, and the woman took a break, until she reached the Kishon river.

On the banks of the Kishon she kept quiet and took samples of the water. She wanted to compare the Haifa stink with the Tel Aviv stink, but there was nothing to compare, both rivers were disgusting, and the woman knew that they had to be dried up once and for all. She got on the air to all kinds of laundry-drying companies, and invited them to bring their giant fans and dry up the Kishon and Yarkon rivers and finish with this stink already. Over the walkie-talkie she commanded the entire operation, and also the paving of the Kishon and the Yarkon with Italian marble, and then, when all the inhabitants of Netanya came to demonstrate and complain about why they didn't do the same thing to the Alexander river, she said she was sorry, it was impossible to leave a whole country without any stinking rivers at all.

After the task was accomplished, she heard the sirens of a police car coming to confiscate her walkie-talkie, in case she suddenly took it into her head to start flooding the Huleh valley over again and destroying the agricultural infrastructure of the kibbutzim.

The woman handed over the walkie-talkie without any problems; she said she was sick of it, she was getting old, and she was going home.

(1993)
—Translated by Dalya Bilu

The Woman Whose Hand Got Stuck in the Mailbox

Orly Castel-Bloom

There was once a woman who waited for years for an important letter. She didn't know who it was from, and perhaps it was actually a check for quite a big sum. The woman waited for this letter eagerly, even though nobody owed her anything.

She was so eager for the letter to arrive, that every day she would open her mailbox and take everything out of it, in other words, mainly cheap flyers advertising fumigation, or the telephone number of a plumber with spelling mistakes.

She would crumple it all into one big ball of colored paper, and throw it into the garden, next to the blooming rose bush, and go upstairs. This had been going on for years: she would get up in the morning, go out for a run, circle the neighborhood, come home, perhaps see the mailman arriving and watch and wait.

One fine day the mailman stopped coming and bringing the mail. This went on for a week until the woman went to the local post office and asked what was happening. They told her that the mailman had been hurt in a traffic accident, and his condition was grave, but stable.

The woman didn't know what to do. She felt an emptiness bordering on despair, and went back to swallowing all kinds of things that she had promised herself never to go near again. For two weeks she received nothing but junk mail, until one day she saw a new mailman coming.

The new mailman was apparently brand new, he kept getting mixed up and putting letters in their mailboxes that had nothing to do with them and belonged to families at the other end of the street.

It was like a nightmare, it was like dreaming about burnt monkeys, and in fact, ever since the muddle with the mail began, the woman had really started dreaming about burnt monkeys, about a fire in the monkey cages of the municipal zoo. In her dreams she looked at black baboons and thought that they were exactly like the shadows of baboons, but they were really burnt baboons.

Weeks passed, the unbearable summer came. No interesting letter came for the woman, only meaningless letters, which weren't meant for her at all, and she stuck them onto the notice board with disgust.

One fine day, she was walking next to a puddle, and the keys to the mailbox fell into it and disappeared. The woman searched for an hour and half, splashing in the stagnant water—but nothing doing.

The woman didn't know what to do. She took it so hard that the idea of breaking into the mailbox didn't even occur to her.

She went home, peeped into the mailbox, and saw something white, which might have been a letter, which might have contained a check or a letter from a distant relative in Uruguay inviting her to come and spend the summer there.

But her hand got stuck, she couldn't get it out. With the tips of her fingers she felt the edge of the envelope and she tried to move them in the splints, hoping to trap the letter between two fingers and snatch it out, and to hurry upstairs to pack.

It didn't work, and she began to sweat, the sweat was really pouring off her, but she was ashamed to ask for help, she was ashamed to be caught waiting for the Messiah.

Luckily for her, her neighbor came past and said that they had to widen the opening of the mailbox, and then she would be able to free herself. The neighbor tried with all her strength, with a plier, and with other tools which she brought from her apartment, but nothing helped.

Suddenly the new mailman arrived, and asked what they thought they were doing. The woman said that it was an accident, and accidents happen, and you had to face it and learn from the experience. The mailman took her at her word, and distributed the mail to all the neighbors, except for her.

"Listen to me for a minute," said the stuck woman. "For seven years I've been checking the mailbox everyday—and I haven't had one important letter. I've got relations in Montevideo, and I'm sure they'd have no objection if I went to stay with them for a month or two."

"Before you go to Montevideo," the mailman sniggered, "you'd better free yourself from your mailbox."

"What do you suggest?" asked the neighbor.

And the mailman rolled up his sleeves, and freed one finger after the other. It took him five hours until he saw that her hand was outside and she was clenching and relaxing to get the blood circulating again.

The neighbor brought pincers, and together all three of them pulled out the letter which was at the bottom of the mailbox. Yes, it was a letter, and the woman opened it in suspense, and inside there was indeed a plane ticket to Montevideo and a check for a few thousand dollars.

"You see?" the woman said, overjoyed.

(1994)
—*Translated by Dalya Bilu*

A Special Section:
Stories Translated from the Russian

" . . . he won't tell me where we're going until I agree to admit I've never been there, even though I was born and raised in this city," says the narrator in Elena Makarova's "Rough Casting." The city is Jerusalem, and the place to which they go—this young woman and her companion, a Russian immigrant whose lanky height makes him stick out "like the site of the Ascension on the Mount of Olives"—is the ancient Greek Orthodox monastery in the Valley of the Cross. It is a place one is not accustomed to enter in Israeli literature. As the monk in "Rough Casting" tells his visitors:

> Sometimes the Israelis come here on Shabbat . . . They litter; they dress immodestly . . . I beg your pardon, not everybody is like that. Take, for example, the Russian Jews, they respect us. If not our faith, then the beauty and purity of these places. . . .

And, indeed, seeing the monastery through her companion's eyes, the narrator muses:

> If one ignores the surroundings—the valley, the cypresses, the palm trees, and looks only into the thick green water—it looks like Russia to him now.

Like much Israeli literature, and more particularly like Yehudit Hendel's novel *The Yard of Momo the Great*, and Nurit Zarchi's "Madame Bovary

212

in Neve Tsedek," the short stories of Russian Jewish new immigrants Elena Makarova and Dina Rubin are narratives of cultural disruption and displacement, of living in what feels like a diaspora though one is now paradoxically in what is supposed to be the "homeland." But whereas the protagonist of Zarchi's story, for one, has come from Russia to the pre-State *yishuv*, the stories by Makarova and Rubin wrestle with the traumas of the Russian Jewish immigrants to the prosperous Israel of today. It is as if we have come full circle: neither the pre-State writer in "Madame Bovary in Neve Tsedek," nor the narrator in "Monologue of a Life Model," nor the immigrant (and even the Jerusalem-born narrator) in "Rough Casting," identify with the collective ideology of Zionism. Rather than perceive Israel as "home," they are all marked by having "feet with no soles."

In Zarchi's story, the protagonist's refusal to participate in "the creation of the New Man!" and her insistence, instead, on writing of the world she had once known and left, estranged her emotionally from her eager and ambitious, as well as more ideological, contemporaries. But there are no ideologues in either Rubin's or Makarova's story. In the former's, disjunction between the Russian past and the Israeli present is less a matter of choice than a result of economics: though an electrical engineer in Russia, the story's narrator works as a cleaning woman and an artist's model in Israel, an experience that reflects the reality of many new Russian immigrants: to earn at least the rudiments of a living, doctors in the former Soviet Union initially became street cleaners or custodians in Israel; members of orchestras became street musicians. But more than loss of economic (and social) status is involved here, for the narrator clearly feels bitterly, cynically, culturally estranged. She dismisses the Moroccan who seeks to help her out as a "*muzhik*"; like the grandmother of an earlier immigration described in "Invisible Mending," she regards him, in Almog's words, as a "parvenu" while "people of culture and learning are cleaning houses."

In English, the word *immigrant* derives from the Latin *immigrans*, "moving into"; in Hebrew, however, the word is *oleh*, from the verb "to move up." The word has ancient sources. The Biblical Ezra leaves Babylon to "go up" to Jerusalem (Ezra 7:6), for example, and in the second century Mishneh to make the pilgrimage to Jerusalem, that "city on a hill," is an *aliyah b'regel*, a "going up by foot." In modern Hebrew, too, a Jew who decides to live in Israel doesn't merely immigrate, in the English sense, but also, "makes *aliyah*," that is, either by implication or by conscious choice acts to fulfill the prophetic and Zionist hope for redemption—spiritual in the one case, national and one might say quasi-spiritual in the other—through an end to the dispersion, an ingathering of the exiles. To leave Israel in order to dwell elsewhere was thus to *choose* exile, to become the prejorative *yored*, one who "goes down."

What is striking about the stories by Dina Rubin and Elena Makarova is how alien this traditionally religious and ideological language is to the experience of immigration they depict. For Rubin's "life model," whether she lives in Amsterdam or Israel is a matter of indifference; all that does matter to her is her relationship with her son. In Makarova's, the family of the Russian Jew is scattered in Corsica, Kiev, and America, and he himself is in Israel only because he has nowhere else to go. He is a drifter in the country. Despite his wearing of a traditionally religious skullcap, he feels closer to the Greek Orthodox monk Basilique, who comes from France, than he does to other Jews. When he walks around Jerusalem, he sticks out above the crowd like "the site of the Ascension on the Mount of Olives." The Israel that the narrator experiences through the Russian Jew's eyes is more Russian than Israeli, more the "Holy Land" of Christianity than the "Promised Land" of either Zionism or Judaism. Indeed, Israelis in the story are portrayed as spiritually vacuous or profane; the rich moshavnik is fixing his car on the Shabbat, Israelis "litter" the Valley of the Cross when they come there for Shabbat "picnics," and they have erected a chicken coop whose odors befoul the air of the monastery. The contempt for religion is echoed in the contempt for nature: the ravine in Ein Kerem, near Hadassah Hospital, is a garbage dump. The dream of the redemption of the people is replaced in this story by the Russian's fantasy of both curing the problem of mildew and staving off decay by casting landmarks of beauty in giant molds.

When the original of Zarchi's "Madame Bovary in Neve Tsedek"—Devora Baron—came to Palestine, she continued writing in Hebrew, as she had done since an early age in eastern Europe. Before emigrating to Israel, however, both Dina Rubin and Elena Makarova had established literary reputations in the former Soviet Union and both continue to write fiction in their native Russian. Partly of course the choice of language is a matter of fluency and of ease; partly an artistic decision. But there is a cultural component as well; while the persecution of Jews in the former Soviet Union helped to drive these writers to emigrate, their enmeshment in and respect for Russian literary culture remain deep. Earlier writers (and, of course, political leaders) believed in casting off the diaspora identity as part of their mission to "create the New Man!" To leave one's native land for Palestine or the new state of Israel once meant a radical rupture with the past; one could not easily ever return if one could return at all. But particularly since the dissolution of communism, moving from one country to another is less dramatic a phenomenon; one can return now and again for a visit; boundaries are fluid. In the cultural heterogeneity/hybridity that results from the relative ease of global communication and travel today, linguistic boundaries, too, have become more fluid. On the one hand, among Hebrew-language writers, the influence of English is becoming increasingly evident. And, on the other, without the ideological or religious passion that perceives "diaspora" identity as exilic—in other words, with a denuding of the spiritual ideological associations of *aliyah*—what then becomes the motivation to give up writing in a major world language in order to write for the much more limited readership of Hebrew?

But if we consider literature written in Russian or English (or in any other language for that matter) also Israeli literature what, then, *is* Israeli literature? Is it literature written only in Hebrew? Literature by those who conceive of their work as written within or in response to the body of Hebrew literature? Or rather, in view of the multiculturality of the country, is it literature in any language produced by writers for whom grappling with Israeli life, culture, society, is a central element of the work? If an Israeli writes in a language other than Hebrew—in Arabic, for example does her or his work belong to the corpus of Arabic, rather than Israeli, literature? At what point does a "Russian Israeli" or an "American Israeli" become, simply, an *Israeli*? If immigrants live on the psychological "edge" of Israeli society, is that edge not also part of what it means to live *in* Israeli society? As so many stories in this collection suggest, the disruptions and displacements of the immigrant experience are themes that echo throughout Israeli literature. It seems to me that in a time such as ours, where linguistic and cultural boundaries are so fluid, and where the assumption of Israeli national identity may no longer be infused with or buttressed by a Zionist or religious ideology of transformation and renewal, and where "diaspora" no longer necessarily is seen as "exile," we will be faced with these questions of hybridity increasingly.

Born in Tashkent in 1953, Dina Rubin was known for writing primarily for and about adolescents before her immigration to Israel. Her early short story, "So When Will It Start Snowing?" written when she was twenty, received major attention after being turned into a radio play. Translations of her works soon appeared in eastern and central Europe. She moved to Moscow in 1984 and then, in 1988, with her husband and two children, emigrated to Israel. Her published works in translation include: "Recapitulation," *SovLit* (1987) 6: 101–116, tr. Alex Miller; "That Strange Man Altukhov," *SovLit* (1989) 3: 14–25, tr. June Goss and Elena Goreva; "The Double-Barreled Name," *Nimrod* 33:2 (Spring/

Summer, 1990), 98–196, tr. Marian Schwartz; "The Blackthorn," *Lives in Transit*, tr. Brittainy Smith (Ann Arbor: University of Michigan Press, 1993).

Born in Baku, Azerbaijan, in 1951, Elena Makarova was raised in Moscow in a literary family; her mother is the well-known poet Inna Lisnianskaia, whose work was banned in the Soviet Union and who lived in internal exile from 1979 to 1988. Makarova graduated from the Gorky Literature Institute, and while teaching art at an experimental school for psychologically disturbed children, published novellas, experimental prose, a collection of essays and many articles, frequently writing about the Holocaust. Makarova became fascinated with the work of Friedl Dicker-Brandeis, who taught art to the children imprisoned in Terezin concentration camp during World War II. She mounted an exhibit in Moscow of Dicker-Brandeis's work, before official harassment spurred her to emigrate to Israel with her family in 1990.

Since settling in Jerusalem, Makarova has taught art and given art therapy lessons to developmentally disabled adults at the Israel Museum; written Holocaust history, screenplays, fiction, and plays; curated exhibits, including "Theresienstadt: Culture and Barbarism" in Scandinavia, as well as participating in the documentary films, *Three Days in Terezin*, a German-Czech production about Terezin cabaretist Karel Svenk (1996); *The Rainbow of Colors* (about Friedl Dicker-Brandeis), an Israeli-Czech production (1995); *Goethe and the Ghetto*, a Swedish poduction about Terezin composer Viktor Ullman (1995), and *Terezin's Children*, a Japanese film (1991).

Works translated into English include: "Herbs from Odessa," *Balancing Acts* (Bloomington: Indiana University Press, 1989), pp. 19–48, tr. Helena Goscilo; "Uncle Pasha," *Nimrod* 33:2 (Spring/Summer, 1990), tr. Lise Brody; "Needlefish," in Susan Aiken et al., *Dialogues\Dialogi* (Durham: University of North Carolina Press, 1993), tr. Lise Brody; and "Rush Job," *Lives in Transit* (Ann Arbor: University of Michigan Press, 1993), tr. Lise Brody.

Monologue of a Life Model

Dina Rubin

Here's the thing. So many times I've wondered why when a naked person stands on a platform in a studio she looks so respectable, as if she were doing something important, but no sooner does she step out into the hall to the fuse box—when a fuse blows—than she's not a model anymore, she's just a naked woman, a former electrical engineer. A naked person truly is a negligible creature.

The fuses at the studio, where I pick up extra cash life modelling, blow all the time. Artists are simple people, great people, but their hands end in brushes. The slightest thing happens and it's "Raya!" Especially since in my past life I *was* an electrical engineer.

As soon as the light goes out, I slip off the platform into the hall, grope my way to the box, and a second later all's well. Then Avi Cohen—he's the director of the studio, such a dear old baldie—gives me his arm, helps me back up onto the platform, and says:

"*Az anakhnu mamshikhim*[66]—so let's get back to where we were."

Fifteen rubles—I mean shekels an hour. That ain't hay. Twice a week, three hours at a crack—figure it out. Before he went into the army, Sergeant and I ate on that—on my naked ass.

They pay Israelis more, of course—twenty-five. But Avi Cohen promised, starting Passover, to slip me another ruble, I mean, shekel.

---

66. *Az anakhnu mamshikhim:* Literally, "so we go on."

Apart from me, though, I don't get it—these artist types—ours, theirs—they're all poor. Especially in the winter when the tourists don't come, so no one's buying pictures. Naturally, they make money any way they can.

Sashka Kornyakin from Voronezh comes to us to draw. He's a real sweet guy, whose connection to Israel is through his ex-wife.

Here's the thing. He grinds flour for matzoh in a small private factory in Mea Shearim for six rubles an hour—shekels, I mean. He hurt his arm a little while ago, his right one—and the blood just spewed, he says. He missed three classes. It's okay, though, he ended up all cheerful. Now, he says, let them try to prove they don't add the blood of Christian boys to the matzoh. Russians here live like Jews in Russia.

We also have Fabritsius van Brauver, a sweetheart of a guy. A great big muzhik, a blond. A Dutch Jew. Actually, he knew he was Dutch, but he found out he was a Jew only six years ago when his mama was dying. She ceremoniously informed him that he came from a family of Marranos—you know, the ones who converted to Christianity five hundred years ago but kept being Jews in secret, even though the Inquisition didn't exactly pat you on the head for that.

So here's his mama explaining to him who he is. And since they lived together—like me and Sergeant—she makes him promise after she dies to sit shiva[67] and then shake a leg to Israel.

That's what someone can have dumped on him in one instant. Just imagine this innocent Dutchman facing these crazy Jewish circumstances. He sat shiva and came and it's okay. He's getting along. He likes it. He just can't manage Hebrew, he's always using English. He himself is such a big strong Dutchman, he says: "My father's a goy."

He works as a guard at the Western Wall.

Then there's Avi Cohen, a fairly well-known avant-gardist, always wearing some ratty sweater. An official from the tax administration showed up at his house a few days ago pretending to be a buyer. Those are their little tricks, you know. . . . So when they'd agreed on a price, the tax man pulls out his I.D. instead of a checkbook, but this doesn't throw our Avi. He gallantly takes this guy by the arm and walks him over to the refrigerator. There, on the nearly empty shelves, lies a crusty piece of cheese on a saucer. The guy from the tax administration stands there and stares at that boring little piece of cheese and goes away without saying a word.

As Avi says in cases like that, "*Az anakhnu mamshikhim!*"

---

67. To *sit shiva:* The week-long traditional Jewish mourning ritual.

As for me, I've always looked well off. Even now I look like I'm well off, even when I'm working on the platform. I have a lifelong rule: never owe anyone anything. You usually sleep much better that way.

A few days ago in the supermarket I was short thirty kopeks—I mean agorot—and some muzhik, a Moroccan obviously, paid it. A hundred percent Moroccan, no doubt about it.

I'd filled my basket—oh, I had good shampoo, a navy blue polka dot cup I liked, ketchup—which Sergeant loves (he was home from the army for Saturday)—and this, that, and the other . . . when I got to the cash register, I suddenly realized I'd left my checkbook at home. And I didn't have enough cash. The cashier at the register is so sweet, she says what you do is, you get rid of what's less important. I'm thinking—all right, the cup, to hell with it, the dietetic crackers, to hell with them, but the shampoo and ketchup, no. She says, well, you're still thirty agorot short.

That's when this muzhik—you could tell he was obviously a Moroccan—he's standing behind me, and he takes out his change purse and says, "How much does the *gveret*[68] owe?"

That throws me for a loop. What do you mean? I say. *Motek,*[69] thank you, of course, but don't you worry about it, I'm very well off. And he counters—oh come on, there's nothing to discuss!—and he throws the change down. He's a classic, a hundred percent, just like they paint them in the Russian papers: gold chains around his neck and wrists . . .

So what I'm thinking is, why is he doing this? Is he trying to humiliate me? Or is he just in a hurry and I'm holding up the line? Or maybe he's just a decent muzhik and I'm making too much of it . . . Anyway . . . there's the milk.

In principle that whole incident doesn't affect me one way or the other. Certainly not. It's funny that what's really been eating at me was that written promise not to leave!

As if I were just about to apply for a visa. First of all, what exactly have I missed seeing over there? Secondly, Sergeant and I have better things to spend our money on. But it's been eating at me! I lie awake at nights and it gnaws at me, it gnaws. What on earth is this, I think? What kind of place have I come to?

Although I should be objective about it. What do the police work from? The facts. But what are the facts? Was I cleaning for that lady? Yes.

---

68. *Gveret.* The "Mrs."

69. *Motek:* Sweetie.

Did she lose her diamonds the way she claimed in her statement? Damned if I know, I guess she did.

At the interrogation I say to the policeman, "Look at me. I even *look* well off. What do I need her diamonds for?"

And he looks at me kindly and says, "Listen, give back what you took and you can go wherever you like."

I say to him, "I'm educated, I'm an electrical engineer. Do you know how many muzhiks like you I had under me at the plant?"

And he says to me, "I don't have time to study your *korot chaim*.[70] Give back what you took from the *gveret* and you can go free. But if you're going to be stubborn, we're going to suggest you take a lie detector test."

That actually made me laugh. Go ahead, I say. Bring on your lie detector. That's really going to scare a Russian Jew. Only that sweet little old bitch has to take the test, too.

This is what he wrote in my file: She agrees to take the test on the *mekhonat emet*.[71] All-l-l right.

Then it turns out my little old lady is refusing to take the lie detector test. Because of her high blood pressure.

Then I start to remember our heart-to-hearts. Sometimes I'd be all bent over bowlegged under the couches and cupboards, and she'd follow me around bemoaning the fact that we Russian Jews had abandoned the great traditions of our people. She'd be stepping on my heels giving me orders about where to wipe and constantly trying to talk me into returning to my traditions.

Well, needless to say, we're pretty lousy on the traditions. Sergeant and I came out pretty confused about the whole thing in general. As soon as we got here, our neighbors gave him a tallith.[72] They knocked at the door one morning, walked in, and ceremoniously draped it over his shoulders. Sergeant was very touched.

"Look, Ma," he says. "Look at the pretty towel they gave us."

So as far as traditions go, it's only right.

After the interrogation I suddenly remembered how just before this incident she'd been trying to show off her diamonds to me. "Look what

---

70. Your *Korot chaim*: Your curriculum vitae, resumé.

71. *Mekhonat emet:* Lie detector.

72. *Tallith:* A prayer shawl.

riches I have!" she says. But I was late for the studio that day, and I was in no mood for diamonds, especially someone else's.

And when I remembered that . . . Well, let's just say it all became crystal clear to me. And I felt like just asking her, What about the great traditions of our people? Just asking—hey, what about those traditions? So I went to see her. She has a smallish house in Kfar-Nof. I rang at the gate, as usual. Her grandson came out on the porch, a boy of about sixteen, real good-looking, wearing an earring.

"Get out of here," he screams, "you Russian thief!" Yeah, except he said *Khushan thiekh*—his attempt at Russian was laughable.

Well, I don't give a damn about that. I'm invulnerable to words like that. . . . At bottom I am not an emotional person.

He also let the dog off its leash, but that was totally stupid. First of all, I'm not afraid of dogs, thank God, I'm not a local, and anyway the dog knows me. She ran up to the gate overjoyed, wagging her tail.

I have to admit, I did pick up a stone. A nice hefty little stone. . . . Then I thought better of it. I might break their window. Then I'd have to pay for the glass myself. So I went away.

The main thing is I'm not telling Sergeant anything. I've never kept him posted on my troubles. Ever since childhood my Sergeant's been a pensive kind of boy. His pensiveness is why I never got married, so as not to give him extra reasons to brood. I just realized it wasn't in his best interests. And now I could care less about marrying. I've seen my fill. They may offer you the same glass of water, but what the price of it is and whether or not you'll ever live to get the glass. . . .

It's a sin to complain. Sergeant brings nothing but official citations back from the army. A little while ago they even rewarded him with a radio. I ask him, "Well, are they going to give you some other kind of material incentive?" And he says, "They did."

"What?"

"The general had me sit next to him at dinner."

"Did you smack your lips?" I ask.

"No," he says. "The general did."

Just a few days ago they suggested he take a test for some kind of officer course. He did. The army psychologist calls him in. "You know," he says, "judging from the results of this test, with your world view not only should you not take officer courses, you shouldn't stay in the army. Go on, in two months you can take another test." Sergeant says to him, "Do you think the world will give me the chance to change my opinion of it in that time?"

He bursts out laughing and says, "I'd never take you for an officer. But I might for a friend."

Sergeant's my first. I mean, my private first-class. He's supposed to be promoted soon. But he's not interested.

He says, "I don't feel like it."

"Why?" I ask.

"Well, you've got to steam off your stripes," he says, "and then sew on new ones."

Well, that's how I live in this not-leaving. Oh well, I don't really need to go.

Only every morning I run to the mail box so that I won't miss a summons from the police.

And here in the studio something's come up. Our Fabritsius, our van Brauver, contracted with a gallery in Amsterdam to exhibit our little fraternity. Now, the pictures have to get there, but there's no one to take them. Sashka Konyakin is grinding flour for matzoh: Passover's right around the corner, it's his busiest season. And Fabritsius is busy giving out kerchiefs to the ladies at his post by the Western Wall and can't get away either.

So, well, they say to me, "Why don't you go, Raya? Why don't you take the pictures? We'll all chip in for your expenses and tell you what to do."

That was all I needed. How many times had I told myself I don't care, I have no plans to go anywhere? And now the least mention and I feel like I'm going to die, I want to go to Amsterdam so bad. I feel like Amsterdam is exactly where I've been wanting to go since my childhood.

I tell them, all well and good. I'm always ready to lend you my friendly padded shoulder, muzhiks, but at the present moment I'm on the books at the police over a little matter of some stolen diamonds. Well, I told them about the old bitch.

My artists were literally blown away. They got on my case and swore at me for not telling them. I have a lifelong rule, I reply, never to owe anybody anything. You usually sleep much better that way.

Avi Cohen actually grimaced at this story, as if he'd bit into something sour. "Visa-shmiza," he says, in Hebrew, of course: *Eize shtuyot!*[73]

He went to the police with me and sat in the supervisor's office for a long time. And I don't know whether he signed some guarantee, but they gave me a three-day pass.

---

73. *Eize shtuyot:* What nonsense!

Avi and I came out on Yaffo Street and we each bought a shvarma.[74] The sun was shining, the crowd was bustling, it felt so good. And he tells me, he says, "It's nothing, Raya, you see? B'Yisrael is just like home, and the main thing you have to know is that there's always somewhere b'Yisrael where people will take care of you."

"You know," he says, "maybe that old lady's crazy. Maybe her grandson's been poking around in boxes and she thought it was you?"

"You know," I tell him, "I wish she and her grandson would just take their boxes and their crazy ideas and go away."

Avi finishes his shvarma and says: "*Az anakhnu mamshikhim.*"

Do I really have to say something about Amsterdam? What's there to say, anyway? I walked around there for three days thinking about Fabritsius van Brauver the whole time. That's how it is, I think, when a man's fate whisks him away. And I tried to picture our flying Dutchman by the Western Wall handing out kerchiefs to the ladies.[75]

What's bad was my English had rotted away. I want to say literally two or three sentences worthy of a human being and flick-flick . . . all of a sudden my Hebrew becomes very strong. The main thing is you get unconsciously irritated at whoever you're talking to: there he is, see, the stupid jerk, flapping his gums, and not a word in ancient Hebrew.

I earned my pay and collected the money for the guys. The gallery owner bought three pictures right away and took five more on commission. I had to take the other four back with me.

I order a taxi to the airport. A Dutchman comes—he smells good, of cologne. He's very elegant. "Excuse me," I say in English. "These pictures I have probably won't fit in the trunk." "Oh," he says, "nonsense. Don't worry, miss!" He takes the pictures back to the trunk, which won't shut, so he gets out a hook of some kind from somewhere and latches it on, secures it, gets in, and we're off. All very quick, precise, and elegant, the foreign snakes.

I tumble out of the plane at Ben Gurion Airport at two in the morning with all my gizmos—paintings, suitcase. I rush over to a shuttlecab:

"How much to Jerusalem?"

The string bean standing there, a gold chain around his neck, is chewing gum and looking at something far away.

---

74. *Shvarma:* Meat-on-a-spit in pita.

75. *Handing out kerchiefs:* Women who pray at the Wall are expected by Orthodox Jewish tradition to cover their heads.

"A hundred shekels."

"What?" I ask. "A hundred shekels flat? For that kind of money I could take that private taxi over there all the way to my house!"

He stops chewing. His face turns to stone and he spits the gum out to one side.

"What?!" he shouts. "A hundred shekels for a taxi to Jerusalem? Come on, show me who's going to take you for that kind of money! I'll give him a hundred shekels myself if he says he'll do it! Get in and don't give me a hard time!"

"Twenty," I say.

"Listen up, you nutty Russian! Eighty and let's go!"

"Twenty," I say.

"Are you making fun of me? Do you think you're back in Russia? Sixty, and say thank you!"

I get in his car. We wait for more passengers, but there aren't any. Ten, twenty minutes. I jump out and scream, "That's it! I'm taking a taxi. There's an empty one waiting."

He grabs me by the arm and shouts:

"You're quitting on me?! Me—a Jerusalemite—you're quitting on me! You want to let that stinking Tel Avivi make the money!"

He points his finger skyward and says with passion:

"Listen to me! The planes are in the air! They're going to be here soon. All the people. Those are our passengers. Get it? Sit still and wait!"

I'm so tired and drained after everything that I don't even notice I've fallen asleep. As I open my eyes it's already growing light and we're sailing over a cloverleaf into Jerusalem. On the left, Ramot spreads out in circles and rocks as if it were under the wing of an airplane.

I'm looking at the driver—Lord, how could I not have recognized him immediately! Of course! It's him—gold chain around the neck, just like they paint them in the Russian papers. We've driven up to my building, I'm getting sixty shekels out of my purse and putting change— three coins, thirty agorot—into his open hand.

He's taken aback: "What's all this?"

"Remember?" I said. "You made up thirty agorot for me in the supermarket. I'm a well-off person and I don't like to owe anything to anyone. That's my lifelong rule."

"Oh," he says. "So it's you? I didn't recognize you."

He helps me drag out the pictures and carry them up to the third floor. He's standing there watching me unlock my door.

"Listen," he says. "Since all that happened, how about inviting me in for a cup of coffee?"

"Oh no," I say. "I have no intention of feeding your local folklore with a story about Russian prostitutes."

Well, he starts going down the stairs, very slowly. On the lower landing he stops and watches me drag the pictures into my apartment.

It's that Sashka Konyakin of ours who works big, whereas Fabritsius—he's just the opposite, like the minor Dutch painters.

Yes . . . He stands on the landing and looks up at me. I've forgotten the last time someone looked at me like that.

All in all, I'm only thirty-nine, and I guess I've still got my figure. But I feel like I'm three hundred and eighty. I was a student back in the age of blotting paper. A little while ago a student sociologist stops me on the street. "We're conducting a flash opinion poll by age groups," he says. "What group do you belong to, the fifty to sixty group or the sixty to seventy group?"

"I belong to the one hundred to one hundred and twenty group," I say.

And I look at his silken cheeks.

Well, he doesn't get humor at that level. He says, "Nut," and walks away.

So you can look at me or not, it has no effect on me. I am not an emotional person at bottom. You usually sleep much better that way. I bring the pictures into the apartment and shut the door.

In the evening Sergeant comes home from the army, and we're sitting, drinking tea with Dutch candies. And all he can say is, "Come on, tell me! Tell me about Amsterdam!"

"Well," I say, "there are houses that look like a drunken model builder cut them out with scissors and glued them together."

"Would you like to live there?" he asks.

I don't say anything. I'm thinking—tomorrow I have to stop by the police station and report that I'm back or else they'll lock me up and throw away the key.

But Sergeant, well, he's like a kid. "And where," he asks, "where would you like to live?"

When you come right down to it, I've already lived my fill. It doesn't matter to me where I live.

But I have Sergeant. . . . And it matters to him.

Az anakhnu mamshikhim!

(1994)
—*Translated by Marian Schwartz*

Rough Casting

Elena Makarova

His father's on Corsica, and his father's relatives are mafiosi; in her letter from Kiev, his mother forbid him, absolutely once and for all, to contact his father, who would only get him mixed up with the mafia, who would use him and then kill him; he can't go to his grandma in America because of his new "motherland's" restrictions—what if this skinny Jew stays there too, never comes back—so he stays put in Israel, carries his lanky body to Jewish sacred sites and to the Judean desert; drinks tea with the Bedouin; acts as his own oral surgeon and treats his own infected gums; offers the girls he knows one long-stemmed rose apiece. He uses his own secret formula to remove mildew from inside the walls of houses, plasters and whitewashes them, cleans up the five-square-meter art studio of a disabled painter from Poland; and he never speaks a word in any of the languages he knows. What's there to talk about?

In Kiev, when he was sixteen, he made up a story; if they'd only made a movie about it then.

Okay, don't torture me, what's the story?

Ah, later, some other time. . . . His awkward height and thin body make him stoop; he's uncomfortable sticking out on a crosswalk like an oversize wick in the crowd, while they wait for the light to turn green; he has large eyes and a big mouth, long hair tied up with a drugstore rubber band, and a long neck whose Adam's apple protrudes. Quiet, modest, in Jerusalem he looks a tourist attraction, the site of the Ascension on the Mount of Olives.[76]

You know, he says after lengthy reflection, the ancient reliefs . . . the limestone . . . —and then his glance sails away somewhere.

We are walking along. It's stuffy; the sun is burning, swallowing up the stones' color and the wild herbs; only the sky's blueness somehow preserves crystals of azure. Monastery of the Cross, constructed with feeling, is to the right; the author of *Tiger Skin Knight*[77] sleeps somewhere within its entrails though that doesn't make the monastery striped; it is monochromatic, small, stolid; shall we stop there?

No, he has a plan of his own, or else he has no plan at all, visiting the monastery is not part of it; we are just walking, with no goal or direction.

One day it will all be over . . .

What "it"?

We have to make a mold of everything; there's a material we can use—a thin layer of plastic, and fixative . . .

To make a casting of the whole world?!

He nods seriously, a deep, grateful, nod of consent. The vertebrae of his neck click.

Or else everything will perish . . .

What would happen if one could make a casting of all the landmarks; where would one keep such gigantic shells; who would pour the plaster (or I don't know what) into them later, to get a copy of the original?

Look, he says, do you see the remains of an ancient relief here?

No.

That's right, because they never cast it. . . . Time levelled it all. . . .

---

76. Jesus is believed to have ascended to heaven from the Mount of Olives, whose highest building is a Russian church.

77. The Monastery of the Cross, in Jerusalem's Valley of the Cross, belongs to the Greek Orthodox Church. According to Christian tradition, the valley was the site where the tree used for the crucifixion of Jesus was prepared. The Monastery belonged to the Georgians in the Middle Ages; the Georgian poet, Shota Rustaveli, lived there in the thirteenth century and wrote his epic *Tiger Skin Knight* (in other translations *Panther Skin*) there. This medieval poem, which glorifies love and friendship, honor and devotion, was translated into Russian and other languages, becoming an inseparable part of the cultural heritage cherished in the multiethnic Russian Empire. Streets and avenues in many cities of the former Soviet Union still bear the name of Shota Rustaveli.

The rumor is he's not quite all there. That I am naive to take him seriously. That he abandoned his wife and children. That he's got a girlfriend in every city. And gives every one of them a gift of a long-stemmed rose. What do I care? I have a husband, and a baby, and I barely understand Russian. . . .

What I do understand ages me.

A lizard sneaks out from under a stone; he stoops and spreads his giant hand over it. The lizard freezes under the five-fingered shade.

We should start with small reliefs. . . . Launch our own business.

He laughs and hugs me. I am no taller than his waistline. And this is the way we walk on, a tall one and a short one, both wondering how to start a business, how to begin, how. We should write a proposal about the need to preserve architectural landmarks which otherwise the heat will destroy. Which will lose their shape and turn into this dumb limestone that lizards sneak out of. . . . It's serious.

Really, he agrees. We'll start today.

The heat has knocked us out. We lie under a stubby olive tree, his green felt hat over his face. He's either sleeping or concocting schemes . . . I'm thirsty. There's a plastic bottle of warm water in his bag. I take a sip and when my mouth is full, I spit the water at him.

He sits up and rubs his eyes with his fists. It dawns on him that he should take me to a place I've never been before, even though I grew up in Jerusalem. It's not more than about seven kilometers from here, but he won't tell me where we're going until I agree to admit I've never been there, even though I was born and raised in this city. I admit it. But how can we get there in such heat, on Shabbat . . .[78]

It's magic!

He takes a white handkerchief out of his pocket, wets it with water from the bottle, puts it on my head. He laughs, plops his green felt hat on my head, and puts the handkerchief on his own. We must look ridiculous, but in this heat it's better for me to cover my head so the sun won't bake me as much.

We buy plums, pitas, and bottles of water in a small Arab shop. The road winds, revealing the steep spurs of cyprus groves, suites of olive trees, an ancient theater where the squat olives don't even glance up to look at our civilization—the concrete highway, multicolored cars, intersections with traffic lights . . .

What kind of movie did he want to shoot?

---

78. That is, when there is no public transportation.

About an artist.

Tell me.

It's stupid. Besides, how could it be translated into Hebrew? But he'll try. This is the way it goes: an artist used to create paintings that he signed either as Chagall, or Klee, or Dali. He kept the paintings in his basement. One day a stranger arrived and saw them. The painter disappeared. The stranger snuck into the basement, grabbed all the works and took them to a museum. The paintings were attributed to famous artists. The stranger grew pretty rich. As for the artist, he was wandering around somewhere and one day, he saw his own painting in a famous gallery hanging alongside Dali originals. Oh, he thought, then I can sign my own name to my paintings. He went back to the basement, signed a lot of paintings with his own name, found the stranger and offered to let him serve as his agent. But not a single painting sold . . .

And how does it end, I ask after a long pause.

As usual, nothing happens . . .

If there's no ending, the movie will never be made.

That's why I never wrote it down. Why should I?

And what about the cast . . . ? It has no cast.

He stops and looks at me with the anguish of a camel. Why a camel? Camels eat prickles. . . . Why did I prick him? It happened on a viewing point overlooking Hadassah Hospital. . . .[79] If instead of facing the city, one looks at the terraces of the curling hills, at the ancient colorless stones—the air over the valley is pure, not as burnt by the sun as the city is—then you can make out everything from here, even flocks of grazing sheep, and they're so far away. . . .

Are we going there?

No. Today, we'll probably not go that far. I'm tired.

But I long to get there. Why don't we rest in the hospital? He refuses. He hates the smell of hospitals. I reassure him that our hospitals don't smell anything like that; the lobby is cool and quiet. No, no, all hospitals smell the same way.

We go a couple of terraces lower, closer to the shade, and there in front of us is the hospital's garbage dump. I see his jaws clench and cheekbones move. He's angry. The angry ones frighten me.

I laugh and shuffle him; I put the hat on his head, but he doesn't look at me. He stares at the dump, his nostrils dilated, his pupils huge

---

79. Hadassah Hospital is on a hill overlooking the valley of Ein Kerem, on the outskirts of Jerusalem.

as if from atropine. Suddenly he runs up and attacks the pile of garbage, kicking around the broken chairs with the toe of his boot. . . .

Maybe everyone's right; I barely know him, I romanticize him, and he can become so full of rage that his wife and children left him. . . . But he's angry at the garbage, not at me. . . .

I call him, and he keeps pushing the trash down the hill—iron bed frames, broken night tables, metal lathes, who knows what else. . . . I'm afraid to get close to him, he might throw me down, too. I make a decision. I'll leave. He doesn't follow me. Maybe the hospital is where he was going to take me? But I've already been here, more than once. I had an appendectomy here, I was in labor here. Have I seen this dump before? I never noticed it. If you set your mind to it, all you'll ever see anywhere are dumps; well, go ahead, dig them out! Weren't there dirty streets in Kiev? If everything was so great there, why come here at all? To show us right and wrong?

I promise myself I won't turn back, but I do. Where is he? Not there. Did he fall down into the ravine together with the garbage? Is he lying there, hurt?

I run back. He's nowhere. I call out. He doesn't respond. At the bottom of the ravine, iron frames stick out of the greenery.

What's going on? Is this where he wanted to take me, is this what I have never seen, though I lived all my life in Jerusalem? Should I go down, fall on the protruding iron bars, plummet to the depth of the ravine after him? Should I call for help? What if he's simply run away because I keep calling him up, it's me who keeps calling him, he never calls me. There is no he. He's never existed. Killed on Corsica. His father got him involved with the mafia and they've done him in. Why does he need to make a mold?

My head whirls, I get more and more frightened. How can I walk back from here alone? I'll take a cab, pay when I get home; what will I tell my husband?

I turn around. Suddenly, he's walking from Hadassah smiling and raising his arms. Maybe they're true, the things people write in books about Russians? But he's Jewish, isn't he?

He sits down at my side, hugs me, and says—We're going there. He points down the hill, below Hadassah.

And what if there's another dump on the way?

He shrugs his shoulders and smiles mysteriously. —Look, it's lovely now, isn't it?

Yes, it's lovely.

And nothing's in the way.

It's true, nothing's in the way.

He strokes my back. I am still shaking with fear. He takes the washed plums out of his bag, he must have gone to the hospital to wash the fruit and to put some water in the bottle. We eat pitas and plums, we drink the water.

And again we are walking along, the tall one and the short one, yet this time we don't dodge along the highway with a white line painted in the middle, we walk down the quiet road into the valley, to a panoramic view of a village with villas, vineyards, roses; it appears abruptly after one of the turns. I have seen this little town on a hill before, with its buildings of white stone covered with greenery. This is a *moshav*—wealthy Israelis.

Is this where we're going?

He shakes his head, No, no. There is nothing to cast in a mold here.

There is one street in the village with villas on both sides. A sleepy man in shorts hanging under his belly is fixing a red car. He salutes us, waving a wrench. Shabbat Shalom! He must be thinking that we're a couple about to be married, we are walking so closely together.

A few steps away from the red car there are stables where one lonely white horse wanders purposelessly behind the gates.

He also signed the works with his own name.

What?

Well, I told you about the artist. Here he is.

The horse comes up to the hedge, puts soft lips into his hand. He gives him a plum from the white sack. Is this where he wanted to take me, to his lonely friend?

This is a pureblood breeding horse, and this car-owner uses him at races.

How do you know?

He makes money off him. That's how he bought the car. And built the villa.

Is that how you think everybody here gets rich?

I don't know, he laughs, throws up his hat and catches it, I don't know. . . . Maybe—he points toward the man—he has mildew to get rid of. Should we ask?

We go back and ask the man whether he or somebody else in the *moshav* would like us to remove mildew from their house, the fungus can cause so many diseases. . . .

No, neither he nor anybody else here has mildew.

It's a shame, he sighs, the rich don't have mildew, and the poor can't pay. I should switch to casting molds before the whole world falls apart.

It is all pure delusion, he thinks; how can he hang on, not give up. . . . He should paint a picture for her, so she can better understand what he means . . . by the word "delusion". . . . He should switch to rock painting. There are so many rocks here. . . . And these ugly shapeless ocherish creations can't possibly be ruined any further. But one never knows. Should he leave for Corsica? On the white horse? Oh, they'd look great together: he dressed up in white riding a white horse.

On the other side of the town a gravel road branches off the concrete highway; it descends sharply, and now they're running along. He's full of joy, waving his hat, talking to himself in Russian. When he speaks to her in Russian, he usually repeats every word, so at least she'll remember something. But now he's speaking freely, one can see how good he's feeling and what a hurry he's in to get there. Where?

The road grows steeper and steeper as they go down; to the left, behind the hedge, are vineyards. A blue door is in front of them. It's closed. To the left are that hedge and the vineyards, to the right of the blue door there's another precipice, a ravine; the *wadi,* as they call it here, with cypresses, olive trees, flocks of sheep.

He rings the bell, there's a low sound heard somewhere deep within. He rings the bell again, the same low sound.

Nobody.

Nobody's there, she says.

There's a spirit there.

What?

A spirit.

Someone you know?

He nods blissfully.

Does it have a big house?

He shakes his head, his hands make an outline—a small one.

Does he really think that I don't understand where he's brought me. It's true, I've never been here. My parents, born in Poland, would never let me step over the threshold of a church. But I'm grown now, though still short; I have a husband and a child.

No one's here, let's go.

Yes, there is!

I better not irritate him, or he'll carry on the way he did at the dump.

The door opens suddenly, a tall monk in habit and cowl greets him cheerfully and extends his hand first to me, then to him; he lets us lead the way and the three of us go along a fragrant lane of roses. We've arrived during the service, so we have to wait, about half an hour, and then we'll talk over coffee. The monk leaves us, opens another door at the end of the lane with his key, and disappears behind it.

There's a little garden behind the door, with stone-cut white benches and a table in the middle. I sit down to rest, but he takes me by the hand and leads me down the narrow winding stone staircase cut into the rock. There's a fish pond at the bottom; on the side, deep under a stone the dampness has turned green and there's a gutter, where the water leaks by. The monotonous music of the water, slow, regular, is the only sound disturbing the quiet there. No, not completely; once you get used to the quiet and the flowing water, you begin to hear the cars, too; they're there, on the other side of the *wadi,* on the highway.

Just imagine, when there was nothing, nothing, he whispers, and on this side, only our monastery up here, in the rock. . . .

Our monastery!

The thick green of the water. The gold fish.

Isn't this algae?—I have squeezed myself under the stone vault and am washing my face with water from the gutter.

He thinks it over. What if we try my formula here? We should talk to Basilique.

That monk?

Yes. His name is Basilique. I call him Vasily in Russian.

Is he from Russia too?

From France.

He's handsome. Really handsome.

He smiles, here, look where I've brought you and who I've shown you. This is the very best I have.

If one ignores the surroundings—the valley, the cypresses, the palm trees, and looks only into the thick green water—it looks like Russia to him now. The thick opaque green.

He takes her to the steps again, this time up the stairs, to an opening behind a white curtain. There's a plaque engraved in languages he cannot read. But she can. She reads and is surprised. That's what he expected, her surprise.

In the semi-darkness of the low deep cave, a lamp is lit under the icon. Some big bottles of a yellowish liquid and two wicker stools stand there.

They sit opposite one another and, obediently, keep silent in the coolness.

He thinks about removing the mildew, about a patent for a formula against mildew, about the casting—there are so many valuable things here that time will destroy. . . . How absurd it is, he thinks, first he becomes a yarmulke-wearing Jew, then he comes here to the monastery, surrenders. . . .

And she, closing her eyes, keeps seeing the dump, the precipice. . . . If she looks at his happy face, everything is fine; if she closes her eyes . . . the iron bars, the beams. . . .

She goes out, out of the cave, into the bright light. It reminds her of the south of France, a kind of picture—the blue sky, the tall palms, the steps, the fish pond; only instead of the sea, the rocky *wadi* is in the background.

Basilique stands there watching her kindly. He has appeared in front of her suddenly, a tall handsome monk, smiling at her, baring his mouth, full of teeth that huddle together out of order like tombstones in an old Jewish cemetery. He raises the curtain and, bending, enters the cave.

What are they talking about? She doesn't even listen. The mildew business?

Then both of them emerge; even Basilique is shorter than he; he has a felt hat, and Basilique has a cowl, an artist and a priest, like a scene from Dostoevsky. But his face is so Jewish. And what was Christ's?

Basilique unlocks the door. We walk along a narrow dark corridor— that's where the mildew is!—to another door; he unlocks it, too, and again we get into a zone of bright light; from there—to a church, with soft light from the narrow windows which look out onto the *wadi*. The landscape, broken into fragments by the narrow windows (a window— a pause, a window—a pause), does not make a whole picture. You can see the panorama from each window, but if you look through all the windows at once, the view is split, scattered.

It's a humble little church with some country-style icons, icon lamps, and a sweet scent. Basilique is glad that folks of a different faith have dropped by, that we seem to like it here, or else he may just feel lonely without visitors.

There are four monks here, he explains, and they take care of every-thing, the service, the garden, the order, quite a bit of work to do.

This is the right time, I think, to mention the patent for removing the mildew fungus.

But he is looking at an icon, his face nears it, his neck turning with a strange twist.

This should be restored, he is saying, or else the mildew will spread.

We do the restorations, all by ourselves, little by little, as you can imagine. The congregation is not big. . . .

Well, he is unlikely to go for it. Try to sell him the idea of casting a mold, I am thinking.

We leave the church and go back to the lane of roses.

What about coffee?

Hold on, I'll be right back.

Basilique disappears and shows up with a little bowl in his hand. He opens an unobtrusive door in the rock for us, and we descend into a spacious clean room. It's a little kitchen; Basilique starts making the coffee right away; he cooks, conjures over the stove, and the spicy smell sneaks upon the two of us sitting at the big oval table made of solid wood. There is one window in the room with the same view of the *wadi*, the hills, the cypresses, the olive trees . . .

Basilique, are you from the south of France?

Yes, yes, he calls back as he stirs the coffee. A bowl of cookies sprinkled with cinnamon is on the table. Basilique brings in a tray with a coffee pot, cups, saucers, spoons; he serves. He thinks a little, goes back to the kitchen, brings out a bowl of sugar. He pours the coffee himself into the cups and sits down.

Help yourselves!

He asks me what I do for a living, laments the negligence of some Israelis—they built a chicken farm next to the monastery, have you seen it over there on the slope?

No, we haven't. We saw a horse.

A horse . . . he repeats . . . a horse would be okay, but a chicken farm. . . . The smell, the dirt . . .

Basilique's face is distorted by a grimace. For a moment. He sips his coffee. Once, about six years ago, some hooligans with "revolutionary" ideas raided us; they wanted to kill all of us, and who is there to kill, just a couple of men, if any at all. . . . Our prior went out to talk to them; he's tall, like you, but husky, and drew them away. Since then we've kept the gates locked, and we're ordered to keep everything closed. It's so unpleasant, we have to go around with a key locking-unlocking things all the time. . . . Sometimes the Israelis come here on Shabbat . . . They litter; they dress immodestly . . . I beg your pardon, not everybody is like that. Take, for example, the Russian Jews, they respect us. If not our faith, then the beauty and purity of these places. . . .

I have patented a formula. . . .

For what?

Removing mildew, the fungus on the walls. . . .

Basilique looks at him as if he has really invented some kind of magic. Wow, what is it? It's nearly impossible to cope with, isn't it?

Well, I have a patent. . . .

I'd like to learn more about it.

Some other time, perhaps. . . . I'll bring the formula and we'll try it in a corner, to begin with. . . .

Is it expensive?

He smiles. Why should you care? It's no sooner said than done.

Business Russian-style, I think. He'll never earn enough even for child support this way.

And if I come here with the formula, will I have a place to stay overnight? I sometimes have problems. . . .

Why not there, Basilique points to a room behind the one we're sitting in. I'll notify the prior. He's tolerant of different faiths. He would be only glad. If you are not upset.

By what?

By our religious beliefs.

But I'm not . . .

An agnostic?

The mildew . . . has nothing to do with it.

It's true, laughs Basilique, not all creations are beautiful. . . .

I am having coffee with a monk and a Russian Jew, and I keep silent. What if it's the devil that lured me to him, what then? Well, I'm not doing anything forbidden, we're just friends, I just walk around town with him. And it's me who keeps following him. . . .

They've both stopped talking and are looking at me. Were they talking about me while I was thinking to myself? They're both serene, no fidgeting, no nervous gestures, but as for me, I scrape my forehead, I scratch my cheek with my nails, I don't know what to do with my hands.

Basilique talks about his recent pilgrimage to Sinai, shows us the illustrations in a book; there, on the summit, is a hut for four, I stayed overnight, watched the sunrise. . . .

He tells Basilique about his idea for casting molds; there's no need to make copies of landmarks, one could cast a rough mold, and after the original is destroyed, you could put together a crude form, cast it, have it back.

Basilique accepts this idea condescendingly; it's not so easy, he says, some things matter only at a particular time. . . .

Those won't be cast, he agrees heatedly.

And who decides what matters and what doesn't?

What do you mean, let everything perish?

I wouldn't say that. There are sophisticated books, modern ones, where philosophers try to define to what extent a person has the right to interfere with the course of history, and at what point one is supposed to say "Stop."

Have such books been written?

Yes, it's all been written. And will be written. I like reading such books before going to bed. Sometimes, when I like something in particular, I copy it on a beautiful sheet of paper, match it with an ornament . . . like the one over there, on the wall.

It's true, there's a page of a French text hanging on the wall, ornamented with flowers, and I interrupt and say it's a Jewish tradition, only we use letters to illuminate the text too.

What's to be done, Basilique says raising his hands, I've been living here for eight years now, surrounded. . . . He laughs; what a row of teeth he has, a mouthful, all askew. Seriously, this is where we come from— he points to the window—everything's legitimate.

We're silent. Basilique offers us more coffee. But I stand up, interpreting the indecisive motion of Basilique's hand toward the coffee pot as a sign that it's time to go.

Come again and bring the formula, we'll try it. I would be obliged, yes.

Do people come here a lot, I ask.

They do, they come. . . . But I don't speak to everyone. Talking to people is work, quite an endeavor; sometimes it's easier to scrub floors in silence all day long than to exchange a word with someone.

Basilique walks us to the blue gate. He asks where we left our car.

On the hill.

You could have driven right here, Basilique laments, to walk up the hill in such heat!

We shake hands.

We leave without turning back.

I ask him why he lied about the car.

So Basilique wouldn't worry. He'll be thinking about us, what, when, how.

But if we said we have a car . . .

He doesn't care whether we have one or not.

Then why lie?

Chill out, he says sharply.

Really, why am I pestering him?

I take his words seriously—go away, don't bother me.

We walk wordlessly along the wall with the vines. He takes big steps—one of his is several of mine—we pass the turn and see the chicken farm, the hens in the cages, the stench, droppings everywhere.

Here it comes. This is the wrong road, the horse should be here and not the hens, the huge wire-mesh coop. How did we get here?

He walks slowly along the railing, very close to it; he watches the hens silently, the cocks, the chickens, he barely moves, is he counting them or what?

He comes up to me, hugs me. Look, he's almost crying! Who is he sorry for now, the birds about to be slaughtered, the monks suffering from the filth and stench?

I keep prodding him, demanding that he explain who exactly he's so sorry for. He shakes his head, slams his hat on my head, and walks past me.

What's upsetting him? That I'm trying to understand him? Or that I'm going home now, and he'll be moving from one friend's house to another's, and I'll be asking them who knows where he is now and nobody will give me any hint?

Could you settle down in the monastery?

He shrugs his shoulders. What's it got to do with me?

But do you like it there?

Yes.

Then why not?

Don't send me to boarding school, I'm not a little boy, he says either jokingly, or in earnest, I can't tell which.

It would be better not to talk now. So we keep silent all along the road, and we no longer embrace as we walk—the heat lessens little by little, but our feet are sore, we climb up and up the hill, up the hill to Hadassah, along the serpentine road, and cars dash by us at high speeds, and the air smells of gasoline, and it gets worse as we near the city, maybe we should wait till sunset when the buses start up again? I drag myself behind him without understanding what's happened, why is it so hard now, is it because of the steep ascent? The lights of the valley go on, darkness falls upon Jerusalem, and now the headlights of the approaching cars hit us, and many-many lights blink, and the valley air shivers with the blinking.

Maybe everything is intensified because of the dusk. . . . I remember the color of the water in the fish pond, and Basilique smiling at me the moment I came out of the cave and he was standing there.

I come up to him and cling to his side. He looks at me kindly, places his hand on my shoulder. That is how we enter the city.

My home is not far from here. I live behind the central bus station. Where is he going?

A siren marks the end of Shabbat. Jews in yarmulkes, wives with flocks of dressed-up children, soldiers—men and women—all our diverse population together at bus stops. The buses will come soon.

On the corner of my street he takes his hat off me, pecks me on the top of my head, says he's sorry there are no flowers nearby, he owes me a rose, and leaves.

Months have passed, but I haven't been able to find him anywhere. Once I persuaded my school girlfriend to give me a lift to the monastery, and wait in the car on top of the hill, while I ran down there for just a second.

I ran by the horse in the pen; I didn't notice the chicken farm, I was even worried I was running the wrong way, and then I saw the blue door and stood in front of it for a long time, afraid to ring the bell. Finally, I pulled myself together and rang it. Nobody will open it, I thought again, and then a monk I didn't know opened the door. I asked about Basilique. Basilique has left for Sinai with some Russian man; I asked if he was tall, with hair tied up by a rubber band, the monk said, yes-yes, that's him. I asked if I could leave a message, he said okay, I hurriedly left only my name and phone number.

He called soon after and told me that the mildew formula worked well. He had found a job in Tel Aviv doing repairs and was going to live there for the time being. He grew silent, either thinking to himself, or looking for the right words in Hebrew. Then he asked me about my son's health, probably sensing that my husband was near me.

Where was he calling from? From a pay phone? From somebody's apartment? From the monastery? I'd have rushed to him without thinking, but I was afraid to ask.

He had once spoken about delusion. Maybe delusion is what's happening to me. Now I, too, would like to cast a mold of everything around, but when I mentioned it to my husband, he had a good laugh; so these days I turn to memories not of casting molds or fighting mildew, but of how fierce he was throwing the garbage down the ravine.

He can't be missed in the Jerusalem crowds, from far off he sticks out like an oversized wick, so whenever I go out for a walk with my son, I sometimes get distracted and glance around, though I know he's in Tel Aviv now. My son doesn't like it; he wants me to belong to him exclusively, and I usually try to pay attention to the questions he pours at me while we walk, but I still lose myself in reverie, and then he frets and pulls at the side of my pants to wake me out of it.

Sometimes I wonder about going to talk to Basilique. What if I just sat silently in the cave?

But I wouldn't be able to walk there on my own, alone.

(1995)
—*Translated by Marina Bereznyak with Miriyam Glazer*

Part II

Poetry

Yona Volach: In Memoriam

Any collection of Israeli women's literature would be inconceivable with-out the work of the late Yona Volach. Born in 1944, Volach became one of Israel's most original voices; in its use of language, tone, and in its content, her poetry is groundbreaking. No other Israeli woman—or man, for that matter—spoke with Volach's kind of boldness. Her work is at once psychologically and spiritually complex, alternately witty, subtle, intensely self-aware, flamboyant, provocative, satiric, startling, and ten-der. Her poems dig into the nuances of identity, emotion, religion, sexu-ality, and sensuality, often responding to the religious and poetic traditions. They play with language and, by doing so undermine gender stereotypes:

> *again you slept with mr no man*
> *you liked his empty look*
> *and you hugged his no body . . .*
>
> *he came out of the old poems he's one of their heroes. . . .*

Her 1983 collection, *Wild Light*, probes civic, religious, familial, and theological expressions of patriarchal authority in poems such as "When You Come Sleep with Me, Come like a Judge," "When You Come Sleep with Me, Come Like God," as well as two included here, "When You Come Sleep with Me, Come Like My Father," and "Tefillin." Her other books are *Things* (1966), *Two Gardens* (1969), *Collected Poems* (1976), *Forms* (1985), *Appearance* (1985), and the posthumous *Selected Poems 1963–1985* (1992), published by Hakibbutz Hameuchad. Translations of her earlier work appear in *Burning Air and a Clear Mind: Contemporary*

243

Israeli Women Poets, ed. Myra (Miriyam) Glazer (Ohio University Press, 1981), among other collections.

Born in a suburb of Tel Aviv, Volach was active in the circle of "Tel Aviv poets" emerging around the journals *Achshav* and *Siman Kriah* in the 1960s. She wrote frequently for Israeli literary periodicals. She wrote for and appeared with an Israeli rock group and in 1982 her poetry was set to music and a record released. After a long illness, she died in 1985. Two very moving poems in Dahlia Ravikovich's collection *Real Love* (1987) speak to the powerful legacy of Volach's death.

Hebrew

Yona Volach

English has all the sexual options
Every I is really
every possible sex
and every *(feminine)* you is *(masculine)* you
and every I is sexless
and there's no difference between *(feminine)* you and *(masculine)* you
and everything is that way—neither man nor woman
and no need to relate to sex at all.

But Hebrew is a sex-maniac
Hebrew discriminates, for better or worse
She begrudges plays favorites
keeps accounts longer than the Exile[80]
in the plural, right of way subtly,
secretly,

The poem explores—and plays with—the fact that Hebrew is a gendered language. Where Volach uses a pronoun such as "you," for example, I have indicated in parentheses whether she's used the masculine or the feminine (or the singular or the plural) in the original Hebrew.

80. That is, the dispersion of the Jews after the fall of the Second Temple in Jerusalem in 70 C.E.

goes to the masculine "they"
chances are equal in the singular, so
who says it's a lost case?

Hebrew is a sex-maniac
She wants to know who's speaking
whose image whose picture
exactly what the whole Torah forbids:
looking at sex
Hebrew peeks through a keyhole
like the way I peek at your mother and you
when you *(plural)* bathed in the cabin
your mother had a big ass
but I never thought of it
the days passed like invisible ink
you stayed a girl, thin and soapy,

later you both blocked up the holes
closed up the cracks
But Hebrew peeks through the keyhole
the language sees you naked

My father wouldn't let me watch
he turned his back when he peed
I never had a really good look at him
he always hid his sex
just like "they" *(masculine)* hides women
like "crowd" is third-person male
"Word" is male and female[81]
Nothing is as sweet as these things.

Hebrew is a woman bathing
A clean Bathsheba
An ineradicable sculpture
with stretch-marks and little dimples
that become more beautiful
as she grows older.
Sometimes her judgment is prehistoric
but a neurosis like that is for the good

---

81. The word *Word* in Hebrew has a feminine ending in the singular, and a masculine
ending in the plural; it is grammatically treated as feminine.

Tell me in the masculine tell me in the feminine
every immature I is an unfertilized egg
sex can be omitted
sex can be given up
Who can tell the sex of a chick?
Only the man nature creates
before implanting with a conjugating verb.

Memory,
the creator of sexes,
is male,[82]
though what matters is generation *(female)*
And Generation is life.

Hebrew is a sex-maniac
What feminists complain about
In authoritative tones,
searching for stimulation outside language
are actually just male and female signs in a sentence
queer sexual relations

Every female has a sign, every male
a different sign
Every verb and conjugation signed
What a man does to a woman
what he receives in return
her power over him
the sign given the body of language
copulatives possessives

Let's consider sex a game of nature
a soul stirring like a young forest
Nature's power play with particulars
of universal natural forces
that might occur, someday

Look what a body language has,
look at what features
I can love her now without
hiding my tongue

(1985)
—*Translated by Miriyam Glazer*

---

82. That is, the word *memory* in Hebrew is male.

I Have a Stage in My Head

Yona Volach

I have a stage in my head
realer than any stage
and when I step down
I'm in the pits.
I have a whole theatre in my head
with me as the hero
and when I turn off the light
I've had it
When I stop acting
my life stops
and when I bring down the curtain
behind my lashes
all my friends
my lovers
are lost.
My memories
my colors
my charms
arrive panicked—
my terrors
My corpse
My shame

(1985)
—*Translated by Miriyam Glazer*

Tefillin

Yona Volach

Come to me.
Don't let me do anything
you do it for me
you do it all for me
everything I even start doing
you do instead of me
I'll lay tefillin
I'll pray
you lay tefillin for me too
wind them around my hands
play them in me
pass them tenderly over my body
rub them into me good

"Put these words of Mine on your heart and on your soul, and bind them for a sign on your hand, and let them be for frontlets between your eyes," commands God in Deuteronomy 11:13–21. The wearing of *tefillin,* the ritual developed to fulfill that commandment, is laden with complex spiritual symbolism, particularly in the midrashic and mystical tradition. The *tefillin,* phylacteries, consist of black leather boxes containing passages from the Torah (Deut. 6:4–9 and 11:13–21; Exodus 13:1–10, 11–16), and are worn on the arm, opposite the heart, and on the head. The *Shel Yad*—for the arm—is threaded with a black leather strap which is tightened to hold fast to the arm, and wound seven times over the arm between the elbow and the wrist. The *Shel Rosh*—for the head—is then placed so that the knot which makes the loop surrounding the head rests on the base of the skull above the nape of the neck. Then the rest of the leather strap is wound around the middle finger and palm. At each stage, a blessing is recited. At the end, one of the "names" of God— *Shaddai*—is seen on the palm. The English expression for this ritual is "to lay tefillin."

249

excite me all over
make me swoon with sensation
pass them over my clitoris
tie them to my hips
so I'll come fast
play them inside me
tie up my hands and legs
do things to me
against my will
turn me over on my belly
put the tefillin in my mouth like reins
ride me—I'm a mare
yank my head back
till I shriek with pain
and you're satisfied
then I'll pass them over your body
with intention my face doesn't hide[83]
oh, what measureless cruelty on my face
I'll pass them over your body slow
slow slow slow
around your neck
I'll twist them a couple of times around your neck first
and then, on the other side, I'll tie them
to something stable
especially heavy maybe twisting
and pull pull
till your soul comes out
till I absolutely choke you
with tefillin
that stretch out the length of the stage
and into the stunned crowd.[84]

(1983)

—Translated by Aryeh Cohen with Miriyam Glazer

---

83. The Hebrew word *kavanah*, translated here as "intention," has layers of meaning. In colloquial Hebrew, it is used to mean simply "on purpose," "intentionally"; within the religious tradition, however, it implies spiritual focus, a depth of intentionality, in prayer.

84. Here, too, in the images of both the "stage" and the "crowd," the Hebrew has a resonance missing in English. *Bamah (Bimah)* means "stage" as in a theatrical setting—but also the raised platform from which prayers are recited in the synagogue. *Kahal* (crowd) also means "congregation." Is the final scene of the poem a theater, or a synagogue, or both?

When You Come Sleep with Me

Yona Volach

When you come and sleep with me
come like my father
come in the dark

speak in his voice
so I won't know it
I'll crawl on all fours
and talk about what I don't have
you'll scold me: "My clay"—
drop me at the gate
saying so long
a thousand times
with all the longings
there are
till God says, "Enough"
I'll let go
and won't sleep
not with God
or my father
I'll want to sleep with you
but you won't let me
along with my father
you'll suddenly be revealed

as the one in charge
of inhibitions
my father will be an angel
Commander of Troops
and you'll both try
to make something of me
I'll feel
like a nothing
and do anything
you tell me to do.
From one point-of-view
you'll be God
and I'll wait till later
and you won't be
the authority and me
just a loser
minding my manners
I'll cut you in two
myself too
part soul
part body
you'll look like two
me too
two seals
one dragging a flipper
bruised
or two women
one forever limping
and you with one face
and another
barely seen.

(1983)
—Translated by
Miriyam Glazer

The Life You Have

Yona Volach

The life you have—
it's the life you're living
look back with understanding
find the moment of genesis
of creation
create yourself
it's the best world
the only one
you could have created
all this is within you
expose it
begin at the beginning
look at your life
as a bad lesson
see what was
as punishment
a standing in the corner
a knockout in the first round
fix it
like one who's recuperating
like one who was sick.

(1985)
—*Translated by Miriyam Glazer*

Bird

Yona Volach

A single bird sang
but not her own song
a different song sang from her throat
her song a different song
the bird didn't recognize
didn't know it was a different song
a different someone speaking from her throat
she always thought it was her
at first she was scared
later on it
didn't matter
it wasn't serious, as what?
as if it were she
who flirted with everyone who went by
and lacked any identity at all
but she didn't connect with anyone
because she didn't have her voice
her voice broke free of her
and spoke from a different throat
which was also unaware
that another spoke from his throat
it didn't matter to him either
it wasn't serious

his voice broke free too
and spoke from a different throat
and so on
and so on
every voice
spoke from some
other throat
and no one
knew
whose

(1985)
—*Translated by Miriyam Glazer*

Dahlia Ravikovitch

Dahlia Ravikovitch has been considered one of the most important voices in Israeli poetry since the publication of her first book, *The Love of an Orange* in 1959, when she was twenty-three. Like the early poems of Adrienne Rich, those of Ravikovitch were formal and tightly structured. Ridden with themes of desolation and loss, her poems incorporated language and metaphors from the liturgy of the Jewish prayer book, Bible, and Midrash, as well as from Greek mythology. Critic Shimon Sandbank, writing in 1977, described the early Dahlia Ravikovitch as exploring "the exotic geography of the unconscious."[85] The images of those early poems range from the Biblical Rachel, Medea's "dress of fire," a potash factory near the Dead Sea, "the land of Cathay/and Madagascar," to the Horns of Hittim, the site of a twelfth-century battle between Moslem and Christian forces.

But that "exotic geography" should be read as a code for what today we can recognize as an excruciating protest against the constraints of women's lives. In one of her most famous poems of the early period, "The Marionette," for example, it is "the judges" who say "This woman is not responsible for her actions"; "The Dress" begins, "You know, she said, they made you a dress of fire." If, with the rise of the right-wing Likud government, and the outbreak of first the Lebanon War and then the *Intifada*, Ravikovitch's poetry became more public, direct, focused

---

85. Shimon Sandbank, "Contemporary Israeli Literature: The Withdrawal from Certainty," *Triquarterly Review* (Spring 1977): 16.

on the present, and overtly political, the changes should be seen not as a break with her poetic past but rather as an evolutionary, if startling, development.

Real Love, her 1987 collection (reprinted in 1993), includes many poems related to the issue of death, including that of the late Yona Volach. But it also includes, "You Can't Kill a Baby Twice," about the massacre by Lebanese Christian forces of Palestinians in the Sabra and Shatilla refugee camps in Lebanon, a massacre in which the Israeli government was implicated, as well as "On the Life of Children during Wartime." "A Mother Walking," from her next collection, *Mother with Child* (1992), describes a child murdered in his mother's stomach for "reasons of political security"; "Stones" is addressed to the children of the *Intifada;* "Associations" bitterly attacks a self-serving Zionism that refuses to acknowledge cruelty and violence. The poems included here are all from her most recent work.

Ravikovitch's poetry appears in English in two collections beautifully translated from the Hebrew by the gifted American poet, Chana Bloch: *A Dress of Fire* (Sheep Meadow Press, 1978) and *The Window* (Sheep Meadow Press, 1989).

Born in a suburb of Tel Aviv, Ravikovitch studied at the Hebrew University and later worked as a journalist. In addition to her poetry, she has published children's books and a collection of short stories, *Death in the Family* (1977). She has translated the poetry of William Butler Yeats and T. S. Eliot, as well as such children's literature as *Mary Poppins* and *Cinderella,* into Hebrew. The recipient of Israel's top literary awards, she lives today in Tel Aviv.

Real Love Isn't What It Seems

Dahlia Ravikovitch

Everybody loved Yona,[86]
all the people in the room loved Yona,
so when the talk turned to books
they said Oh that Yona, may her memory be blessed!
but the memory of Yona kept getting smaller
—maybe because we didn't really love her.
Besides, it's natural that a memory is eaten away
like dust eating away a dead body.

Do we love our friends?
We don't really love our friends.
And do we love our children?
Sometimes we love our children, and even that
mostly in a limited way,
as a citrus tree loves an orange.
Beyond that, a whole range of misunderstandings
greedily eat away at real love.

---

86. "Yona" is the poet Yona Volach (d. 1985). The phrase "May her memory be blessed!"
is a traditional one spoken when one mentions the dead.

Do we love ourselves
really, the way Jonathan loved David?[87]
Better to speak the truth now,
not mourn over Jonathan like David.
Ourselves we love unstintingly,
tune in to ourselves with absolute attention.
But even that is a real improvement,
for just a few months ago
our body was seized by a terrible longing
to throw itself urgently from the roof.

(1987/1983)
—*Translated by Chana Bloch*

---

87. The powerful love between David and King Saul's son Jonathan is related in I Samuel 18–20. Jonathan is slain in I Samuel 31:2; David mourns his death in II Samuel 1:18ff: "The beauty of Israel is slain on thy high places: how are the mighty fallen!"

An Unusual Autumn

Dahlia Ravikovitch

Little by little it becomes clear to me
how I got trapped here
Ten in the morning, a country-quiet
following a night of no sleep.
Flowerpots bloom wherever you look.
Little woven doilies cover every corner
and the kettle and the cluttered houseware
conspicuously austere
and the quiet inside
and the voice of a demanding child in the yard.
They took his swing.

The scene of the poem is a kibbutz—a collective settlement—where, in the pre-State days
and up until the recent collapse of Israeli socialism and the industrialization of the kibbut-
zim, "manual labor" and agriculture were primary values. Many of the kibbutzim belonged
to the leftist/moderate Labor movement—the party of Yitzhak Rabin, Shimon Peres, and
Ehud Barak—which dominated Israeli politics until the election, first, of Menahem Begin
in the 1970s, and subsequently Yitzhak Shamir and Benjamin Netanyahu (the three of
whom were from the right-wing Likud); Netanyahu lost the 1999 election to Ehud Barak.
Lines twenty-three and twenty-four adapt *Pirke Avot [Sayings of the Fathers]* 3:2: "Pray for
the welfare of the government; if not for the fear thereof, men would eat each other alive."

Someone is digging with a simple farm tool,
I forgot what it's called
(I forgot? Never mind).
A rhythmic beating,
the rustling of a hose dragged along the ground.
Everyone here is raking and tending
the flora and fauna.
The women also knit a lot,
manual labor is the top priority.
This diligence, this urge to be useful,
make it all seem idyllic.
If not for the dreaded awe of Labor Movement values
men would swallow each other alive.

For three days now my mother has been sleeping
the sleep of the just.
I tell Ido: Grandma is sleeping in peace and quiet.
And Ido says: Isn't that the eternal rest.
God forbid, I say, not eternal,
just peace and quiet.
And yet, so as not to frighten anyone,
I tell myself
that eternal rest is the best sleep of all.

(1992)
—*Translated by Chana Bloch*

Hovering at a Low Altitude

Dahlia Ravikovitch

I am not here.
I am on those craggy eastern hills
streaked with ice,
where grass doesn't grow
and a wide shadow lies over the slope.
A shepherd girl appears
from an invisible tent,
leading a herd of black goats to pasture.
She won't live out the day,
that girl.

I am not here.
From the deep mountain gorge
a red globe floats up,
not yet a sun.
A patch of frost, reddish, inflamed,
flickers inside the gorge.

The girl gets up early to go to the pasture.
She doesn't walk with neck outstretched

and wanton glances.[88]
She doesn't ask, Whence cometh my help.[89]

I am not here.
I've been in the mountains many days now.
The light will not burn me, the frost
won't touch me.
Why be astonished now?
I've seen worse things in my life.

I gather my skirt and hover
very close to the ground.
What is she thinking, that girl?

Wild to look at, unwashed.
For a moment she crouches down,
her cheeks flushed,
frostbite on the back of her hands.
She seems distracted, but no,
she's alert.

She still has a few hours left.
But that's not what I'm thinking about.
My thoughts cushion me gently, comfortably.
I've found a very simple method,
not with my feet on the ground, and not flying—
hovering
at a low altitude.

Then at noon,
many hours after sunrise,
that man goes up the mountain.
He looks innocent enough.

---

88. *With neck outstretched and wanton glances:* A reference to Isaiah 3: 16–20.

89. *Whence cometh my help:* "I lift up mine eyes to the hills/From whence comest my help" (Psalm 121).

The girl is right there,
no one else around.
And if she runs for cover, or cries out—
there's no place to hide in the mountains.

I am not here.
I'm above those jagged mountain ranges
in the farthest reaches of the east.
No need to elaborate.
With one strong push I can hover and whirl around
with the speed of the wind.
I can get away and say to myself:
I haven't seen a thing.
And the girl, her palate is dry as a potsherd,
her eyes bulge,
when that hand closes over her hair, grasping it
without a shred of pity.

(1987/1993)
—*Translated by Ariel Bloch and Chana Bloch*

Blood Heifer

Dahlia Ravikovitch

He took one step,
then a few steps more.
His glasses fell to the ground,
his skullcap.
Managed another step,
bloody, dragging his feet.
Ten steps
and he's not a Jew anymore,
not an Arab—
in limbo.

Havoc in the marketplace; people shouting, Why
are you murdering us?
Others rushing
to take revenge.

The title is based on Deut. 21: 1–9, in which the law states that if a body is found in a
field and the killer is unknown, the elders of the nearest city are to take a heifer and break
its neck. All the elders shall wash their hands over the heifer and say, "Our hands have not
shed this blood, neither have our eyes seen it. . . ." And the death shall be forgiven them.
    The poem is based on an actual incident that took place in Hebron, the only city (to
date) which is under the aegis of the Palestinian Authority but also home to a Jewish
enclave of settlers. A yeshiva student was shot in the marketplace and left to die because
no one knew his identity; the Jews assumed he was an Arab, and the Arabs, a Jew.

And he lies on the ground: a death rattle,
a body torn open,
blood streaming out of the flesh,
streaming
out of the flesh.

He died here, or there—
no one knows for sure.
What do we know?
A dead body lying in the field.

Suffering cleanseth from sin, it is said,
man is like dust in the wind,
but who was that man
lying there lonely in his blood?
What did he see,
what did he hear
with all that commotion around him?
If thou seest even thine enemy's ass[90]
lying under its burden,
it is said, thou shalt surely help.

If a dead body is found lying in the field
if a body is found in the open,
let your elders go out and slaughter a heifer
and scatter its ashes in the river.[91]

(1987/1993)
—*Translated by Ariel Bloch and Chana Bloch*

---

90. See Exodus 23:5.

91. See Numbers 19.

Hedva Harechavi

Hedva Harechavi is a poet and painter whose work bears a visionary stamp. Her voice is often passionate, obsessive, unrelenting. Though others have seen a creative debt to Yona Volach in Harechavi's poetry, she herself regards her own inner life as her most profound influence.

Harechavi grew up in Kibbutz Degania Bet, near the Kinneret (the Sea of Galilee), and later moved to Jerusalem, where she earned her B.A. from the Bezalel Academy of Art and has lived ever since. Her paintings have been exhibited in solo and group shows, and her poetry translated into English, Russian, and Arabic, set to music and performed by singers both in Israel and abroad. She has received numerous literary awards—including, twice, the Eshkol Award for Creativity in Poetry.

Hedva Harechavi works at the Jerusalem Municipality as an Advisor on Art and edits a journal for the arts within the "Unite for Arts" project at the municipality. Though she has participated in the International Poetry Festivals held in Jerusalem, and occasionally in conferences and workshops, her passion is for concentrating on her own work.

She is the single mother to her son, Elisha.

Her books, all in Hebrew, include *Because He Is King* (Newman, 1973), awarded Prize for First Publication; *Adi* (Sifriat Poalim, 1981); *All I Want Is to Tell You* (Sifriat Poalim, 1985); and *The Other* (Bitan, 1993).

Translations of her earlier work appear in *Burning Air and a Clear Mind: Contemporary Israeli Women Poets.*

1 x 2

Hedva Harechavi

"Decide. I suggest you decide. Only after you decide" (Dr. Moses)

A.

The illogical logic of life is exactly
the illogical logic of the lottery

B.

And now some sound
the room has turned into a meadow, the cows and sheep
are mine
and I in a white velvet dress
dance in the meadow
dancing with the cows and sheep
dancing inside
outside
forward
backward right left
right or left, dancing backward

"1 x 2" describes the soccer-betting card (the Israeli "Totto"), which the bettor marks. "1" means the home team wins; "x" that the game is a tie; "2" that the visiting team wins. "Totto" in the poem has been translated as "lottery."

this way or that
adapting herself to the dance
the same dance, always the same dance that she always
danced anew, always wrapping herself around me, dancing moist
dancing sticky dancing closed dancing being danced dancing being
danced
being made to dance something like desire
dancing the desire of "what, when, how did I get here"
dancing as one should, dancing quick, clear, colorful, dancing white
or
this way or another and
being danced with desire
being danced heavy being danced slow, or just
being danced this for so
long
really, just how long
Have I been dancing this.
Ever since. Dancing on the table, over flashing neon lights
over the moon
over over the moon
and yet let them gush over her, to dance rough hairy
with eyes closed, no, no, the opposite: just so
to dance this as if
I came to dance with what goes on here and what
can turn this disquiet into tenderness
into gentleness
and this smile
like this dance
a dance she's barely dancing

dancing as it's clear, just so
dancing clear
what is clear. Dancing being danced being made to dance
dancing the desire of "what is clear"
the kind of dance that begins
at birth
before birth
before they were still dripping from the rocks
lying in a closed circle
on the dry mud, while they disappear
all at once, of course, I love them
of course, I love to dance, dance, dance
with all that comes to hand to dance

with reds with yellows with golden blonds
green blues, to dance
with opponents with potential, with
favored champions revolutionaries musketeers merchants samurai
to dance with pimps, with things like these, of course
with all that comes to hand, of course, I love them, of course
I love to dance, or

what you call "what's this absurdity"
to dance "what a wonderful absurdity"
to dance every possible argument
in every matter,
to dance every possible matter
in my name, clearly

in my name, to dance "in my name"
only in my name, actually just so
to dance just someone resembling me
dancing in my name
all the time;
what can I say, things like these, with these, like these
things, with other things, with the beings
with lands, in all sort of stadiums, in balconies
in wardrobes in showers in bars in public parks
in parkings in second-hand car lots
in garages, just so
with tender street cleaners
especially with beggars,

hotheads who need a hair cut, and yes
oh yes,
to dance with the dirt
with the lice at noon
or in the evening or in the morning or
at night, to dance
in the heart of the night
along a tiny stream
a wounded animal along a tiny stream
trying to reenter
the arena, to dance
a wounded animal
kneeling

tears flowing from her eyes
on the body of her beloved. To dance
a dead animal.
And now some sound.
Tell me about me
what's my name,
my family name,
where do I live,
who do I know.
Of course, I love them. A lot. I love
to dance.
To dance
is to dance. Or

just to dance with one stained with blood
and so it will be: stained with blood
propping her head on my shoulder
dancing with me
in my yard, no
theirs, no
mine, mine, theirs, mine, theirs
theirs, mine, actually
it doesn't matter any more
if I dance here, and there is
a dog stained with blood
covered with rain, between the falling of rain
dancing with the fall of the rain

I with the fall of the rain
I with the lightning
I with God
God and I with new dogs
near a one-story house
near the city park
and I don't care what it takes and if
she's just dancing there
dancing with
dancing without
my blemished one,
my beautiful one,
you pampered power, dance, now, dance,

something like
in a lit-up show window
with the back to the crowd with the face to the crowd
dancing in a lit-up shop window
polishing her nails
wetting the tips of her fingers
blinking her eyes
waving her tyrant rod and dancing, dancing
dancing "the other image is me," just
dancing sensitive wise courageous exact
and only my lack of decisiveness suddenly, like when
there was a danger of a thin crack

and all eyes were shut
and danced around me
and everyone had to dance
careful orderly methodical or
so just dancing wild
instinctuitively associative free
it's so evident, to dance
in time for a while for ever
for a while.
To dance what was.
I call this exaltation of the spirit
pleasure
disgust

to dance behind those rags, no
no, just in the front
return to the front and dance
in front,
to put my hands around your neck and dance.
To put your hands around my neck and dance.
And suddenly everything changes.
The dance floor is dying.
I smile glisten shine
and someone near me is suddenly excited
because of me and dances and we dance in the evening in the night
in the morning and dance and dance
and his dance which is actually my dance

your dance which is actually my dance
what does putting your hands

around my neck mean and dance dance
and dance, no, to decide, no, to dance, to decide, yes, to decide
to decide, no, to dance
whatever you decide
whatever you dance
decide
dance dancing the desire of "decide. I suggest you decide. Only
after you decide"
imagine a woman of 1,000 years living alone in a ruin and dance
on my own, no, together, no,
1, solo, no,
2, together, no

1 is 2
2 is 1
3 is a triangle
4 is a double, or a triangle
5 is balanced
6 is a decision
7, the guest
8, the hostess breathes down the neck of the guest who gets just a
bit ahead of her
9, the guest runs at the top
10, the hostess has pretensions of running at the top
11, the hostess leads
12, now the guest leads
13, the Queen of Stalemate ended in a stalemate with the lead

14, the guest is staying in the neighborhood, and that smile
like this dance
dancing where
dancing what matter
dancing in huge quantities
to dance gigantic
to dance and just heap hallucinations
to dance imagination
any kind of imagination, and yes
you should not be harmed, and yes,
what's yes,
15, this time the guest will be careful

(1993)
—*Translated by Miriyam Glazer*

And It Is Still That Way

Hedva Harechavi

Beside me a memory of every detail and
possible detail
I say to myself "Hedva, you must go on
waiting. Wait and wait. Wait and wait
and wait."
1000
years
a day.
One difficult moment reminds me
of the cry of a bird soaring
over the unknown
and it is still so,
still each utterance of mine is accompanied
by the smell of blood.
Desire all the time.
And all in absent-mindedness.
Nerves, nerves cracking
a fear of heights looking at me in fear, this
or another. Another rumor,
another reflecting thing.

I know that this is the room
in which black winds gallop every night

and from all the walls, from all the floor,
a smile echoes as
small as an insect
crying

I am afraid, Ruth,
the door is open
and it is still that way.

(1985)
—Translated by Miriyam Glazer

Already Night, Already Day

Hedva Harechavi

My mother is a whore without a dagger
Her dead body without defense.
A dead power.

When she deceived me the first time
I turned to stone. Voices
laughed. Murderous smoke spread
like a sea of rust
on my forehead, my eyes, my neck,
around the palms of my hands, the soles of my feet.
Every fragment of thought capable
of knowing
froze and wept
froze and wept.

(Sometimes, when I'd smile like
a robot a shape resembling me
would soar and crawl, soar and crawl
but there was a lawn and in the lawn a mountain, and in
the mountain a garden,
and in the garden, darkness, and in the darkness
blood, and in the blood

a white boat
that I drew
went beserk
for the benefit
of no one.
Sometimes, I'd be killed off right away
like some old worn-out bitch.)

Now, every gesture of mine is broadcast
now, every sound of mine reported
now I am, I am not
watching stray black cats
that I hear between my fingers.

My dead power,
mother, mother, mother,
I spit on common sense
I no longer care about your messy death
in your damp hole.

One thing only matters to me: your eyes,
with what red
did you make up your eyes?
People ask me about you.
I have to toss out a word. Or two.
Already evening, already night, already day, already noon
I want wings, ...wings
I want wings
and to fly

(1985)
—*Translated by Miriyam Glazer*

Raquel Chalfi

Raquel Chalfi's often visionary and dramatic poetry has been acclaimed for its independence and daring by leading Israeli literary critics. Born in Israel, Chalfi spent several years of her childhood in Mexico, a landscape, language, and culture whose influence made itself felt in her early work. While a student at Hebrew University, Chalfi worked as a documentary film maker for Israeli television, and later did graduate work at Berkeley in playwriting. She has published five books of poetry: *Submarine* (1975), *Free Fall* (1979), *Zikit* (1986), *Chomer* (1990), and most recently, *The Love of a Dragon* (1995).

Chalfi won the 1989 Prime Minister's Award for Literature as well as winning several awards for her scripts from the Israeli Film Institute. She lives in Tel Aviv.

Reading the I Ching

Raquel Chalfi

So, it's like this:
Tiny bumps of fear on my flesh
because of a journey to the other side of the globe
a journey hanging over my head
like a black cloud before the break
and I'm intently debating whether to go or not
and I fall from weakness
every time I think of that voyage—this voyage
and my heart falls from weakness
when I think of leaving behind
my Love
my lovely Love my rickety Love
whose black eyes will pounce on every woman on all of them
when I am not here

So it's like this: I throw three coins
and ask the I Ching in my heart
the question that strikes fear in my heart
and Chien comes out six strong lines of Chien
I already see it is something
very positive and strong I already see
this ancient book is winking mischievously

So it's like this: "above—the creative Chien. Sky.
below—the creative Chien. Sky."

These six whole lines, says the I Ching, stand for the power
primal light-giving strong active power of the spirit.
    "A strong hexagram. Without weakness. Its essence
is power. Its image is heaven.
The strong person moves forward." Oh yes. Should I go?
And the I Ching continues in an ancient Chinese voice:
    "Nine in the beginning means: Hidden dragon. Do
not act."
The images flicker in my mind. My heart muddles. After
all, "The strong one
moves forward." So why "Do not act"? And what of my
Love?
A hundred ancient Chinese chant into my burning ears:
    "The dragon the dragon the dragon is the symbol of
motivating power.
    The electrical force that is revealed in thunder storms.
    Thus too is the great man still unrecognized
diffident."
And what of my rickety Love? Should I not go?
The second line means: "Dragon appearing in the field."
The third is not relevant.
The fourth line says: "Wavering flight over the depths. No
blame."
And onward, to the fifth: "Flying dragon in the heavens."
The sixth line, the last, warns: "Arrogant dragon
will have cause to repent." Dragon claw stirs in my hair. I
run to flip through another version of the ancient book.
Ho hee. The I Ching continues to preach. All the lines
together say:
    "There appears a flight of dragons without heads.
    Good fortune.
    The severed heads will soften the strength of the
dragon.
    Strength and mildness join in good fortune."
Am I hallucinating the I Ching? Is it hallucinating me?
Seeking, seeking explanations. Dragons in China. Half a
feverish yellow night passes over me with a virginal pile of
books books unopened
until tonight. And here is a dragonfly miracle: "In China
dragon teeth heal
convulsions. Dragon teeth will comfort the heart, will
soothe melancholy."

Dragon teeth? Where shall I find them? Should I hunt
dragon?
And I go on reading: In the days of the reign of Huang-
Dee, who began his rule
two thousand seven hundred years B.C.,
"The Bamboo Chronicle" tells of the dragon ch'i-lin:
"The noblest of creatures. Of divine origin. The
emblem of serenity
"Never would it eat a living thing. Never place a
hoof on growing grass."
A-ha. And what of my beloved? And if China, then I must
have India too.
Now I bend over a portrait of Buddha's sculpture. Even he
is protected by the Naga, the good snake-dragons. Aha.
Naga. Buddha.
Not enough. So it's like this: "In the drawing before us
is Ananda the eternal the giant dragon snake.
The symbol of cosmic energy. The god Vishnu rests
upon him."
Here is Vishnu with eyes shut resting in Nirvana
his reclining body and four on the body of Ananda
sailing in cosmic waters.
My head sails in cosmic waters my body wants to go back
to my bed my tumbled bed
my insomniac bed How will I understand How will I
understand the I Ching
How will the I Ching understand me?

So it's like this:
A halo of radiant-black dragons whole and headless
electric soft-hard good-evil terrible noble divine
round my head
my little head
searching trembling through the pages of the I Ching
while the electric sparked eyes of my beloved
are shut
and he sleeps calmly
as his mouth emits the snore
of a lightning-stormed night

(1995)
—Translated by Karen Alkalay-Gut

Night Hair

Raquel Chalfi

1.

To braid the locks of the dark
a heavy braid on earth's soft nape
To mold with wet hands
longing's dark clay
trees knitted of trembling
thick boughs of bonding
and a wide field waiting
in vain

2.

Night combs his long hair like a woman
seated in the window at night

3.

Night—hungry—runs barefoot through streets
leaving gossiping grasses behind

4.

Night will beget day what will day beget
Night, his dreams tangled,
tears into the city's heart
rips the street to bites.

How I would want to dye
the hair of night
shocking red!

5.

How we wanted a flame of twigs to break out
into sprouts that shoot like flame
to sweep away straw words
to leave the dance floor empty, smooth
for dense feelings to be whirled
into an enormous ball

6.

How I wanted the air of the big she-night
to wrap me around like pythons. Warm ones.

7.

Truth like this and even the down of the evening bristles.
Shutters of the brain slam wildly
Shock of darkness
saves a night entangled in her own hair

8.

Dreams, heart's sweat,
on the stretched skin of night
his hair gathered
his temples damp
secretions of dreams drip
drop
cool
salty
drop

9.

Such an old night
his peals still clear
We crawl on his belly
and he takes us inside him
like a mad satyr who falls asleep
in grace

(1979)
—*Translated by Karen Alkalay-Gut*

Maya Bejerano

A prolific poet, Maya Bejerano's works include *Ostrich* (1978), *The Heat and the Cold* (1981), *Data Processing* (1983), *Song of Birds* (1985), *Voice* (1987), *Selected Poems* (1987), *Whale* (1993), and *The Hymns of Job* (1996)—a variety of titles that suggests the breadth and complexity of her poetic range. Her interest in photography is reflected in her use of film techniques: she has been called "adept at . . . the quick cut, the voice-over, the juxtaposition of incongruous imagery and the sudden panoramic sweep."[92] Other critics have described her as the heir of Yona Volach, perhaps in part because of the disruptions, dislocations, and brilliant use of satire in her poetry, as well as the linguistic, philosophical, psychological, intellectual, and aesthetic challenges it poses. In *The Hymns of Job,* for example, as critic Yael Feldman has pointed out, Bejerano moves "from the mundane to the sublime, 'from the cash machine' to 'the power to sing,' from the intimacy of conversational Hebrew to the sonorous tone of the poetic monologue" in a manner that "bespeaks the unredeemed pain of life at the end of the second millenium."[93]

Born in Kibbutz Ayalon near Haifa, Maya Bejerano lived in Jerusalem before settling in Tel Aviv. She has a B.A. in Hebrew Literature and Philosophy, studied violin and flute, and has a special interest in the history of the Second Temple era. She is a librarian at Ariela House. She lives with her companion and daughter.

---

92. Gershon Shaked, ed., *Hebrew Winters* (Tel Aviv: Institute for Translation of Hebrew Literature, 1993), p. 29.

93. In "The Ability to Speak Entirely New Phrases," *Seneca Review* (27:1), 1997: 36.

I Made a New Memory for You
For Avot Yeshurun

Maya Bejerano

I made a new memory for you
that will stand at the end of the tower of your memories
like the tip of a distant bough
and I made a memory for me:
an empty closet
ready to store new clothes;
an 80-plus-year old man, a poet, sitting
all head and mouth and Johann Sebastian Bach mane
and blue eyes burning in their red rims
finding nowhere to rest
sliding, sliding, down the slippery greyish cream walls,
the color of oil.
Noon in Ichilov Hospital.
Leftover chicken and soup in plastic dishes.

A meeting, in which, in equal measure,
in equal measure, my desire was

Avot Yeshurun was a major innovative Israeli poet, a regular contributor to the literary journal *Siman Kriah*, who died in Tel Aviv in 1992 and was posthumously awarded the Israel Prize.

to see and my desire to be seen
to linger in the receptive space
of the old eye combing like radar
to get entangled in the cocktail of scenes and voices
of a man born at the beginning of the century,
a king stirring love for the world.

For a moment I was myself the world
in the image of a woman without even flowers or sweets
(superfluous surely).
Not a physical therapist, no, no,
Alas, a dear familiar image
who goes on sitting, speaking perhaps,
forcing opacity into words
teasing the heavy distant hands and feet
of this giant proud personality
with a cotton bathrobe on his shoulders
and a daily thermometer in his mouth.

(1993)
—*Translated by Miriyam Glazer*

States of War

Maya Bejerano

The structure of the soul,
the geology of the human soul,
always includes fiery lava
always bubbles of war,
war, persistently present
in the disintegration of matter.

From beneath the dizzying colors of the carousels,
to the gauzy dim cafes where hands hurl
something sweet, intoxicating tastes—even a baby—
under stages, auditoriums, schoolroom desks and blackboards—
under sleepy sheets, to clear trails, to clocks

under life
there is always heard
disintegrating matter battling to be present
under mountains of aggressive forgetting
under the mountain of the city dressed in addresses
what nerve and arrogance overturned it, gave it a wide open escape

---

The poem was written during the Gulf War.

let it be seen and heard
at the will of the missile-man, the sort that brags about lethal weapons—
one-dimensional creatures with weapons for trespassing borders,
    deceiving borders,
churning us up from our guts, faceless men in uniforms
without dignity or distinction, with experience fleeing which
is the experience of trying to save their human face
but doomed to failure

war insinuates itself in every pore
war is found in the air
and the shattered mouth sings it at any price

(1993)
—*Translated by Miriyam Glazer*

From The Hymns of Job

Maya Bejerano

1.

From morning slumber a stir a shift a spinning motion of tossing
rising from a single bed strewn with black and white cotton squares
       seven o'clock
the cat already howling since four to hug her feed her egg and milk
why feed and hug her what do I owe her why the need to attend to
her
a beautiful useless dot a white queen a bride
an executive secretary of lofty pedigree
shedding Persian fur everywhere completing with jerky motions my
       grooming routine
preparing for a new morning.

There's no escaping this body and a new day in spite of us
is not to be postponed for even a second
what else what else, I was and will be,
and all I wish for without lifting a finger
is to glimpse the bull's eye of this dazzling driving order that rules
       me with its vulgar beauty
indolent in the very essence of diligence, force of habit,
       or whatever you want to call it
and already the feet are in the shoes
and I must, with all the mule power that I possess,

wake my daughter from her sweet sticky sleep.
Where to where to now?
"Out out girls" be quick[94]
calls the neighbor with his Hungarian voice that croaks like an old
          radio—don't linger
it is crowded indeed but one must find a spot in the long procession
of the morning boxcars

Have I mentioned already that I was weaned of distant markets?
A weaned baby—I was never weaned and never will be
of my wish to strike the root of my soul in distant lands
squander my capital on the beautiful, study the meaning of pleasure
on the Seine, the Arno,
on the banks of the Ganges, the fountains of Rome.
And the sands of Jerusalem I wished to forget for I have yet to be
          weaned of distant markets
of beauty wealth and health
at my heels only the litter of stillness, of memories.
I walked up to the marketplace hurried to the glittering pit of the
          automatic teller
to withdraw my money to draw power to me, I slipped my hand,
as if asked in marriage I gave my hand to the automatic teller,
a hand bedecked and heavy with diamonds, sapphires,
wrapped like an injured limb in a black bandage spotted with first
   red stains
I drew my hand toward me out of there.

2.

Suddenly I was stabbed from behind,
and before me stood a black angel, a talking stone,
and he took me into his crackling wings
like an elevator shaft in an invisible tower
and I alighted with him, ascended with him, descended with him, I
was consumed,
disgorged, discharged, and came back to myself with open eyes;
my dear ones hung over me, the more I smiled at them,
the more they blew my nose, wiped my tears that absolutely

---

94. *Out out girls,* a joyous march sung by the early pioneers and still popular today.

weren't flowing from anywhere, but
in the main we successfully recognized one another, namely,
we took a picture together;
once again I was suddenly stabbed from behind, and an angel,
darker than the first of talking stone,
stood before me and took me into his crackling wings;
in a sweet-bitter flavor his knowledge was transmitted to me,
seeped into my ears, and I turned a dark tint,
smooth and glistening,
we alighted ascended descended as if in an elevator in an invisible
          tower
his thick knowledge transmitted to me
received and absorbed and instantly squeezed
into a slimy fluid that dripped from the pores
of my black skin, as mentioned,
I was gleaming like a stone and all the other angels sang with me
in a discordant voice that infuriated me,
how can angels be so off-key,
they've been out of practice for thousands of years, emissaries of
divine bidding

For years they've been fossilized
steeped in graves, in veins,
in coloring books, albums, carved in marble, steel
and cardboard, etched in glass
they tore themselves loose rose to sing with me
calling as one: come come
and I did I came I obeyed knowing
they'd take me to him
and they took me to him

4.

In a slick, black bodysuit Job stood before me
fixed in the dance of his blessed passing princehood
unwilling to numb the great sufferings
that subdue him with an awful grip,
Job a happy prince—
a couple of flat obscenities and it'll all be over
a few ornaments, colored ship, several delightful pets
will make you forget—
unwilling to let go of his afflictions they clung to him

like his lost assets, the negative print of reality's luster
he's been waiting for with the infinite persistence of the philosopher
      of pain;
it's a tunnel joining the everlasting human future
to the infinitely mysterious universe of the other,
the knowledge of other
is godliness from its primordial beginning to its end;
in a black bodysuit in a spot of light he waited for me
in his pistol with a tiny muzzle ravenous as a child's,
very near me near me in the shade
at dusk he calls my name in hushed tenderness: M M M
and when I say: yes yes here I am
he'll shoot once and vanish, I'll vanish with him
in a black bodysuit
into the void.

5.

Interlude
Truth is I was kidnapped;
don't take me to an abandoned field
I implored
don't stash me away in the stripped rocky field
on such a hot day;
sharp yellowish rocks, thorns, scorched greenish shrubs,
hills, only hills and, of course, sparkling skies,
I'm not interested in skies, I screamed,
the earth,
my life on earth—its affairs
not the rough ground not an abandoned field
I'm here with people;
you're acting blindly, understand!
I begged, Don't! Don't! I yelled, mariner,
such a vulgar sailor he tied me to his boat and left.
Won't you take pity on my children, my beautiful creatures?
Won't you spare my thriving undertakings,
my wife, my husband,
a momentary silence, a murmur pounded in me,
I know my heart murmurs and I'm frightened

Truth is I was kidnapped
and I too have kidnapped, between me and myself

all is done willfully knowingly
with no coercion only surprise
a hell of a surprise
truth is I expected him
truth is I resembled him
he was the reflection of my own death
in the looking glass of my future, waiting
until I reach it fully realized
and resembling it at the end of my days perhaps at the beginning
perhaps in mid-life—your time is up,
sorry, say the angels,
we've sent you a sailor's lifeboat
to sail in the opposite direction—upward
come come, they chant
and I did, I came knowing
they'd take me to him
and they did . . .

6.

Noon. 12:45 already
12:45 and I'm starved because
at twelve forty-five I'm starved
in need of *cash*
children, please get off the monument, get off the monument
children
it's lunchtime, we'll eat downstairs
at Illforno's near the beach for
lunch we eat at Illforno's!

Please release me
my stomach is churning listen listen what a nothing commotion
my plate is set outside ready
like a dark brimming eyeball
on a white washed-off table
and now I must dash off
down there,
they're waiting with the meal . . .

And to how many souls have I told the following story
over noodles, wide as elephant's ears, drenched in red sauce
and served with a greenish broccoli pie stuffed and crusted

with a layer of fatty yellow cheese
cubes of cabbage and beets and baby carrots
in the shelter of wilted lettuce, and Thousand Island dressing and
tahini sauce
embrace the boundaries of this presence:
"Over there we were people over here asses"
Dear Mr. Naguetta hold on a minute
it is not yet time for you to die
you have no right (it is a right)[95]

Naguetta, a devoted Ethiopian father,
an artisan, the tribe's blacksmith,
a respectable homeowner in his village;
the ivory smile that was still his gleamed
like a cat's hanging from a tree
Oh the miraculous holy land
Oh the land of hardship, of gallows . . .

For a moment I listened: there were sounds, statues, pictures all
         around me on the walls
in the air-conditioned restaurant by the sea, restoring the jolt of
         horror back to its place,
under the eyebrows, the tongue, behind the ears, in the roots of hair
and gossipy laughter, fondling pendulous earrings, yellow stubs
for those entitled to food and shelter,
but the black paint slowly dripped
like chocolate coating in the noon sun
and the proud Ethiopian's skin was stripped
and delivered to a maker of happy stiffs.

9.

It has all begun with still waters
Satan emerged from God's bowels
with a sort of claim:
Job Job is too mellow, content, an inhuman naif,
he absolutely needs to be pushed pinched
to see what will happen

---

95. Rachamim Naguetta, a new immigrant from Ethiopia who committed suicide (newspaper article, 7/4/91).

to fool around a bit on the beach
I the devil devise experiments out of blissful boredom
provide the doubt, hills upon hills of sharp investigations
stinging positions of lethal voltage and scabs
with a might that won't crust
with an actual steep ascent
toward a thing confidential a thing terminal
up to the advent to return to plumpness
after the oblivion and the obeying
upward upward
downward downward.
But
nights someone unstitches your garments,
Job, and days—
it is all in your heart all in your name,
God and Satan too cavort in Uz
(Uz Puz Tuz Guz),
and Uz is the paper land that spins with the times

paper cuts and paper ailments
paper outcries
paper scolding
and recollections of wealth lawns and banquets
praise and flattery on paper,
paper.
And yet the touch of God scalds you badly
black on white
the leprous back
an electric fence fences you in
an alarm system
let humanity hear
let human hear
because

nights someone unstitches your clothes,
your garments, days, Job,
it is all in your heart your name
God and Satan cavort in the land of Uz
land of Uz land of Puz
they toy with your legacy, Job, your misfortune,
your fate bisected like the two hemispheres of a fruit

corresponding twins, black and white and tender,
between your temples—God and his negative print,
I tell him that,
I stand before him—he stands
in a black bodysuit
after I've been stabbed from behind.

11.

Oh spare me, spare me
for the hand of God has touched me
pinched my ass his hand all over my body, mercy,
Oh my ass
I was calm and he shook me held my neck and cracked me
such crack crack will split my kidneys he won't take pity
I can't anymore I can't
the shadow of death upon my lids, my prayer
purifies, this is the poem of death (or) a cozy life poem
but I am in poetry—all times all days
I'm in metaphors;
he who holds in his hand heads, hearts,
rules them with a remote-control, merges in them,
misleads them,
confounds moderators, kings, ministers,
editors, judges, youths;
spins the drivers' life wheel
like a pleasant illusory seductive tune
and finally like a rusty screw in the ass
and me he leaves without a clue to the changing code
the unexpected code—right or wrong
without my box in hand
my box of precious jewels, of alms and obligations,
has turned into a box of disgusting insects
my loathsome deeds—spare me
negative negatives

16.

Job: I was cast onto a new life cycle
an immaculate youth in the gentle light of morning
I awake naked as on the day of my birth
wish to begin my life afresh

only my great pensive eye contemplates the past
my pensive gloomy eye
it sees ahead
like the upside-down memory of an infant;
I've rejected all my former treasures
to return here
naked and young cast into a new life
after I've emerged from God's belly, the belly of pain
I roam the gulf of my soul
enter the recess of my person, the recess of my ocean,
up to the small reef that opens in the folds of my familiar brain,
I'm lit,
my consciousness before me like a set table.[96]

> "Hast thou entered into the springs of the sea?
> or hast thou walked in search of its depth?"
> (Job 38:16)

(1993)
—*Translated by Tsipi Keller*

---

96. *Set table*, in the Hebrew, also refers to the code of Jewish laws, *Shulhan Arukh* (the "Prepared Table"), written by Joseph Caro (1488–1575).

Esther Ettinger

"Most of my childhood and youth was spent in the shadow of war," writes Esther Ettinger. Born in Poland, Esther Ettinger's parents came to Israel as pioneers before World War II. But the rest of their family stayed in Poland. "When I was born in Jerusalem during the war, my parents named me 'Esther' after my father's late grandmother, not knowing whether anyone else in the family was alive or dead." The stories of her family's experience during the Holocaust found their way into her first book of poetry, *Possible Green* (1981), which won the Neuman Prize awarded by the Jerusalem Writers House.

Ettinger's second and third books, *Before the Music* (1986) and *Leant by the Artist* (1991), as their names suggest, probe the relationship of words to music and the plastic arts, reflecting her own interest in drawing. Her work was exhibited in the Jerusalem Artists House in a group show of "Poets Drawing." *Leant by the Artist* won the Jerusalem Fund Prize; she won the Prime Minister's Prize for Creativity the following year. With Ruth Almog, she collaborated on writing a best-selling novel, *A Full Love*, in 1995. Her work frequently appears in Israeli literary journals.

Most of Esther Ettinger's poetry is infused with her own religious sensibility, drawing on associations from the world of Bible, Midrash, traditional liturgy, and Talmud. Such associations enrich and deepen the language of poetry, and one of her abiding concerns is the ways tensions between secular and observant Israelis in social, cultural, and political life, and debates about how "Jewish" the Jewish state should be, are cutting off much of the Israeli public from these traditional Jewish sources.

The result is a growing gulf between writer and audience, particularly with the younger generation.

Esther Ettinger studied Hebrew Literature and the History of Israel at the Hebrew University and earned a graduate degree in Library Science. She is a librarian at the Law Faculty at Hebrew University and edits programs on literature for Israeli radio. The mother of four children and grandmother of five, she lives in Jerusalem with her husband, Aharon Ettinger.

Excerpts from the Sabbath Dream Book

Esther Ettinger

The book of the Sabbath is sealed like an unwritten dream
what arises in the dream is elegant and noble,
an angel will reveal a tip of its wing
a rush of sound
and give a fine, familiar smile
and you'll try to hold on to the fleeting, the forgotten,
dipping in the morning shadows,
the leftovers
on the table.
The Book of the Sabbath is like an unwritten dream,
the most beautiful of books:
all of it filled with electricity
the second soul drawn like a bridal train

The poem is rich with allusions about the holiness of the Sabbath drawn from the Jewish mystical tradition. The Sabbath is a time of transfiguration, set apart from all other days, suffused with spiritual joy; celebrating the original day of rest after the creation of the universe, it is the day God, envisioned as King, is reunited with his Queen (the *Shekhinah*), the Divine Bridegroom with His Bride, and the day on which each person's soul *(neshama)* receives an "additional" soul or spirit *(ru'ah)*. The mystical tradition also envisions the sexual union of male and female on the Sabbath as an enactment of the Divine union.

asking with glowing grace
for a touch in hollow places.[97]
But there are prohibitions and forbidden labors[98]
and what remains till the coming of the stars
is as flawed as the moon.[99]

From the dawn of Sabbath, a dream:
the Maharaja watches me with unveiled desire,
with amber eyes seated on ivory
where all his darkness is.
Truthfully, though I desired him
I preferred the servant's wing,
the infinite prattle
over coffee and strawberry jam.
Every once in a while,
particularly when the moon is full and
a lit-up soap bubble considers bursting,
adorned in black I would reciprocate
the look of this Eastern Prince
and, I must admit,
a few flashes of thunder would fly, or more,
and silence, not without waves of spasms,
till the coming moon would return
and, in between, the flaws.

(1991)

—*Translated by Mariana Barr*

---

97. In Gen. 32:22, Jacob wrestles with an angel; when the angel cannot prevail, he wrenches Jacob's hip at the socket ("a hollow place") and Jacob demands a blessing. The angel responds by changing Jacob's name to "Israel" ("the God-wrestler").

98. That is, there are laws designed to separate the Sabbath from the rest of the week—laws, for example, to prevent laboring.

99. According to tradition, the appearance of three stars on Saturday night heralds the end of the Sabbath.

Micrographic Manuscript, Miniature (I)

Esther Ettinger

Bible. Spain. Saragossa. Fourteen hundred and something,
a few years before the expulsion, miniature, micrographic writing.
Who ruined his days and turned his nights into days
to write so minutely, in the city of Saragossa, so and so
many years before the discovery of America and the treasures of the Inca.
A few hundred years after Ibn Gabirol was banished from the city,[100]
his throat parched as he yelled, standing in the midst of the times, a scribe
bending over parchment, dipping a feather in ink black as a beak,
ploughing in gold, sowing letters like flights of birds in winter
rushing to become Bible. Spain. Saragossa. Aye,
we're here, bent over the glass cover to see,
to read, immense, immense

(1991)
—*Translated by Mariana Barr*

---

100. Solomon Ibn Gabirol (1020–c.1057) was a Neoplatonic philosopher and one of the
most important writers of Hebrew religious and secular poetry during the Jewish Golden
Age in Moorish Spain. See his poem, "On Leaving Saragossa," translated by Nicholas de
Lange, in the *Jerusalem Review* (April 1997): 61–64.

Micrographic Manuscript, Miniature (II)

Esther Ettinger

Bible. Poland. Lodz Ghetto. Nineteen hundred forty one.[101]
Eighty five pages in such smallness, written in the night.
The woman and child went to bed and Shlomo Knobel writes Bible
for the sake of the child in the beginning God created for the sake of
    the child Exodus
and Second Kings then the child was taken and Shlomo Knobel
stops and continues Job and Chronicles
continue by themselves fastening and stuffing letters in the thick night
insect-like letter next to insect-like letter
in an insect-like world, while the soul grows smaller and smaller
and its breadth is impossible and we are not here
and it is impossible, immense, immense

(1991)
—*Translated by Mariana Barr*

---

101. That is, during the Holocaust. The Lodz Ghetto was entirely liquidated in 1944.

The Glass

Esther Ettinger

I didn't know whether from Phoenician sands
some Zedonian took it to his mouth like a flute
and blew till he was out of breath,
the air from his nose preserved in the greenish bubbles
dancing in the jug.
Later, I was a member of the glassmakers' guild
and the glassblowers in sixteenth century Prague,
perhaps even the honorary president
shaping and dissolving it at my will
for I'm an expert on running meetings
when the matter is solid and thin and ephemeral
and made to splinter.
I walked in the streets of Jerusalem as well
imitating the heavy accent of my Bulgarian glassmaker
with his small chest and thick eyebrows
calling glassmaker glassmaker

The poem takes off from the prayer recited at the evening service for Yom Kippur, the Day of Atonement, during the Days of Awe: "Behold, like glass in the hand of the glassmaker, who, when he pleases forms it and when he pleases melts it down, so are we in Your hand."

waiting for a housewife to lean out of her window
and wave to me to come up,
my fragile merchandise melted into big sheets
under my arm, summoned to put glass everywhere
to gather the fragments piling up with a bruising sound
to lay a transparent sheet before the world
to treasure the spinning wind.

(1991)
—*Translated by Mariana Barr*

Believe Me

Esther Ettinger

Believe me, she grew more beautiful from moment to moment
her face poised, calm
from contraction to contraction, peaks of pleasure and pain
known in love.
The air was full and thick
and the spotlight upsetting the peace piercing
but she was so beautiful, rose of a perfect rose
till the child's head broke forth from within her, his shoulders, his body
and the umbilical cord wriggled and shone with light bluer
than the bottom of the sea.[102]
I don't want to ease over the agony and the blood
only to tell you she was the essence of beauty
becoming elation when the child was placed on her belly.
And I who stood there cried with him, a first cry
clean of joy, clean of pain,
the purity of crying.

---

102. The word here translated as "bottom of the sea" is *te'hom*, from Gen. 1:2, which is traditionally translated "And the earth was waste and void, and darkness was upon *the face of the deep*." Along with the strong word used for "light" it conjures up the biblical moment of creation.

How is it that she went from beauty to beauty
like memory to memory
to the place of love where you say
you grow more beautiful as you go, more beautiful as you go
just as it is written
"weeping as he goes, weeping . . . "[103]

(1986)
—*Translated by Mariana Barr*

---

103. The last line comes from Psalm 126, a psalm celebrating the return from exile and the promise of joy after great sorrow ("We were like them that dream"). "They that sow in tears, shall reap in joy," says the psalm. "He that goes forth weeping scattering his seed shall return in rejoicing, bringing his sheaves with him." In the Hebrew, the line describing the woman's growing beauty in the last stanza grammatically echoes the last line, "becoming beautiful" with a verb parallel to the "weeping."

Chava Pinchas-Cohen

Born in 1955, Chava Pinchas-Cohen has published three books of poetry, the prize-winning *The Essence of Color* (1989), *The Journey of the Doe* (1994), and her most recent, *A River and Forgetfulness* (1998). Her poems have been honored for their linguistic and imaginative richness, as well as their spiritual depth and human understanding. The poems of Chava Pinchas-Cohen, in their content, metaphors, symbolism, language, and feeling, draw at once on the present and the personal and on the wells of Jewish tradition: on Midrash, Bible, Talmud, Jewish history, ceremony, and ritual.

Chava Pinchas-Cohen is also a literary critic and edits the periodical *Dimui*, devoted to literature, art, and Jewish culture, which she is passionately engaged in seeking to define in the context of contemporary Israel. She lives in Rehovot with her family.

Remembering Our Fathers

Chava Pinchas-Cohen

On Rosh Hashanah, I didn't bow
for the prayer extolling the kingship of God. I was giving birth.
The King was there alone.
Memories wrapped me. My father, my father—
he carried me on his shoulders like a knight
so I could see through the window of the Sephardic synagogue
at the end of "Seven Mills" Street near the Yarkon,
so I could be part of the congregation

The poem juxtaposes two prayers of the New Year (Rosh Hashanah) service; imagery of labor and giving birth; *Tru'ah,* the call for the blowing of the Shofar—the ram's horn—during the service; loss of the father, and, finally, the promise of redemption in the Biblical book of Jeremiah. During the *Malkuyot* (Kingship) prayer, one is reminded that all creation stands before God to be recorded in "The Book of Life" for life or for death in the coming year.

The words "My father, my father," echo II Kings 2:11, the cry of Elisha when Elijah is taken into heaven.

"The hour of opening/and closing": Imagery of labor and of birth is juxtaposed with the blowing of the Shofar, and the opening and closing of the "Gates of Life" during the Days of Awe, beginning with Rosh Hashanah and ending with Yom Kippur (the Day of Atonement). The "closing of the gates" is the name of the final prayer of the Days of Awe.

309

in white, breathing,
at the moment of *Tru'ah*
blowing, contracting,
at the hour of opening
and closing.

In the yard, jasmine flowers,
tangerines, and guava bore the fall with a purity of heart.[104]
Rain has no fragrance; it's the earth that gives forth
the fragrance of roots and of rot.
The rose petals flowing onto the airy soil
already knew that even if the wind sweeps away signs
remembrance will come
of happiness, of grace,
and above all, of mercy,
lovingkindness.
Did my father know then
not to leave a child alone
near a window noisy
from the sounding Shofar within?
Did he know?

My father left
in a snatched moment of the month of Elul[105]

---

104. Rosh Hashanah occurs in the early fall (in the Hebrew month of Tishri); hence line 15. It is often the time of the first rains. The phrase, *"rose petals flowing onto the airy soil"* evokes, in Hebrew, both the Rosh Hashanah service, and Jeremiah 31:11: "For the Lord will ransom Jacob [Israel], Redeem him from one too strong for him. . . . They shall fare like a watered garden, They shall never languish again."

The references to "grace . . . mercy . . . lovingkindness" recall the traditional attributes of God.

105. Elul is the month before Tishri, on the first two days of which Rosh Hashanah falls. Traditionally, Elul is a month of spiritual introspection that ends with special penitential prayers.

and even when I turn against him
my thoughts dwell on him still.[106]

That is why—
though it's not in accord with the world's order—
so many years later
at the moment of nursing
my heart yearns
       for him still.

(1990)
—Translated by Miriyam Glazer

---

106. "*Even when I turned against him . . .*": The first five lines, and the last two, of this
stanza come from the *Zichronot* (Remembrance) verses that follow those extolling God's
sovereignty (the *Malkuyot*) during the Rosh Hashanah service. The English includes alter-
nate translations of Jeremiah 31: 14–19 (spoken during the Remembrance prayers), in
which the prophet speaks in the name of God of his son Ephraim (Israel), promising
redemption. Here it is reversed: juxtaposed into the words of the prayer is the image of
the daughter remembering her father as she nurses her own baby. In the book of Jeremiah
(31: 14–15), the matriarch Rachel is portrayed as the archetypal mother of Israel, imagined
"weeping for her children" and "refusing to be comforted" because they are gone (dis-
persed). "Restrain your voice from weeping," declares the prophet, "Your eyes from shed-
ding tears; For there is a reward for your labor . . . there is hope for your future." Perhaps
that hope is evoked in this poem through the image of the mother not weeping, but giving
birth and nursing her newborn.

Her, Me, and Yochanan

Chava Pinchas-Cohen

she whispers to me she says to me she says to me says to me she
  whispers to me says to me whispers to me whispers to me that she
    says drills
      into me says to me whispers to me again says to me whispers to me
        In the language that women who live in the land know
        but men who are born here do not speak
      in the language of the kitchen
    and the tub of dirty laundry
  of the family
who's disappearing

The poem draws from a rich well of ancient sources to explore the world of womanly intimacy and sensuality. "Yochanan" is a reference to Rabbi Yochanan of the Babylonian Talmud (Baba Metsia, 81a), known for his extraordinary beauty. He is depicted bathing in the Jordan. In the Hebrew original, the lines italicized here are in "Rashi script"—that is, in the typeface used for the Biblical and Talmudic commentary by Rabbi Solomon ben Isaac ("Rashi"), 1040–1105, when his commentaries were printed in 1465. The translations of lines four and five add the words "women" and "men" to convey the poet's use of feminine and masculine verb forms. Finally, " . . . the day she opens your eyes . . . you will know you are naked" is based on Genesis 3:7. "And the eyes of them both were opened, and they knew that they were naked"; the Biblical text, of course, refers to Adam and Eve.

she whispers to me says to me
she says to me says to me whispers to me
drills into me says to me
whispers to me says to me says to me says to me

and her words overflow
  on my eyes my shoulders
    and why do I polish the lens of my eye
      till it is a strange, cold, mirror of her
        for the day she opens your eyes oh my mother oh my daughter
          you know you are naked. You're alone. You're alone. You're alone.
            An untamed animal.

I'll jump into the river to the beautiful white
arms of Yochanan
who, too, is not of this world
and I will drown
in his loins.

(1994)
—*Translated by Miriyam Glazer*

My English Teacher

Chava Pinchas-Cohen

My English teacher is a journalist
for the gossip page of a woman's magazine
My English teacher—*A, B, C.*
Her fat husband
learns a new word
from the dictionary
every day.
Every passing day I say
I could have learned
a new word
from the dictionary.

My English teacher told us about
San Francisco—it was good there—
and taught us a lullaby:
Sweet dreams my dear
We are all pioneers
How is it then that I emerged
from all this split as
the asphalt in Tel Aviv—
a cross-walk

for words
from language
to language.

(1990)
—*Translated by Miriyam Glazer*

The Yearning of Karakashian

Chava Pinchas-Cohen

I carry in the vases the yearning
of Karakashian from Via Dolorosa 15, *Old City*.
All the yearning for Armenia, painted blue. (Since then all
the flowers of those distant hills
have been flattened, made identical. Six sky-blue petals,
orange stamens, and what might be pale-orange tulips from the hills,
reach up to the lips of the vase whose neck decorated
in a symmetrical pattern of pattern of green triangles.)

White does run in a slow, softly tinted, glorious gait
in golden-crowned grasses with a tongue of black fire.
And leaves, too, droplets, stalactites.
Oh, *Jerusalem Pottery*, the Armenian is in *Yerushalayim*[107]
dreaming of his green hills and drawing and I
fabricate a sound-track of footsteps
on the sidewalk of Valley Street,
beat the dust out of a goat-hair Bedouin carpet,

Long a landmark in the Old City of Jerusalem, the shop "Jerusalem Pottery" at Via Dolorosa 15 is owned by the Karakashian family, who are Armenian Christians.

107. *Yerushalayim* is Hebrew for "Jerusalem." The italicized "Jerusalem Pottery" appears in the poem in English (as do the words "Old City").

and a plate of Hebron glass (in that blue)
captures the uncommon light.

And to all these crying out like a wild dove
cooing on an antenna—

my land.

(1994)
—*Translated by Miriyam Glazer*

The Ineffable Name

Chava Pinchas-Cohen

Everyone's gone to the mount already and they're waiting,
waiting to see, waiting in great quiet—
even, strangely, the camels and the donkeys—
In this quiet not a bird twitters
or children on their fathers' shoulders.
An overwhelming quiet, as if before some
wondrous thing. Still—I wanted time
to hang out the laundry,
time for myself to freshen up
and I warmed the baby's milk so he won't get hungry—
and God forbid, cry at the wrong moment,
however long till then. You can expect

Based on the allusions in the poem, the "mount" referred to in line one is Mount Sinai.
" ... in this quiet not a bird twitters" comes from the Midrash: when the Holy One,
Blessed be He, gave the Torah at Mount Sinai, "not a bird twittered, no fowl flew, the bull
did not low ... the world was silent ... mute." The image of doing laundry is based on
Exodus 19:10: "The Lord said to Moses: 'Go unto the people, and sanctify them today
and tomorrow, and let them wash their garments'" to prepare to receive the Law. In lines
six and seven, the Hebrew for the word "thing" has a double meaning: *davar* can mean
"word" or "thing" and the Ten Commandments themselves are in Hebrew the ten *dib'rot*,
the ten "speakings." Finally, the title, "The Ineffable Name" is a traditional phrase to
describe God.

the laundry to dry—but the baby?
No one knew.
And I saw that a soft breeze, like the breath of a sleeping man, passed
through the laundry and ballooned the belly
of my nightgown and the Sabbath tablecloth
was a white sail in the middle of the desert
and we left there on the sky-blue
far away to the place where

we'll split open pomegranates and eat their juice
to the place where
love is
the ineffable name.

(1994)
—*Translated by Miriyam Glazer*

Introduction to Chava Pinchas-Cohen's "Journey of a Doe"

As if reconstructing Jerusalem throughout history, Pinchas-Cohen's "Journey of a Doe" is an ambitious poem covering a vast terrain. It incorporates language and images in a palimpset of voices from archeology, myth, history, Talmud, Kabbalah, and Bible (including Deuteronomy, Prophets, Lamentations, and the Song of Songs). The poem is replete with the names of streets and neighborhoods that also evoke Jewish history and the Jewish religious tradition. "Talpiot," for example, means "turrets"; the open air market in the heart of downtown Jerusalem, *Mahane Yehuda*, literally means "The Camp of Judah." "Shiloh" is the name of the religious center of the Tribes of Israel prior to the conquest of Jerusalem. At one point in the poem, the poet describes herself as standing on "Ramban and King George." "Ramban" Street was named in honor of the rabbinic sage Moshe ben Nahmon [Nachmanides] who, when first reaching Jerusalem in 1267, sent a message to his family back in Spain bewailing the plight of the city; "King George" was named for the British monarch during whose reign, in 1917, the Balfour Declaration was issued "looking with favor on the establishment of a home for the Jewish people in Palestine." To stand on "Ramban and King George" is thus spiritually to stand between the ancient desolation of the city during the Exile and the hope for return and redemption in the modern age. But just as the Shulamith of the Song of Songs is beaten and bruised by the "watchmen" as she searches the city for her beloved (Song of Songs 5:6‑7), so the poet is attacked by modern-day "Security Guards" as she stands between Exile and Redemption.

The tensions of the poem are most vividly evident in the way it is visually split. On the right side of the page is a voice at once arrogant, powerful, monarchical, and reminiscent of Shelley's Ozymandias. It is the voice of the Moabite king Mesha (c. 850 B.C.E.), whose words, in fact, appear on a stele unearthed in the nineteenth century which enumerates his wars with the Israelites and the architectural accomplishments of his reign. The voice of Mesha culminates in stone: the description of a monument "with my name in gold/ for eternity." But his countervoice is on the left side of the page, where the lines begin with an account of the effort made during the reign of King Hezekiah (700 B.C.E.) to *break through* stone. That is, drawing on the words from an inscription found by archeologists, the poet describes the attempt to hammer out through limestone rock a conduit of water from the Springs of Gihon (also known as "the Virgin's Spring") to the Pool of Siloam, within the walls of Jerusalem near where the Temple stood. The original inscription reads:

> . . . and this way the breach was made. While [the masons] were wielding their picks, one gang toward another, and while there were still three cubits to be [cut through], a man's voice [was heard] calling to his mate: for there was a fissure in the rock running from south to north.[108]

If the "Mesha" side of the page is dominated by the trope of stone, the voice of this side is as fluid as the water that the tunnel freed to flow into ancient Jerusalem. This voice is mythic, mystic, and female, one that moves in and out of the city's present and its many pasts. Stone is the visible and material; water, the hidden, underground, spiritual. It is resonant with meanings drawn from tradition. "Behold the day of the Lord cometh," says the prophet Zechariah, for example. "And on that day a fountain will be opened to the house of David and to the inhabitants of Jerusalem for the purification of sin. . . . And living waters shall go out from Jerusalem: half of them toward the eastern sea, and half of them toward the western sea: in summer and in winter" (13:1; 14:8). If the "source of living water" was cut off when the Jews went into exile, according to the Zohar, the return of the "living waters" to Jerusalem, and the "fountain" opened to the "house of David" are images of return and messianic redemption.

---

108. John C. L. Gibson, *Textbook of Syrian Semitic Inscriptions* (Oxford: Clarendon Press, 1971), p. 23.

The voice of Mesha slices through time and contexts. It is as if the same arrogance that built the "high place" of "Qarho" mentioned in the original stele built, in this century, the *Armon Ha'Natziv*, the Palace of the High Commissioner of the British mandate and later the headquarters of the United Nations on what was, prior to the Six Day War of 1967, the Israeli-Jordanian border. For Pinchas-Cohen, such (foreign) male powers have imprisoned the "King's Daughter," that is, the vessel of light variously identified in the mystical tradition as the soul, the Torah, the Shulamith of the Song of Songs, and the Divine Presence, the *Shekhinah.*

The core question of the poem thus becomes whether, in our generation, the "King's Daughter" can be set free. On the left side of the page the poem moves through time and space as it moves, too, toward an answer. She draws in architect Richard Kaufman (1887–1958), who was responsible for building what became German-Jewish enclaves in modern Jerusalem, and Moses Mendelssohn (1729–1786), the Jewish Enlightenment philosopher who distinguished between Jewish nationality and religious belief, authored the book *Jerusalem,* rejected a plan to establish a Jewish state in Palestine, and whose own descendants (including his grandson, the composer Felix) converted to Christianity. The poet evokes the book of Lamentations, describing the violence and suffering during the Roman siege of Jerusalem and the destruction of the Temple, though "her princes were purer than snow, whiter than milk" (Lam. 4:7). And then, just as, across the page, the voice of Mesha brags of his "powerful turrets" *(Talpiot),* she moves to the disaster of the ancient dispersion. It is from that moment in the poem on, that the doe begins to tread "the streets of the city."

The doe whose journey through history and through Jerusalem the poem maps evokes associations with the doe of the midrashic commentary on the Psalms who is described as worrying about the rain on behalf of all living creatures. She is the doe of the Kabbalah whose narrow womb, and thus difficulty in giving birth, serves as a figuration of the "birthpangs" of the messianic age and who, as *ayelet ha'shachar* ("the doe of the dawn," the morning star), was seen as a sign of the promised Redemption. And, finally, she is the doe of the Song of Songs who is cautioned by the bride "not to wake love till it is ripe" (3:5)—as if the Redemption cannot come until the people are ready.

Interwoven in this vast textual, mythic, and historical landscape is the voice of the poet. She traces the hoofprints of the doe as it seeks the scent of water. She witnesses its labored birth and the blood of its "afterbirth." Like the Shulamith, she wanders all over the city in search of her true spouse—that is, the true "spouse" of Jerusalem. She seeks the name of the son, the husband, the redeemer—that is, she seeks the pathway to the water. For if indeed she *could* find the water, if the hard materiality of the stony visible Jerusalem were to fuse with the underground life-giving water, there would be a sacred marriage. The people of Israel would end their exile, the King and the *Shekhinah* would reunite, God and the people Israel would become one.

But finally, in the poem, the doe is silent. The prophetic voice is muffled. The whispered name of the one who will bring about the messianic redemption for *Eretz Yisrael* goes ultimately unnamed. Toward the end of the poem, the left and the right sides of the poem are bridged just as they come into the present. And, in its closing lines, the poet reveals that the voices of this era are incapable of creating the *sukkah*, or tabernacle, in which, as the tradition teaches, the Divine Presence would then dwell.

If they cannot build a tabernacle, they cannot celebrate the Feast of Tabernacles—the festival on which the words of the prophet Zechariah are read: the vision of living waters going forth from Jerusalem, of the redemption of the Land, of Jerusalem itself dwelling "in safety" (Zech. 14:11). They will not hear of the building of Temple by King Solomon, nor of Joshua's promise after the death of Moses to enter the Land. At the end, it is as if Pinchas-Cohen is suggesting that our own era of cultural confusion and cacophony can erect only a tabernacle "without beams"—one, that is, inevitably doomed to fall.

Journey of a Doe

Chava Pinchas-Cohen

The pineneedles cast a quivering shadow on
   the stone   *I myself built*
House, and on the sounds of hammers beating it
   beating it beating
(till we heard a man's voice calling   *Qarho, the*
                                                      parkland

to his mate in the darkness, "Listen!").
And they exposed capillaries capillaries of red iron
   in the limestone   *walls and Jacob's*
                                                      Pasture

and the games of Mendelssohn or Richard Kaufman
with the cruel sun (in those days still   *and the walls of the*
tender and guileless,   *acropolis*
a virginal sun on the Jerusalem hills).

                                                      And Mamilla,
                                                      with its
                                                      pools and I
                                                      myself

About the breach. As if forever and always water
Would flow underground to Siloam and the City—   *built her gates*
a parable of the hidden, the fresh,
the full of promise.   *and her*
                                                     approaches
                                                     and I
                                                     myself

And in the upper city the pleasure of festivals
And the mulberry touched the ficus,
The olive tree near the overladen fig bending
   to the ground

built Talpiot:
her great

and powerful
turrets

(those were the first days of Tammuz)
night after night screams rose from the city,
the terror of the hunted.

And I built the
Palace

for the High
Commissioners
inside
a room for the

The doe treads the streets of the city
The doe of dawn, the doe of night, on the
   courtyard walls
and in-between doorways of Prophets' Street

glory
of the
imprisoned
King's
Daughter

she whispers her name—
she follows the scent of the water (oh the touch

whom the
media still

of maidenhair fern, the "Shulamith's Hair"
in the humid merciful dusk)
from the source to the pool
in the footprints of feet scorched from
   walking barefoot

haven't
discovered
and
Mount

From dawn-prayers to nightfall
And behind her, in silent strides, dressed in white,

Gilo Nature
Reserve

Princes and maidens of the city gather her whispers
to hoard in clay pots that quiver

for lovers of
her pines

with liquid twilight
like the sound of coins in beggars' tin cups

and her caves
and her
memories-
And I myself

And I was there the night
Blood of her afterbirth streamed down
   between her thighs

I opened her
pathways

And she cried that a stranger's tongue was licking
   the streets
And I called to her: *And I bruised*
                                      her bruises

"Doe, doe, whose womb is narrow, who is
   wholly love,
where is your child?

                                      To the
                                      heavens. And
                                      houses

"Doe, doe, whose womb is narrow and whose
   thighs are white,
where is your lover?" *of glass I*
                                      made for her

And I called her till I was found by Security Guards *so they will*
                                      come and see

Between Ramban Street and King George
they beat and bruised me, *and write and*
                                      photograph

but the maddening smell of her blood and the
   beauty of the soles
of her feet on the sidewalks gave me no rest *and there will*
                                      be nothing

I was beside myself—
And I called her in the Mahane Yehuda market
   and on Shiloh Street: they never heard of her
"Doe, doe, whose name are you whispering?

                                      and I made one day a
                                      year holy and

"Where is your son?
"Doe, doe, who is your husband? *I sanctified*
                                      a stone
                                      monument

"Doe, doe, doe *with my name on it*
                                      in gold

what road shall I take to the water?"

                                      for eternity.

         And this era is like a *sukkah* without beams
             concealing the city from her.

                                      (1994)
                           —*Translated by Miriyam Glazer*

Hamutal Bar Yosef

A professor of Hebrew Literature at Ben Gurion University in Beersheba, Hamutal Bar Yosef has published five books of poetry: *If Only I Had to Hurry* (1971); *To Take in Air* (1978); *Only the Green* (1981); *Jumping Jacks* (1984); and *Crowded* (1990). *Crowded* was awarded the Municipality of Tel Aviv Prize for Literature, as well as the prize of the Association of Writers and Composers in Israel.

Fluent in English, French, Russian, Yiddish, and German, as well as her native Hebrew, Hamutal Bar Yosef has studied the influence of Russian literature on the "New Hebrew Literature" of the nineteenth and twentieth centuries, Jewish literature written in Russian between 1870 and 1930; she has a special interest in both feminism and religion in Hebrew poetry. She has translated stories by Isaac Babel from the Russian, the poetry of Verlaine and Mallarme from the French, and, from English, the poetry of Esther Cameron and Shirley Kaufman (the latter of whom translated Bar Yosef's poetry for *Dreaming the Actual*).

Born on a kibbutz, Hamutal Bar Yosef earned her doctorate in Hebrew Literature at the Hebrew University in Jerusalem, lived in Tel Aviv, and later settled in Jerusalem. She is the mother of three children.

Jaffa, July 1948

Hamutal Bar Yosef

No one notices what I am doing by the border fence.
In the meantime people are busy moving pianos, carpets,
boiling the suspicious drinking water.
Behind the fence other people walk with their hands up.
This is not a dream. My mouth is dry
and the water not yet lukewarm, so in the meantime
through the border fence I am doing business with an Arab girl,
bubble gum from wet mouth to dry, for a slice of bread
with salty American butter, and the flies on her pus-filled
eyes settle on mine, in the meantime
import, export, a first taste of tourism.

That's how it was in Jaffa in July, 1948
When women and children were evacuated to occupied Jaffa
and refugees from the whole world were milling around
both sides of the fence.

(1981)
—*Translated by Shirley Kaufman*

Jaffa is the port city on the Mediterranean, south of Tel Aviv. Prior to the War of Independence in 1948, it was the gateway for Jewish immigration, though its population was primarily Arab. Heavy fighting raged on the Jaffa Tel Aviv border during the Independence War; the city fell to Jewish units in May 1948, on the eve of the declaration of the state of Israel.

Reflections on a Dove

Hamutal Bar Yosef

A blowzy dove. Beak wide open, on a *khamsin* day
next to the dog's leftover meat.
Pecks, crackles, brawls with the ants.

1.

You were fantastic
with your fluttering eyelashes
and delicate neck
all covered in pure
silver.

2.

An angel by nature?
It's easy like that
with a dreamy hand
to float *shalom*.
Why did you of all people want to leave through the hatch?
To bring home a medal?
Were you pulled by the pale blue emptiness

In Genesis 8: 8–12 Noah sends a dove out from the ark to see if the flood-waters have
abated. The dove brings back an olive leaf in its beak (8:11).

that looked like purity?
Was it great to faint from the absolute?

3.

Your skin is too white.
Jerusalem's sun
will touch you all day.
You won't be able to sleep for a week from the sunburn.

4.

Two by two they came out of the ark
blinking.
They didn't start praying right away.

5.

You proved the flood did not destroy the roots of the olive trees.
The root of evil goes deeper into this earth.
On what apple of Sodom do you make love?
On what are you building?

6.

To build a nest
to guard the fledglings
from owls
from hawks
from wind in the trees
from lightning
from bees
from the evil eye
from disease
from the plague of the first-born
from death in war
from other doves
from their fledgling brothers
and from themselves.

7.

And the earth is full of ants,
some flying, some writing, some building nests.

Come in, they'll spread their wings over you
so you can join their acid conversation
and find a family.

8.

Count how many children are left.
Learn how to scream.
Your throat will get tougher.
Your voice thick.

9.

They said she managed to look like a dove
even in the emergency ward, in spite of
the radiation, the infusions, and all that.
Others spoke of screams
when the treatment ended.

10.

Get out of yourself. Spoiled dove!
Be sharp and piercing.
Vote with your head to the wall.
They taught you to trust only madness.

11.

Now turn on the TV,
faces denounce you,
shouting *Arabieh Falastin!*[109]
They are younger, more fastidious than you.
There you are, speaking into your mirror,
ranting about love and peace in a hoarse voice,
pecking, cackling, brawling.

12.

When did I sit on the warm stairs,
the air full of dandelion seeds,
the dog stretched out next to me well fed and petted.
A blowzy dove, beak wide open, shifting the tin plate
with her beak
very close to me.

(1990)
—*Translated by Shirley Kaufman*

---

109. *Arabieh Falastin:* "Palestine for Arabs!"

In the Library

Hamutal Bar Yosef

1.

I got up. My legs too. Was I here? Yes.
Make me blind, foreign books
with your stinging chalk pages
and artificial light.
Help me to be
fog.

2.

Light crouches cool on gray windows.
Breath of elaborate manuscripts, bright
pages like orchids illuminated in gold
on the glittering tips of my fingers
rose lacquer leaves shut tight.
Are these hands
that made me glad to clean, to hug, to bake, to mend?

3.

Just today, more than two years already,
and the drills seem to be calmer,
sounds of things falling hard into wagons at night
have softened, only random images still trigger a gun,
every stain from the distance flows red.

Just today in the library behind a row of bent backs
catching a glimpse of a pattern
that I had once knitted—
not for you, no,
for you I never knitted a sweater—
and how is it I never knitted even one sweater for you?
Didn't I kiss you more than I kissed your big brothers?
And didn't I speak to you more words of love than I spoke
to your brothers, grieve with you, give you
more room than to each of your brothers?
But a sweater, I never knitted a single sweater for you:
I had not even thought of it till now.

(1990)
—Translated by Shirley Kaufman

An Angel on the Beach

Hamutal Bar Yosef

Now the wings of our thoughts belong to one angel
and the words before sleep or walking on the beach
and the moments we're filled and emptied
belong to the same mildly sexed angel
the one we've been fighting day and night
swearing to accomplish something heroic or sinful
as long as it won't catch us
and join our legs and our heads
and we've run away from each other to the ends of hell
burned our most precious possession
become ashes and dust and a spring of tears
given birth to mud. And we've drowned in the mud
and floundered till we were kneaded into a sort of soft angel
swaying on its feet not knowing the neighborhood
like a goose walking on the beach
when the sky has no color the sea no horizon
thinking it over, longing for one another with two beaks.

(1990)
—*Translated by Shirley Kaufman*

Agi Mishol

Drawing often on the images of everyday life, the poems of Agi Mishol have been variously described as lively, conversational, blunt, spontaneous, meditative, humorous, and characterized by a line from her own poem, "Estate": the ability to speak "entirely new phrases." Like Hedva Harechavi and Maya Bejerano, Mishol has been called one of the most important poets of her generation.[110]

On the editorial board of the literary journal *Helicon*, Agi Mishol was born in 1947 in Hungary, the only child of survivors of the Holocaust. The family immigrated to Israel in 1950, settling in the town of Gedera. After serving in the Israel Defense Forces, she studied Hebrew Literature at the Hebrew University in Jerusalem. She now teaches creative writing workshops as well as literature at Ben Gurion University, appears in the programs of "Art for the Nation," and participates in international festivals of poetry. She lives in the rural community of Kfar Mordecai.

Her first book of poetry was published in 1971; since then, she has published six more, most recently *Fax Pigeon* (Hakibbutz Hameuchad, 1991), and *The Interior Plain* (Hakibbutz Hameuchad, 1995), which won the Prime Minister's prize. For additional translations of her work, see *Modern Hebrew Literature* 6 (Spring/Summer 1991), and *Modern Hebrew Literature* 19 (Fall/Winter 1997).

---

110. See *Modern Hebrew Literature: Women's Writing in the 1980s* 6 (Spring-Summer 1991): 20, 33, and Yael Feldman, "The Ability to Speak Entirely New Phrases," *Seneca Review* 27:1 (Spring 1997): 36.

Estate

Agi Mishol

No peacocks will strut in my yard.
It's enough that this morning I rose from the sink
to the triptych of my face in the mirror,
too pink to my liking, what with the honey-blond hairdo,
too curly to boot, God, how tacky I've become.
So, no peacocks.

I'll purchase a pig
purchase a pig so I can speak
entirely new phrases, such as:
go check on the pig, or:
the cost of pigs has risen.
But no peacocks.

I am that pig from the previous stanza,
splayed on my side in a puddle of hurt.
So shove your "my tomboy my muffin
my soft cheese tomato" for words
aside and you aside,
I'm the cute hedgehog turned porcupine,
the livid porcupine
multiplying in every pupil of our pupils;
I'm the metallic green fly rubbing

its forelegs before your face
spinning malice
even if behind my back
clovers have begun to chatter spring,
reporting on my impressionistic life
and on the clear pink I show the world
when I yawn.

(1995)
—*Translated by Tsipi Keller*

The Sacred Cow of Hardship

Agi Mishol

In the hour between wolf and dog the sacred cow of hardship
promenades in my yard as if this were India. A mottled bow,
fat cow, cow, hey cow, what are you looking for here
where the *oy* blooms, can't you see how weary I am,
unable to tell if it's sleep I seek or death.
The weed of eking out a living wraps around me, draws a slash
of silence across me; I have nothing except
the brown stupor of your eyes. I, too,
am not at my best, am wrapped around the void
like a pretzel round its hole; my laughter exhales vanity,
my face the vanity of vanities, my body the folly of follies;[111]
on the one hand, oh, the fear of death, and on the other,
your bewilderment. One thing is clear, oh Lord, my shepherd,[112]
I am done for here,
and I have yet to decide
whether to slaughter or write about you
as you squat at the asterisk between the stanzas,
take life impersonally like a morning erection.

---

111. The phrase "vanity of vanities" is the traditional translation of Ecclesiastes 1:2.

112. See Psalm 23:1, 4.

Already lines leap at me to tell me about the gorgeous pink
packed in the contour of your teats,
as I build upon you verbal towers,
even if there's no hardship in the word hardship,
and in the end I'll be pierced by the two-edged sword
my poem directs upon itself.

(1995)
—*Translated by Tsipi Keller*

Gravity, Death

Agi Mishol

How weak his will to resist has become.
The hair falls out, the jaw drops,
the foot no longer lifts up
from the ground;
the drained body inclines toward it;
only the walking stick—an extension of sorts—
stands between them.

He sits before me
wrapped in his rent phrases
his skin a garment someone hastily left
behind on the chair.

For a moment I sit with my father
and for a moment I sit with my death
that befriends me through my crumbling father
who has begun to give back
to spirit what is spirit
to ashes what is ash.

(1995)
—*Translated by Tsipi Keller*

Shopping

Agi Mishol

1.

Through the supermarket aisles I push a cart,
as if I were the mother of two heads of cauliflower,
and navigate according to the verse-list
I composed this morning over coffee.
Sale banners wave to shoppers
studying labels on packaged foods
as Muzak entertains the frozen birds.
And I, too, whose life is made of life,
stroll down the dog-food aisle
toward Mr. Flinker who confides in my ear
that only the body crumbles but the spirit forever
remains young, believe me. I believe, but now let me turn
to Granny Smith and MacIntosh;
hurry, hurry, folks, to the coriander,
hurry, hurry, I'm the supermarket bard,
I'll sing the rustle of cornflakes,
the arch of mutinous gherkins,
until the register will hand me
the final printed version
of my poem.

2.

I'm clad in the essence of my housewifery
when suddenly, near the pickles,
you kid me, "Agi-Bagi,"
and then complicitly
pinch my ass
near the delicatessen counter
while your wife
among the dairy products
hunts for you
for the final ruling:
Lowfat?
Nonfat?

3.

(In the lingerie department
I heard a woman say:
I have nice legs
but my breasts are a flop.
With me, said another,
it's just the opposite.
My breasts are a knockout
but my legs are a flop.)

4.

I hugged you
and you hugged a watermelon.
I loved you and you didn't
know what to do
with the watermelon;
your hands wanted
to hug me but couldn't
let go of the watermelon;
on the other hand
what could you say,
wait, let me just
put down
the watermelon?

(1995)
—*Translated by Tsipi Keller*

Devorah Amir

Devorah Amir was born in Jerusalem during the 1948 War of Independence to parents who had immigrated to Israel from Poland. She studied Hebrew Literature, Jewish Philosophy, and Jewish Mysticism at the Hebrew University of Jerusalem after the Six Day War of 1967, and in the 1970s was at the University of Illinois, studying English Literature.

She has described her poems as "whispers against forgetfulness," a way of dulling the pain of separation and capturing the vanishing world of her mother and the Polish-Russian immigration to Israel. "It is difficult to describe the poems," she says. "They write themselves." Her book, *Slow Burning (B'irah Eeteet)*, was published in 1994 by Hakibbutz Hameuchad.

Devorah Amir works at the Center for Educational Technology writing programs on language and literature.

After Fall, 1956

Devorah Amir

Strips of adhesive tape criss-crossed the windowpane cutting
checkerboards with Margosa branches.
Thin strings burst out of the branches like sheaves of fireworks,
dropping lanterns of golden fruit at their tips—ammunition for the
children's wars.
After that fall mother took a basin of hot water and scraped off the
windowpane.
She tore the strips, warp and woof, that made crosses in her eyes,
saw
her Dovid caught on the fence
and as if bandaging a dead man's wounds to revive him
she whispered, "The war is over."

(1994)
—*Translated by Miriyam Glazer*

Following the British and French, the Israelis invaded the Sinai desert and Gaza on October 29, 1956 (in what is often called the "Suez War"); by November 5, the Israeli operation ended; 180 Israelis soldiers were killed and four taken prisoner. (The troops, however, did not withdraw until March 15, 1957.)

I Have Longings for My Dead

Devorah Amir

I have longings for my dead
I haven't erected even the tip of an obelisk for them
and I haven't made rituals with stones.
They travel with me light, transportable,
to Egypt, to the sea, to hotels, weddings, the emergency room,
the delivery room, bed.

(1994)
—*Translated by Miriyam Glazer*

What Seeps In

Devorah Amir

In every photo in your album the women workers huddle
so closely together their temples touch each other,
a brazen, direct, look, just like the photographer wanted.
Bending on your knee, you sort sugar beets in the corner
as if refusing to take part in the proletarian pose.

The day I glanced gently at your beautiful legs,
I discovered bite marks on your calves.
So by chance does a child discover
traces of a parent's scars.
All those years you strode about this country—a world
foreign to me clung to your legs
like a forbidden garden, a cruel landlord,
guard dogs, a girl attacked.
Once on George Eliot Lane near "Sisters of Zion" convent
fear overwhelmed me suddenly—they would drag me inside,
dress me in orphans' clothes, lock me in a cellar
steeped in the smells of crucifixes
and from the dark folds of a monk's robes
I would be bitten by Satan's dogs.

(1994)
—*Translated by Miriyam Glazer*

Thoughts about Sari's Jump

Devorah Amir

The silouette of a woman appears in my mind as if from a
      sixteen millimeter film.
A celluloid image in black and white, a hoarse, weak, sound track, a poor
copy of an old movie. A beautiful young woman from Botticelli's
   drawings.
Her face like the faces of the girls in the drawing "The Libel,"
      her body enveloped in black,
more tortured and emaciated than their plump bodies. And she walks
   on Givat Ram.

Once, in the "Tales of Rabbi Nachman,"[113] we read together
      of the amazing memory
of someone who remembers when he was a mere drop
at the moment of conception.
You said, "I'd like forgetfulness as large as his memory,"
because one who remembers nothing, "is above it all and remembers
even what comes before Self, Spirit, Soul."

---

113. The tales of Rabbi Nachman of Bratslav are parable-like kabbalistic and mystical
stories told by the Hasidic master (1772–1810).

God, where is the impulse from, to touch death with trembling fingers
yellow from cheap cigarettes?
And so, at the end of her perfectly starched cuffs
her bandaged wrists were exposed. She was like a bird marked with a ring.
In the morning she announced that she was jumping and she went to
    the Old City.[114]
Her black dress spread like wide wings in the air.

(1994)
—*Translated by Miriyam Glazer*

---

114. The walled Old City of Jerusalem.

The "Nightingale" of Uncle Yair

Devorah Amir

Uncle Yair, against a white ceramic wall in my mother's kitchen,
pressed his head
to cool off stormy pink bays on his brow.
And mother said, "Yair, you need a home. You know, a wife and work."
And Yair asked for tea. And when the cookies were gone he sucked
a cube of sugar to the last grain
"so the tears won't be salty" and thought, *wo bin ich in der Welt—*
where am I in the world.
And mother said, "Zvi thank God has gotten along, Roite Malech
too, has found something, maybe
we'll find something by Schmil at the "Stone & Limestone" quarry."[115]
Uncle Yair didn't answer, he started singing.
"The nightingale, the nightingale don't interrupt with song,
don't wake don't wake . . . soldiers at the front,
again at the front spring breathes free, but the soldier doesn't sleep . . . "[116]
Such a longing for that spring scorched in him, for the soldiers that
    came to free,
and mother said, *"Yair, du bist nicht alleine in der Welt,"*
and afterward, in Hebrew, "we are all alone."

(1994)
—*Translated by Linda Zisquit*

---

115. The "Stone and Limestone" *(Ehven va Sid)* was a quarry owned by the construction
cooperative Solel Boneh, once responsible for much of the building in Israel.

116. A popular nationalist Russian song. After he sings the song, the mother's Yiddish
response is, "Yair, you are not alone in the world."

One Girl's Dance

Leah Aini

One girl's dance
in an alley.
A spidery arc of movement above,
in front,
arms climbing
intoxicating bubbles
of her murmured song.
Just so.
Not to rain,
not to love, not
to God.
A cleaving
to a dream of the actual,
breathing touch
spinning the self
and the shadow.

(1991)
—Translated by Miriyam Glazer

For an introduction to the work of Leah Aini, see Part One, p. 90 ff.

Liquidation

Leah Aini

The Ramat Gan houseware shop
was liquidating the old woman
to her great sorrow, which
hovered over the chaos of customers,
aborting kiddish cups,
making a clatter of the rusty bed-pans.
Her family rushed to sell
a blue Chinese vase
before it shattered on its own.
I chose a horse, red and thin,
and a candlestick in the shape of a child.
With my own hands I paid the old woman
who rattled hopelessly with cutlery fingers
and bleated in the steam that wept
from a tin kettle.
When I came home I read Psalms
and invited the old woman
to come, from time to time to ride
the horse that holds letters,
to touch the child,
and to kindle the light of the Yahrzeit candle[117]
when she sees my soul stumble
on the hands of the old clock.

(1990)

—*Translated by Miriyam Glazer*

---

117. *Yahrzeit candle:* A memorial candle lit in honor of the dead.

350

In Their House

Leah Aini

In their house some door is always
left open
Maybe he'll drop in for a visit
from the land of the dead
stretch out on his short youth bed
and fall asleep
for half an hour, an hour,
not more.
They'll come in, all quiet,
gasping for breath,
to wipe gray sweat from his forehead,
a mole, a worm,
And to feel, O God,
again,
just once more,
with stiff, frozen fingers
his temples—pounding
the stone-face,
shouting.

(1990)
—*Translated by Miriyam Glazer*

Shower

Leah Aini

The combing of my hair by grandma . . .
still today pleasure-combs
sting me into memory

In the small shower room in the yard
a mirror like a belly spilling over
on a wall swollen from steam
the color of split sky—
On the side a tank of boiling water breathes
clouds of foam on the cement floor
All the sky bathed there, a cloud and a cloudlet,
childhood and me,
Two by two grandma brought us in
to the shower
I am keeping the touch of this picture, keeping it like a bitch
over a bone

Years later
a man combed my hair
his touch was soft, the strokes
of the hand warm
passion bubbles foamed on it
but it had nothing to do with
cleanliness.

My second grandmother
entered the shower alone
without me
(many years before I was born)
the gas combed the cement walls
to find sky
but the sky of Auschwitz
refused to be bathed
unless my grandmother turned first into
soap
Here too I think it had nothing to do with cleanliness
but I also saved this picture
I save it like a bitch
and already a long time ago, a long time ago, I buried
the bone of the murder
and the bone of bathing
in the garden of life.

(1990)
—Translated by Linda Zisquit

The Empress of Imagined Fertility

Leah Aini

A baby carriage abandoned
in the stairwell
A colorful napkin staining
the strip of grass behind me.
In the yard
mothers on one leg
lighting butt from butt,
baby slings strapped
round their hips,
creatures kicking in their bellies.
And I, mad, on the roof
nestle in snowing laundry
pregnant with pain.
Nine stars
and not one moon
around me,
empress
of imagined
fertility.

(1990)
—*Translated by Miriyam Glazer*

Nidaa Khoury

Nidaa Khoury is a Palestinian poet who was born in the Upper Galilee village of Fassouta in 1959. She has published five books of poetry in Arabic, including a second edition of *The Belt of Wind*, published in Beirut, Lebanon, in 1993, and *The Culture of Wine*, published in Nazareth (Al Nahda), also in 1993. Her collection, *The Barefoot River* (Jerusalem, Ishkolot Publishing) was published in Arabic and Hebrew in 1990. Her latest collection, *The Bitter Crown*, was censored by the Jordanians, who prevented its publication in 1997.

Nidaa Khoury's poetry has been the subject of studies at the University of Haifa and the Hebrew University and has been reviewed by the Arab press. She currently teaches Creative Writing in the town of Tarshiha, and works for The Association of Forty, an organization for Human Rights and for the full acceptance of the "Unrecognized Villages" in Israel.

She has been an active participant in international poetry conferences, including the Conference of Arab Poets held in Amsterdam, and the Conference of Human Rights and Solidarity with the Third World, in Paris.

She lives in the village of Fassouta. She is married and the mother of four children.

Death Is Your Salvation

In Memory of Rashid Husein

Nidaa Khoury

Get out of me a little
so that I'll see you as half an orange.
Get out of me you squeezed one,
color of drunkenness.

Get out of my walls:
their sorrow breeds pain,
their swords fire my rage.
Get out and tell them about me.
Say to them I am a death-bed,
Say to them I am . . . you.

Come back to me as a sea
from the sand, from the rocks,

Rashid Husein (1936–1977) was a poet from an Arab Muslim village near Haifa who spent many years in Israeli prisons for his political beliefs. He was an editor of the Arab journal *Al-Fajr* (The Dawn), which was banned in 1962. He translated the poetry of Hayim Nahman Bialik from Hebrew into Arabic, and translated Palestinian folk songs into Hebrew. After the Six Day War in June 1967, Husein left Israel and settled in New York City, where he died in a fire in his apartment. Most of his poetry was concerned with the predicament of the Palestinians both in Israel and in the Palestinian diaspora.

come back from the desert
to my sea,
come back from each chapter,
each verse of the exile.
Come back to the land of sorrow,
you, a man whose blood is different,
whose white blood has
another taste.

Come back to my desert,
you, sand of all shores—come back.
Strip off the waves,
put on your own surf
and come to my rage,
quit the kisses of all the seas
that kiss whenever you leave
and come to my cloudburst,
those kisses
hidden by sister
lover
mother, flooding the seas . . . with seas.
In each dot of rain

there are kisses hidden for you
in the name of the fire in your body,
in your name, in your time,
death is a salvation.

(1987)

—Translated by Shirley Kaufman
and Roger Tavor

People of Fire

Nidaa Khoury

Burn generations,
burn the olive leaves
raise incense.
Burn their fingertips.
Smoke.
Burn their farewells
and go.
Burn their cookbooks
burn the kindling.
Infuse their wheat
and scatter it
on the rooftops.
They burn the candle's end
illuminate the shame of graves.
Dress in ashes and lie down like coals.

(1994)
—Translation from the Hebrew
translation of Sasson Somech
by Karen Alkalay-Gut

People of Pomegranates

Nidaa Khoury

Roll within themselves
seeds of love and liberty
from the dawn of time.
And now they break up
in the mother's hips
into wedges wedges
and she bursts
this is the land
narrow of womb
the place erupts.

(1994)
—*Translation from the Hebrew*
translation of Sasson Somech
by Karen Alkalay-Gut

People of Figs

Nidaa Khoury

In the land of milk and honey
whenever they pick unripe dates
and children in their dawn
the pain dries
like curdled milk
rivers in my land will drip
the land of milk and honey

(1994)
*—Translation from the Hebrew
translation of Sasson Somech
by Karen Alkalay-Gut*

People of Olives

Nidaa Khoury

They come and are pressed
like those impressed with a Mission.
Thus thought the crushed:
In the crushing is most of the oil.
Our oil has been sold like our blood
to the holy places
for we are poor
our land is holy
and our palace is the Mount of Olives.

(1994)
—*Translation from the Hebrew
translation of Sasson Somech
by Karen Alkalay-Gut*

A Special Section: American Israeli Poets Writing in English

> *. . . though*
> *the pilot explains the rocking of the plane*
> *as turbulence, I know it is that cord*
> *pulling*
> —Karen Alkalay-Gut, "Transportation"

I doubt whether there are other countries—even ones bigger than Israel—that have separate professional associations for Romanian, Georgian, Polish, Russian, Arab, Spanish, English—as well as Hebrew—writers, or where other writers also produce poetry in Ladino and Yiddish. Transculturality is woven into the fabric of thousands of Israelis' lives. In the past, great ideological pressure was exerted to cast off the language and culture of the diaspora, Hebraicize one's name, and pour oneself wholeheartedly into the enterprise of creating a new Hebrew literature. But in our day, with its waning ideological hold and its much greater global fluidity, that pressure has all but disappeared. Instead, transculturality is embraced as an asset. As the fiction of Dina Rubin and Elena Makarova suggests, many Russian writers in Israel continue to write in their native language. The same is true for a group of American writers whom readers may find particularly intriguing: American-born poets in Israel who, after many years in the country, continue their dedication to writing in English.

Shirley Kaufman, Rachel Tzvia Back, Linda Zisquit, and Karen Alkalay-Gut all live transcultural and translingual lives. They actively participate

362

in the Israeli literary scene and often translate poetry from the Hebrew, while continuing to write their own poetry in English (which, in turn, has been translated into Hebrew). The "cord" pulls both ways—toward Israel, and toward the States. Perhaps for the first time in history, one no longer has to choose between them.

Shirley Kaufman

Once a first-generation American who grew up in an assimilating family in Seattle and who lived for many years in San Francisco, Shirley Kaufman has been "an American hyphen Israeli" since making her home in Jerusalem in 1973. Her first poem—published in 1945—was a protest against the British White Paper that prevented Jewish refugees from entering Palestine; her most recent book, *Roots in the Air: New and Selected Poems* (Copper Canyon Press, 1996), captures her own sense of living between cultures, languages, and identities. Acts of translation are part of her life: her own work has been translated into Chinese, Arabic, Danish, and Dutch, as well as into Hebrew, appearing in Israeli journals and newspapers, and collected in book form (*Selected and New Poems*, trans. Aharon Shabtai [Bialik Press, 1995]). She has translated the poetry of Israelis Abba Kovner and Amir Gilboa, and she collaborated with Judith Herzberg on the award-winning translation of the latter's poems from the Dutch.

Shirley Kaufman's books of poetry include *The Floor Keeps Turning, Gold Country, From One Life to Another, Looking at Henry Moore's Etchings in Jerusalem During the War* (with the Moore etchings), *Claims, Rivers of Salt,* as well as her newest *Roots in the Air,* from which many of the poems that appear here have been taken. She is also coeditor, with Galit Hasan-Rokem, of *The Defiant Muse: Hebrew Feminist Poems from Antiquity to the Present* (Feminist Press, 1999).

Déjà Vu

Shirley Kaufman

Whatever they wanted for their sons
will be wanted forever, success,
the right wife, they should be
good to their mothers.

One day they meet at the rock[118]
where Isaac was cut free
at the last minute. Sara stands
with her shoes off under the dome
showing the tourists with their Minoltas
around their necks the place
where Mohammed flew up to heaven.
Hagar is on her knees
in the women's section praying.

They bump into each other at the door,
the dark still heavy on their backs
like the future always coming after them.
Sara wants to find out what happened

---

118. Mount Moriah in Jerusalem is the legendary site of the *Akedah*, the Binding of Isaac, and since the seventh century, C.E., also the site of the Mosque of Omar (Dome of the Rock); from the rock on which tradition teaches Isaac was bound, and from which Mohammed is believed to have ascended into heaven.

to Ishmael but is afraid to ask.
Hagar's lips make a crooked seam
over her accusations.

They know that the world is flat,
and if they move to the edge
they're sure to fall over. They know
they can only follow their own feet
the way they came.
Jet planes fly over their heads
as they walk out of each other's lives
like the last time, silent, not mentioning
the angels of god and the bright
miracles of birth and water. Not telling
that the boys are gone.

The air ticks slowly. It's August
and the heat is sick of itself
waiting all summer for rain.
Sarah is in her cool villa.
She keeps her eyes on the pot
so it won't boil over.
She brings the food to the table
where he's already seated
reading the afternoon paper
or listening to the news,
the common corruptions they don't
even speak about now.
Guess who I met she says talking
across the desert.

Hagar shops in the market.
There's a run on chickens, the grapes
are finished and the plums are soft.
She fills her bag with warm bread
fresh from the oven thinking
there's nothing to forgive,
I got what I wanted from the old man.
The flight in the wilderness
is a morning stroll.
She buys a kilo of ripe figs. She
climbs the dusty path home.

                                        (1996)

Stones

Shirley Kaufman

When you live in Jerusalem you begin
to feel the weight of stones.
You begin to know the word
was made stone, not flesh.

They dwell among us. They crawl
up the hillsides and lie down
on each other to build a wall.
They don't care about prayers,
the small slips of paper
we feed them between the cracks.

They stamp at the earth
until the air runs out
and nothing can grow.

They stare at the sun without blinking
and when they've had enough,
make holes in the sky
so the rain will run down their faces.

They sprawl all over the town
with their pitted bodies. They want
to be water, but nobody
strikes them anymore.

Sometimes at night I hear them
licking the wind to drive it crazy.
There's a huge rock lying on my chest
and I can't get up.

(1996)

Security

Shirley Kaufman

If only she could make herself
shuffle the papers on her desk
and sort out what to deal with
and what to dump and what to fill out
and who to thank and when to pay. If only
she could arrange them neatly
the way he arranges his pills each morning.
If only she had a system of priorities—
most, more, least
terribly, very, oh well—
especially since mail had been accumulating
for weeks, months, even before it happened,
even a year. If only he went out sometimes.
If only he weren't hurting all day,
all night from the gash
in the middle of his shaved chest
and the split of his rib cage,
from the two slits up the sides
of his hairless legs. His patched body.
His pain. If only she could complain.
If only he'd answer the phone. If only
he wouldn't say didn't you make soup.
If only she could lie down alone

369

and sleep for ten hours. If only she could
stop complaining. If only he ate yoghurt.
If only she could cook. If only
she could find his glasses. If only she could
write a poem. If only they could stop watching
the news. If only they could stop looking
at the cut-up faces. If only twenty-two people
weren't blown up in the bus yesterday.
If only they could turn it off.
If only they could stop talking
about security.

(1996)

Job's Wife

Shirley Kaufman

She has to pity him after what happened,
rocking alone like that in the rubble,
covered with boils. She's watched him scrape
his sores with anything broken, half naked
and bleeding, scraping his soul.

And if she staggers out of the dark
to hound him when he is busy
with his own grief, surely he'll speak
for her too, three daughters, seven sons,
aren't they in this together?

She's wearing the slip she had on
when the house was blitzed and everything
with it: children, donkeys, we know
how many. And how, with nothing to lose,
She begs him to damn God and die.

He's all that's left, beyond what they
used to be for each other, abuse
or solace. He scratches his scabs
and tells her she's foolish. She stares
at the rancid sky.

(1996)

371

The Mount of Olives

Shirley Kaufman

The hills slide eastward into the desert
from the Mount of Olives,
a slow process the natives ignore.
The coffee is sweet and bitter
in the small cups.

What are you doing in Jerusalem?

A donkey staggers over the slope
of the cemetery, carrying a load of rocks.
Everything glitters.
Everything's hammered by the sun
into bright mica.

Only the dead are dull.
They have all the answers.

It's a clear day. When I turn
I can see the mountains of Moab
renewing themselves in the blue distance
on the other side.

The Dead Sea shines at the bottom of the world
like the black, original water.

(1996)

Linda Zisquit

Originally from Buffalo, New York, Linda Stern Zisquit was educated at Tufts, Harvard, and SUNY Buffalo, before moving to Israel, where she has made her home in Jerusalem with her husband and family since 1978. She writes, translates, teaches Poetry and Creative Writing at Hebrew University and at the Wesleyan University Overseas Program in Israel, as well as running an art gallery in Jerusalem that represents leading Israeli artists.

After two decades of living in Jerusalem, Linda Zisquit perceives herself as an Israeli poet who writes in English (for what happens in Israel matters to her and nourishes her; her five children are Israeli, and she translates the work of Israeli poets) and, at the same time, as an American poet living in Israel (because she writes in English, publishes in the States, and returns frequently to help care for her aging parents, as well as feeling deeply connected to beloved people and places here).

Her books of poetry are *Ritual Bath* (Broken Moon Press, 1993) and *Unopened Letters* (Sheep Meadow Press, 1996); *Wild Light: Selected Poems of Yona Volach* (Sheep Meadow Press, 1997), her translations from the Hebrew, received a National Endowment for the Arts translation fellowship. Her translations of Israeli poets frequently appear in the journal *Modern Hebrew Literature in Translation*.

From Unopened Letters

Linda Zisquit

An unopened letter is like an uninterpreted dream.
—Talmud

1.

Because passion is the silence we share
your absence must find my tongue.
To speak of love—that generous garden—
is to speak of borders overgrown, erased,
torn down. And a woman without borders
belongs to anyone. I see myself
in this brutal light: halved, hugging
yellow margins, whoring after man
and gods whose weight and sore inform
by days uncertain. On trial, hooded faces
before and behind. You ask what can it
matter in this world, this iron wall?
I ride through this question as though
it were a woods given to any vision.

2.

Because passion is the absence we speak
I am seeking another silence
to trace my transgressions,

step outside the frame of experience,
inform a book with divinity.
I know that dark descends.
As I know the back of an honest man.
From the way he stands he is faithful,
free, face to face (with God?)
A mere back, yet I envy his
connection, so real the projection
of my loss. I stand in my own rejection,
remember what closeness would be like,
and know the faces I've lost.

6.

There is always a sound
in the pine trees
and because I was there with you
I can't tell anyone.
Always a wind
through the pines
on a hill
at the edge.
Is it the sound
coming back from the muezzin
to the pines?
Or my mouth,
and inside the throat,
nothing?
Not for any other utterance
or any other punishment
though all I love now
will be cut off from me.
No future future
but those pines, this wind.

(1996)

After Years of Feasting and No Sacrifice

Linda Zisquit

I can see how Abraham answered.
Even the plodding walk up a mountain,
that slow-motion-holding-back
of a soul anxious to encounter
what luminous task awaits it.
After these things,
how could I not have suffered
hot oil behind my eyes,
the smack across my face to wake me?

(1996)

A Word before the Last about Loss

For I will go into the grave unto my son mourning.
—Genesis 37:35

Precisely because you are alive
there is no comfort in this world.
Because wherever you are not
I search, and where I hear your step
you have not been or left a mark.
So the roads are trampled by one,
not two. And the past is maimed
by remembering more. Just as
an old man cannot live at peace
clutching a rag of stripes as proof
without a swish of snakes underneath,
without imagining profoundest dis-
ease that follows him—a body
of bones, a soul clanking around—
it is asking for comfort where
there is none, possessing the one
thing alive that has no end.

(1996)

377

Rachel Tzvia Back

Born in Buffalo, New York in 1960, Rachel Tzvia Back was raised in a family who felt profoundly connected to Israel, a connection, she believes, that was "clearly transmitted to their five children and became a crucial factor in our developing identities." Living in Israel intermittently during her childhood, she immigrated to the country on her own in 1981, living first on a kibbutz in the Golan Heights and subsequently moving to Jerusalem.

After serving in the Israel Defense Forces, she completed her B.A. in English Literature and Psychology at the Hebrew University of Jerusalem. Later she returned to the States for an M.A. in Creative Writing at Temple University, where she studied with postmodern poets Rachel Blau DuPlessis and Susan Howe. "Howe, an Irish-American and a poet strongly identified with the landscapes of her past and present, later wrote me how happy she was I had returned to Israel, for a poet . . . must be in the place where the spirits speak to her. It was clear to her that Israel was that place for me," writes Back. Connecting her cultural crossings once again, Back has recently completed a Ph.D. dissertation on the poetry and poetics of Susan Howe.

From 1990 to 1998, Rachel Tzvia Back taught English literature courses at the Hebrew University in Jerusalem, where she also initiated, developed, and taught an English-language poetry workshop. She currently works as the Israeli director of the Wesleyan University Overseas Program on Israeli and Palestinian Studies. In addition, she is involved in research into the iconoclastic poetry of contemporary American women poets and she translates the work of contemporary Israeli poets.

Back's poetry has appeared in numerous journals in Israel and the United States, including *The American Poetry Review, Sulfur, Tikkun, Tyuonyi, The Painted Bride Quarterly, Modern Poetry in Translation. ARC, Ariel, The Tel-Aviv Review, Bridges,* and *Apex of the M.* Her chapbook entitled *Litany* was published by Meow Press in 1995, and she was a 1996 recipient of the Israeli Minister of Absorption's Award for Immigrant Writers. A collection of her work translated into Hebrew by Israeli poets Aharon Shabtai and Zali Gurevitch is forthcoming from Ha'Kibbutz Ha'Meuchad Press. Some of her translations of contemporary Israeli women poets are included in the Feminist Press anthology entitled *The Defiant Muse: Hebrew Feminist Poems from Antiquity to the Present.*

Rachel Tzvia Back has recently moved to the village of Ya'ad in the Lower Galilee, where she lives with her husband and children.

Notes: From the Wait

Rachel Tzvia Back

1.

No namable danger to the season.
The heat an absence of air absence
of desire. Behind the doors we painted
blue we pull shades low move slow:

let others stake out their territory.

What we have lost will stay lost
last half moon buried under.

I know now we belong
to no part of this landscape.

2.

At night the road to the capital
disappears.

Mountains bulldozed and abandoned
open to the sun and slow deaths
move together to console.
Displaced dirt red at first
unearthing returns dry and dark
in gathering of the exiled

All our markings sword to stone
are vanishing

3.

We of a scorched generation
while night nets in its stars

And the half-drained swamp
returns to swamp.

Musk smell of hot trees in water
thickening like fire: land
of pale wood pyres.

Through smoke darkness I hear
drum murmurs over the valley:

the sacrifice done not done

4.

Dawn
White hillside boulders
gather forces to storm city walls:

stone on stone on marked stone.
Last deafening insurrection
as splintered city gates burn.

Far from home at home no one
speaks now of exiles
that will end

5.

You are right to stay away.
Those prayers on the doorpost
will protect no one.

As to why we remain:
we're busy now
Waiting

behind blue doors
for the season that will not pass
to pass

(1992)

Untitled

Rachel Tzvia Back

                    you ask
why here, in the high north,
perched on peaks and slopes,
open to the sky's full weight
of fringed clouds
and bombs, why here?
We stopped on our way to the sea
and stayed: I remember
no more but the stars
told stories, pointed
nowhere. We built homes
on stilts, terraced the hillside
and the mountain now wears rings
of red dirt paths round her,
wedded as we are.
We bathe in these mists,
our salt is of stone, and we carry
this sky on our shoulders, heavy
and warm. In winter, wrapped in shrouds
of white silence and space, there is
no escape: god follows, bears down
with the weight of a child
in your arms, on your mind.

Our youngest carried dreams
of a side unseen, climbed over
a barbed wire fence last spring
and in the valley stepped on a mine.
The soil is not fertile, too many rocks,
and too many years are meager.
Muscles ache and the heart,
but we are mountain people,
we cannot live on flat land.

(1989)

Abu Salim, Healer

Rachel Tzvia Back

Speaks to spirits
in crowned black letters
strange language a gift of angels in green
he says he remembers only when healing.

Abu Salim touches
those who ache from a spirit
holding to the heart
twisting blood or bone.

For the girl
with a yellow spirit
behind her dry eyes
he burns the dust of red stone

Seven days
in flames, has her breathe
the bitter smoke
to loosen the *jin*

Sways
them both in an orange smoke
until the half-built hut tilts
toward the dry river.

While she sleeps
he bargains with the spirit, says:
Leave through her shoulders
and they will be yours—she will bend.

Leave through her thighs
and she will wander.
But not through her eyes.
They are no good

To you who looked
and back again
on fire. Ash in the air.
She wants water.

Abu Salim says
the spirits can be reasonable
(when she wakes, her back aches,
alone in a goat skin tent beside the hut)

Says the dry river
will flood this winter
(and she is crying)
but there is no telling when.

(1996)

Gaza, Undated

Rachel Tzvia Back

1.

After the final heave, house collapsing
in and all the prayers that had held
the ceiling up for years rushing
through dust with a low moan
but leaving, you have seen her
sifting through the rubble,
sandaled foot striking an iron
bed frame, splintered picture
of a prophet's resting place.
With no tears you have seen her,
dry like stone, like tile, and alone.

Then understand the Law as I did not:
we tore her house down and she may not rebuild
there or elsewhere. *Her kitchen smelled of zatar
and of bread.* She will have no home here, no home.

2.

Consider the prayer's desertion and our faith
crushed where it had been tucked neatly
between headscarves in the top drawer

even as our walls still stand: *there is
no believing now. Only children in alleys,
their blood darkening the dirt.*

After the rains, this mound will settle, sink
in on itself and forget what it was.
But she will not forget.

                                        (1989)

After Eden

Rachel Tzvia Back

We slept on the edge of town, in the last building
before desert. Freight trains carried salt
all night through our sleep, rusted boxcars
from forty years before clanging north, then south
at the edge of town. We could have forgotten
that wandering, but there were still dreams
of thirst and yellow winds.

By dark morning, our car parked in the last light
of the last street lamp, our eyes narrowing,
we saw late the side window shattered
around a hole at the center: Cain's splintered
web across our foreheads in the glass.
We could have forgotten that mark, still
stunned to be so far from Eden.

(1997)

Karen Alkalay-Gut

Born in London during the last night of the Blitz to parents who were ardent Zionists, had escaped Hitler and been granted temporary visas in England, Karen Alkalay-Gut was brought to the States in 1948, and raised in Rochester, New York. Her own belief in the necessity of a homeland for the Jews and in the socialist spirit of the then still-new country led her to immigrate to Israel thirty-five years ago.

"Am I American? Am I Israeli?" asks Alkalay-Gut. She has taught American Poetry at Tel Aviv University since 1977; her two children have returned to the States, to live in New York. "But I exist in Israel, my experiences are here, and so are my subjects," she says. "So I am an Israeli poet who writes in English, with an American poetic context."

The transculturality of Alkalay-Gut's work is evident in her publications. Though written in English, three of her books, *Butter Sculptures* (1983), *I\Thou and Other War Poems* (1994), and *Paranormal Poems* (1997) have been published in Hebrew, with a fourth due in 1998; *Making Love* (1980), *Ignorant Armies* (1992), *Between Bombardments* (1992), *Love Soup* (1992), *High School Girls* (1992), and *Recipes* (1994) were published in Israel, and in 1997, *Life in Israel: November 1995–1996* was published on the Internet. She is also actively engaged in translation; more than three hundred poems from the Hebrew have appeared in journals, books, and anthologies (including her translations of the poetry of Raquel Chalfi, which appear in *Dreaming the Actual*). Alkalay-Gut serves on the editorial board of the *Tel Aviv Review* and as the Hebrew Poetry Editor in the dual-language Cross Cultural Communication series. She has been the co-editor of the *Pen Israel Anthology 1997*, *Jerusalem Review 1996*, and the *Anthology of English Writing in Israel, 1997.*

She lives in Ramat Aviv.

From Between Bombardments:
A Journal

Karen Alkalay-Gut

1.

Unable to move
waiting to be sprung
into action, we anticipate the sirens:
remembering the missiles of last night
targeting the people we love—
missing, missing, yet striking the heart:
the child choking on her vomit in her mask,
the old woman suffocating in unavoidable ignorance,
the psychotic whose nightmares came true.

8.

"Think of the children in Baghdad"
the radio announcer tells the kids,
"how frightened they must be
—hiding in their shelters—
by the unrelenting bombing."

The title refers to the missile bombardments by Iraq during the Gulf War, 1991. Because of the threat of chemical weapons, Israelis were supplied with gas masks and instructed to remain in sealed rooms once the sirens were heard.

The news is on next—celebrations
high on Palestinian roofs
that our time to die has come.

16 CUSTOM

Tonight we wait for the alarm.
Who wants to get caught in the shower
or the toilet or in the middle of love?
You say, "I'll wash my hair after
the attack" and I decide to put off
lacquering my nails, read
short poems about decadence instead
into the night—And it doesn't come -
And we take off our shoes and lie down
fully clothed, alert, prepared
for the sudden race to the shelter.
Even towards morning while the radio clock
shines out 3 and 4, illuminating
the passing minutes, we wait,
remember the shock of the 7:00 A.M. surprise.

Although I try to weary us with chapters from Jeremiah,
"I need my nightly missile," you say, "to fall asleep."

23.

Instead of his leash
the dog brings my mask
to remind me of his walk.

27.

Some people terrified for their lives cut
themselves off in times like these. Even I
spent hours in my room, unable to face the rest
of the family those first days of war. Weeks
later we meet our friends like wary dogs,
sniffing from behind, asking about sex
and digestion before we can kiss and smell
the sweat that emerges now from deep inside.

39.

So we begin to plan
our adult Purim costumes[119]
as if back into the swing of things.
Diane paints formulas on her face
to parade with me down the street
as a chemical warhead, and I can't think
of how to conceal what I have become
even though I expect to drink

(1993)

---

119. Among the celebrations of the festive holiday of Purim, which commemorates the deliverance of the Jews of the Perisan Empire from the threat of extermination in the fifth century B.C.E., are the wearing of costumes and the fulfilling of the custom of getting so drunk one cannot distinguish between Haman, the villain of Purim, and Mordecai, who along with Queen Esther, is its hero.

Kitzbuhl Church

Karen Alkalay-Gut

Let us say I was sitting in this place
50 years ago. Let us say I have heard
of the camps—have felt the disappearance
of the minority population.
Let us say I prayed to the only one who knew
with me that it was wrong and with the only one
who could commiserate in our impotence.
Oh indeed thou art just

Let us say I believe
there were people in this town
who sat in this church
and prayed
for the end of Anschluss
for the lives of the jews
for the souls of their soldiers

Public Outcry

Karen Alkalay-Gut

Literature is not innocent. It is guilty and should admit iself so.

—Georges Bataille

1.

Why are you silent, poets of Israel?
How can you write of anything but
the war we are careening toward like
children on a water slide screaming
for the moment they will hit the sea?

How do we let ourselves believe
that poetry is innocent and we
mere victims of circumstances
that may work themselves out,
if we just continue to concentrate on beauty
and the truths that can only mean something
in a land that is free?

2.

"Where will you go for the war?"
Simon asks on his first night in this country,
throwing us all into total confusion—as if

we hadn't realized the implications of our own dire predictions,
the logical conclusions of the facts to which we too
have played our convictionless part, watching
those full of passionate intensity
destroy a dream-coming true while shaking our sensible heads.

3.

"We should have the courage of our beliefs," I say
to my friends who having been discussing
computer programs, international bargains, Internet sites,
and how they use technology to escape,
escape this narrow world.
They all agree something must be done,
then we slip back into the usual petty complaints

4.

All we have left is a public outcry—
we must speak
of nothing else,
write only of peace,
obsessively
whispering,
clamoring it
until there is so much noise
someone at last
must hear.

5.

As long as poets believe
they must write of little beauties and wars
that mean nothing to the world outside
and that only this
is poetry,
there will be no one to listen.

6.

Perhaps it is true
that all we write is in vain—
But the silence, the silence
thunders through me like a train.

Transportation

Karen Alkalay-Gut

There are always ties of responsibility—
Try to fly, you remember you owe something
to the earth. Now we are in a plane
on that long, stuffy ride from New York
emptying our wallets of credit cards to make room
for identity folders, health clinic booklets, army
releases, special permission passes for everything.

The first time I left America for Israel my mother
spurted blood all over the rug. I knew
it was because she could endure no more losses.
But she lived through it, fifteen years ago.
Today she is a new widow, with everyone she loves
in the ground or in the air, and though
the pilot explains the rocking of the plane
as turbulence, I know it is that cord
pulling

(1993)